CITIES, SUBURBS AND BLACKS
A Study of Concerns, Distrust and Alienation

CITIES, SUBURBS AND BLACKS
A Study of Concerns, Distrust and Alienation

GENERAL HALL, INC.
23–45 Corporal Kennedy Street
Bayside, New York 11360

Publisher: Ravi Mehra
Editor: Susan Cohen

Composition: *Graphics Division,* General Hall, Inc.

LIBRARY OF CONGRESS CATALOG CARD NUMBER: 82–80239
ISBN: 0–930390–46–6 [paper]
    0–930390–45–8 [cloth]

Manufactured in the United States of America

CITIES, SUBURBS AND BLACKS
A Study of Concerns, Distrust and Alienation

James E. Blackwell
  University of Massachusetts/Boston

Philip S. Hart
  University of Massachusetts/Boston

GENERAL HALL, Inc.
Publishers
23–45 Corporal Kennedy Street
Bayside, New York 11360

For Myrt and Tanya

CONTENTS

LIST OF TABLES

List of Figures

Preface

America is in a dismal state. It is besieged by the most serious economic crisis faced by this nation since the Great Depression of the 1930's. Millions of able-bodied Americans, young and old, blue-collar and white-collar, are unemployed because they cannot find a job. More than a million are so discouraged from their inability to find work that they have retreated into a world of their own — away from the daily struggle, concerned more often than not about how to survive from day to day. For those fortunate enough to be employed, wages are not keeping pace with inflation; consequently, not only is it difficult to keep one's head above water, the possibility of saving for the future is increasingly remote for more and more Americans. As a result of policies implemented by the Reagan Administration, several social and economic programs, from which millions of previously qualified Americans benefited, have been eviscerated. Consequently, poverty deepens. Economic disability is widespread. Thousands line up at unemployment offices, join the welfare rolls or seek food at Salvation Army facilities or other social service centers. Some school children are fed "leftovers" because they no longer qualify for participation in the school lunch program and have no money to buy even a carton of milk. From city to city, all across the nation, thousands of Americans cannot be assured of one nutritious meal per day. Discontent mounts. Bitterness spreads. Blame becomes diffused and sometimes directed toward less fortunate scapegoats. America stands on the brink of perhaps its most cataclysmic period of social unrest and racial turmoil since the long hot summers of the 1960's.

Cities, Suburbs and Blacks addresses some of the specific problems facing American society. Although its focal point is toward black Americans, a great deal of what is said about blacks may describe the conditions of other groups in American society. Without question, all racial groups are affected by the economic crisis and the serious curtailment in federally sponsored programs. The sixty percent cutback in CETA funds, the twenty-two percent reduction in health services, the thirty-one percent loss of funds to support nutrition or other aid programs to children — all imposed by the Reagan Administration in 1981 — affect broad segments of American society. However, blacks, other minorities, and poor whites suffer most from such cutbacks in federal support. It is they who comprise a large segment of the central cities, and there is no evidence that their city governments are anxious to compensate for the debilitating economic and social upheaval created in their lives by Reagan Administration policies. Although poor Americans and discriminated against blacks may fiercely compete for shrinking resources, now is the time to recognize that these groups may coalesce in their perceptions of an Administration whose policies favor the rich and well-to-do as their common enemy. This situation could portend both racial and class turmoil and/or a major political upheaval directed against conservative policies and politicians.

Cities, Suburbs and Blacks was not undertaken to address such probabilities. It was initiated to ascertain the major priorities and most urgent concerns identified by black Americans and to determine ways in which these have changed, if at all, since Gunnar Myrdal described his rank order of discrimination in 1944. Initially this study also sought to understand the relationship between blacks and the power structure within five metropolitan areas. It aimed to interpret their feelings about themselves, their prospects for the future, their social and economic conditions, and their relationships with others within their communities. Differentiations were made between two broad classes of priorities — micro- and macro-community issues — that appeared to characterize residents of metropolitan areas. *Micro-community* issues were conceptualized as community-specific and quality of life concerns such as street lighting, garbage collection, police protection, conditions of roads and sidewalks, and selected health isssues. On the other hand, *macro-community* issues were characterized as those which transcended a specific community and probably cut across lines within the black population (i.e., education, job opportunities, economic life and so forth.) This study also examined the question of alienation and its manifestations among blacks in cities and suburbs.

In essence, *Cities, Suburbs and Blacks* was designed to address the following ten questions: (1) What are the health needs, priorities, and concerns that black Americans identify as important to them and why are they important? (2) What micro-community issues do black Americans regard as having high salience? (3) What macro-community issues do black Americans regard as critical? (4) How pervasive is a sense of alienation and social isolation in the black community in the late 1970's and early 1980's? What accounts for this sense of alienation and isolation? (5) To what extent do suburban blacks maintain social bonds with blacks in urban neighborhoods, break off relationships and establish new ones with blacks or whites in suburban communities, feel socially integrated or isolated in suburbia? (6) How do black suburban parents assess the quality of suburban life in terms of establishing significant social bonds for their children or affecting their own sense of well being? (7) What is the level of distrust in the power structure among black Americans in cities and suburbs? (8) How do black Americans perceive their accessibility to and availability of health services in their respective communities? (9) To what extent do racism and persistent discrimination continue to have impact on perceptions of health care delivery, alienation, isolation and distrust among black Americans? To what extent does class membership affect such perceptions? and (10) What impact are Reagan Administration policies and programs having on black Americans in cities and suburbs?

Near the end of the data collection period, a major political change occurred in the United States. This change was signalled most dramatically in 1980 by the election of Ronald Reagan as President of the United States. The authors decided to add a new chapter to this study which would assess the impact of the Reagan Administration on black Americans. Although the Reagan Administration had been in power one year by the time this book went to press, and despite possible criticisms that the assessment offered might be premature, it seems evident that certain policy changes have had disturbing consequences for blacks and the urban poor.

President Reagan has set this nation on a course which will, if unchecked by the Courts, escalate racial and class enmity, terminate the bloodstained national commitment to achieve racial harmony and equality, and broaden the condition of racial apartheid that exists in so many institutions and metropolitan areas. At news conferences in January 1982, President Reagan vehemently denied allegations of racism and asserted that he was opposed to racial discrimination with "every fiber of his being." Such protestations are extremely difficult for many black Americans to accept when the policies he encourages or acquiesces to appear to be anti-black. They seem likely to rescind those major gains toward a modicum of equal opportunity and integrated education achieved during the Civil Rights Movement.

The Reagan Administration seems unconcerned about the conditions of racial minorities and the poor. It seems unaffected by the possibilities of turmoil propelled by economic disability, want, insecurity or racial antagonisms. It is probable that the bitterness expressed by "people in the street" might be far more pervasive than envisioned by governmental leaders who are insensitive to the life chances of the poor and racial minorities.

The indignation expressed by civil rights groups, private citizens, and the major newspapers across the country over the efforts of the Reagan Administration to change a long-standing policy against tax exempt status to schools and nonprofit institutions that racially discriminate should be evidence that fair-minded Americans expect an American president to *exercise moral leadership* as well as political acumen. The nation cannot afford to turn its back on any of its citizens, irrespective of race, color, religion or national origin. We still have time to continue to make progress toward equality of opportunity and racial justice. *Do we have the resolve?* Can it again become a national priority? Those are the central questions in the 1980's.

Acknowledgments

Projects of this scope can never be completed without the assistance of others. The authors of this book, in recognition of that reality, deeply appreciate the help given by those persons identified below.

We especially thank the 1,000 black men and women in Atlanta, Boston, Cleveland, Houston and Los Angeles who consented to be interviewed. Their views, concerns, and general comments were the primary data source for *Cities, Suburbs and Blacks*. We sincerely appreciate the thoroughness of the work performed by the interviewers on this project. Our profound gratitude is acknowledged to the on-site supervisors who monitored and facilitated data collection in the five cities studied: Professor Wiley Bolden of Georgia State University in Atlanta, Professor James Kelsaw of the University of Houston, Professor Butler Jones of Cleveland State University, Dr. Andrea Baker of Case Western Reserve University, and Professor Belinda Tucker of the University of California at Los Angeles. In addition, we thank those persons who assisted in sample selection and others who served as research assistants in the cities studied. In Boston, Dr. Michael Forte assisted in the statistical design and computer programming, Kathleen Murray and Patricia Garrity were diligent in the typing of the manuscript.

We also acknowledge the financial support for research provided by the Center for Minority Group Mental Health Programs of NIMH on which the first seven chapters of this book are based. The critical comments of four blind readers on earlier drafts of the book were particularly invaluable since they helped to strengthen our focus, organization, and approach to the issues discussed. Above all, we deeply appreciate the contributions of our wives, Myrt Blackwell and Tanya Hart. They offered timely advice, important suggestions and constructive criticisms.

ABOUT THE AUTHORS

James E. Blackwell (Ph.D., Washington State University) is currently Professor of Sociology at the University of Massachusetts/Boston. He is the 1981-82 President of the Eastern Sociological Society, 1980-81 President of the Society for the Study of Social Problems, and founding President of the Caucus of Black Sociologists. He has held teaching positions at Case Western Reserve University, San Jose State University, Washington State University and Grambling State University. His most recent books include *Mainstreaming Outsiders: The Production of Black Professionals, Health Needs of Urban Blacks* (with Philip Hart and Robert Sharpley), *The Black Community: Diversity and Unity,* and *Black Sociologists: Historical and Contemporary Perspectives* (with Morris Janowitz).

Philip S. Hart (Ph.D., Michigan State University) is presently an Associate Professor of Sociology, College of Public and Community Service, University of Massachusetts/Boston. Dr. Hart is a Denver native and is a graduate of the University of Colorado (BA, 1966), where he was a varsity athlete and received cum laude honors. Dr. Hart is a specialist in mass communications and has headed his own firm since 1974. Dr. Hart has produced award-winning films, and has films in national distribution. Dr. Hart was elected as one of the Outstanding Young Men in the United States in 1978; Who's Who in the East, 1981; International Book of Honor, 1982; and Men of Achievement, 1982.

CHAPTER 1

Overview of the Study

For more than a century black Americans have sought complete assimilation and integration into American life. In terms of health care and other societal opportunities, large segments of the black population have not realized the goal of complete assimilation and integration. "While black Americans are linguistically acculturated, the process of developing a sense of 'peoplehood' with other Americans is threatened by daily confrontations with prejudice and discrimination, and their adverse effects."[1] Thus, even with some degree of structural assimilation occurring everyday, it is difficult to convince some groups of blacks outside the system that the opportunity structure is changing. For others, the ultimate dream of two-way assimilation, in which the contributions of both entrants and members of the new society or culture are equally valued, has not been fulfilled.[2]

Conditions such as these create ambivalence among many black Americans concerning their ethnic identity. Historical examples of this ambivalence to the U.S. include Marcus Garvey's United Negro Improvement Association which championed "Back to Africa" movements beginning with Garvey's Black Power movement, and pan-Africanism. Hence, many black Americans tend to view their experiences from the dual perspective of "two souls" — one black, and the other American.[3] This dual perspective persists because millions of black Americans have experiences which make them feel they have not gained sufficient entitlements as full and equal citizens of the United States. There are many black Americans who do not feel that even their most pressing needs are being met. Many do not believe that they are able to secure employment equal to their training and ability or that they will experience equal opportunity for upward occupational mobility. Many blacks feel that segregation and discrimination persist within school systems and districts, despite legal remedies established to

1

alleviate such problems.[4] Many blacks also believe that they are being denied the right to decent housing despite their income. Further, many black Americans believe that access to adequate health care is almost non-existent. "In essence, their expectations as American citizens have not been sufficiently realized to make their prospects for the future optimistic."[5]

The apparent failure of these basic expectations to be realized has produced myriad stresses among a significant segment of the black population. Manifestations of stress may be found in several arenas of daily life. For instance, stress may manifest itself in health problems such as hypertension,[6] or hostile interpersonal relations,[7] which, in turn, can reflect on the overall quality of mental health. Stress may also be manifested in a pervasive sense of powerlessness or in degrees of alienation, anomie, and social isolation. The impact of stress can be observed in ideological polarity of the sort that finds "assimilationists" and "integrationists" at one end of the spectrum and "nationalists" and "separatists" at the other.[8] In addition, the impact of stress may be observed in diverse perceptions of black Americans' most urgent concerns and priorities. The concerns and priorities of American blacks can be classified as micro-community and macro-community in scope. Blackwell, Sharpley and Hart wrote:

> *Micro-community issues* are affective and impact on daily neighborhood life and on community specific issues. These concerns include better police protection and street lighting, more frequent garbage collection, better access to community health centers and medical services, and improved transportation facilities. *Macro-community issues* transcend a particular community and are more universal in scope. Macro-community issues include the broad problems of economic disabilities, high rates of black unemployment, mechanisms for achieving quality education at the elementary and secondary school levels, and inequality of access to graduate and professional schools. Both types of concerns can and do contribute to mental health problems which may be manifested in varying degrees of alienation, anomie, powerlessness, social isolation, and distrust of decision-makers or the authority structure."[9]

The persistence of such issues points to the fact that neither equality of opportunity nor equality of result has been achieved by all segments of the American population despite major changes in the American social, political, and economic fabric during the past thirty years. Since 1948, the U.S. Supreme Court has ordered graduate and professional schools to admit students of all races, declared segregation and discrimination in public institutions unconstitutional, and ruled against discriminatory practices in housing, and on prohibitions against marriage across racial lines. The U.S. Congress has created a Civil Rights Commission, and Equal Employment

Opportunity Commission, and has enacted Voting Rights Bills as well as far-reaching Civil Rights Bills in 1964 and 1968. Congress has also enacted a number of measures under "Great Society Legislation" which have promoted major improvements in the delivery of health care services to a broad portion of the American population.

Despite these changes, black Americans continue to articulate certain urgencies and priorities. These unmet concerns point up the weakness in the implementation and enforcement of various court decrees and corrective legislation. The black unemployment rate is still close to double the white unemployment rate, according to the Bureau of Labor Statistics. The black labor force remains largely employed in lower level occupational roles, and the median black family income is less than three-fifths of the median family income of white Americans.*

Among black teenagers, unemployment is acknowledged by the Labor Department to be in excess of 40 percent. The National Urban League Research Department reports an unemployment rate among black teenagers in excess of 60 percent in some areas of the nation. The NUL Research Department further claims the overall rate of unemployment among black adults is close to 25 percent. The persistence of high rates of unemployment among blacks tends to create and perpetuate a class of "black lumpen-proletarians," or underclass standing outside the system with minimal possibilities for becoming a part of the labor force. For some segments of the black population who are prepared only for labor intensive occupational roles, their unemployment is partially explained by technological demands which render their skills obsolete.[10] Blackwell, Sharpley, and Hart note:

> These conditions also find partial explanation in affirmative action guidelines which fail to include appropriate means of enforcement. This failure enhances the penchant of employers towards lengthy legalistic negotiation rather than direct implementation of processes which insure equality of opportunity. It further permits some employers to hinder black employment. Nevertheless, many Black Americans have benefitted either from the threat of enforcement of equal employment opportunity policies or from particularistic practices which followed some employers' heightened sensitivity to the problems of inequality.[11]

Often housing ordinances have made it possible for more blacks to move into formerly all-white urban and suburban enclaves. Without question, the Omnibus Housing Bill or the Civil Rights Act of 1968 spurred the movement of some 800,000 blacks into suburbia between 1970 and 1977 but the total number of blacks in suburban communities represents only

---

*It has been argued by some scholars that part of the explanation for lower black family income compared to white families is that blacks are younger.

about 6 percent of the suburban population. Although blacks can legally rent and purchase housing in areas formerly off limits, if they can afford such locales, they still face the possibility of discrimination and violence. The number of these incidents of violence seemed to have increased during the latter part of the seventies and some of them received national attention (e.g., the burning of the homes of middle-class blacks in suburban New York City and the abuse of an elderly black family who moved into a formerly all-white neighborhood in Great Barrington, Massachussets in 1980).

In terms of employment, housing, health and other aspects of daily living, it has usually taken governmental intervention or prodding of the market-mechanisms in order for black Americans to achieve the improvements observable in their life patterns today. Oftentimes, even this public sector intervention has been slow, reluctant and induced by pressures mounted by formal organizations in the black community. This situation has the effect of reinforcing within the black population a sense of alienation, despair, and distrust of the power structure.

These observations, and other evidence, led this team of researchers to explore in more depth the following questions: what are the present urgent concerns and priorities of urban and suburban black Americans in the late 1970's and early 1980's?

Have these concerns and priorities changed during the past three decades? If so, how have they changed? Do these urgent concerns differ across social class lines, do they differ depending upon place of residence, income differentials, education, or with regard to age and sex variables? Is there a sense of alienation,[12] anomie, and distrust of the power structure among black Americans? To what extent are urban and suburban black Americans oriented to the future and do they differ in this orientation? To what extent are macro-community and micro-community issues of salience to black Americans of different socio-economic background? To what extent do suburban black Americans feel estranged from the concerns of those in predominantly black neighborhoods? To what extent are there differences and similarities between residents of the five cities included in this national study in terms of health care, alienation, distrust, orientation to the future, macro- and micro-community concerns?

Research Objectives

In order to answer these questions with more specificity, the researchers secured two separate grants [13] and conducted field work in Boston, Atlanta, Cleveland, Houston, and Los Angeles, between early 1977 and mid-1980. In the research monograph [14] published after completion of the metropolitan Boston pilot study, the authors state the principal study objectives: (1) to obtain general and specific information that would serve as the basis for policy decisions affecting the quality of life in metropolitan communities, particularly among urban blacks, (2) to identify in a systematic manner the perceptions of blacks (in urban ghetto and suburban areas) on what constitutes their most urgent needs in the mid-eighties, (3) to systematically determine the accessibility and utilization or deterrents to utilization of services in predominantly black communities capable of meeting the identified needs of the population, (4) to identify those factors which affect the realization of identified priorities, (5) to examine the effects of goal attainment or lack of goal attainment on their mental health needs, and (6) to examine the mental health needs of youth and the resources used for treating mental health problems. In general, these objectives guided the four-city study which followed the metropolitan Boston study.

These research objectives are rooted in empirical research concerned with the priorities and basic expectations of black Americans begun almost four decades ago. Myrdal pioneered in the field with the highly influential publication, *An American Dilemma (1944),* in which he identified a dual "rank order of discrimination" among the black and white population. In reviewing the divergent perspective of the two racial groups, it is important to take into account the social, political, and legal climate of the late 1930's and the early 1940's. During these years, racial prejudice, discrimination and segregation reinforced an inequality which pervaded the institutional fabric of life in the United States. White Americans were preoccupied with the perpetuation of a boundary-maintenance system that would protect their privileges and their sense of entitlement which both law and social custom guaranteed to them. [15]

Myrdal's rank order of discrimination, which in our view constitutes the major concerns and priorities of black Americans, was the exact opposite of the rank order described for white Americans. Thus, listed from most to least urgent, blacks had as their concerns: (1) better economic conditions which included jobs, credit, land, and an end to discrimination in public relief and social welfare, (2) equality before the law or an end to discrimination by the courts, police, and law enforcement agencies in general, (3) political enfranchisement, (4) access to public accommodations without discrimination, (5) an end to discrimination in social and personal relations, and (6) the right to intermarry. [16]

In 1944, the same year that *An American Dilemma* was published, a group of fourteen prominent black leaders came together to discuss the interests, concerns, and priority needs of black Americans. This discussion resulted in the publication of the anthology, *What the Negro Wants*.[17] The contributors to this anthology included renowned scholars, academic administrators, civic leaders, and literary notables such as W.E.B. DuBois, Charles Wesley, Leslie Pinckney Hill, Mary McCleod Bethune, Roy Wilkins, Langston Hughes, and Sterling Brown.

What the Negro Wants brought to the fore, the urgent concerns and priorities of black Americans. These focal concerns and priorities were expressed in such phrases as: "we want first-class citizenship;" "we want 'freedom,' 'power,' 'certain inalienable rights,' 'full equality';" or simply "we want to be counted in."[18] Even though this anthology cannot be assessed as empirical research, one can hardly dispute its contributors' conventional wisdom, insights, and ability to pinpoint and articulate the fundamental defects in their contemporary social structure. "Clearly, they called attention to the urgent priorities of a tenth of America's population whose members continued to be treated as social, legal and political pariahs."[19]

There have been several empirical studies on Myrdal's findings of a rank order of discrimination. W.S.M. Banks was the first to conduct a systematic study in Columbus, Ohio, in 1950 with a sample of 200 blacks. Banks did not make a black-white comparison as did Myrdal. He concluded that the rank order proposed by Myrdal was generally supported. However, his findings showed that economic matters dropped from first to third in priority.[20] This change may have reflected post WW II improvements in the economic life of black Americans.

Edwin R. Edmunds studied a sample of 443 blacks and 522 whites in Texas and Oklahoma in 1954. His study provided evidence that the rank order postulated by Myrdal was not completely supported. However, the top four variables, remained in that category even if rearranged, suggesting that black Americans continued to seek major transformations within the system that would lead to improvements in their condition within the society.[21]

Lewis Killian and Charles Grigg in a sample of 225 blacks and 225 whites in Jacksonville, Florida in 1961, sought to ascertain whether a modified rank order of discrimination existed. The rank order developed by Myrdal was supported in the black population.

A careful reading of each of these studies reveals a common theoretical thread. It is abundantly clear that, at least for the last four decades, black Americans have primarily expressed concern about economic betterment through attainment of dependable jobs and higher incomes. Such a change in economic conditions would have innumerable ramifications for millions of black Americans. Economic disabilities affect from one-third to one-half of the black population. Continual recessive economic conditions are generally thought to affect crime rates, health care, and other quality of life measures.[22] As the studies of Myrdal, Banks, Blackwell, et al., and other theoretically significant works demonstrate, it is the prevalence of adverse economic conditions which lessen black Americans' chances for a rewarding life, sound health, and substantial improvements in their life chances, or to gain entry into mainstream American life.

Although useful in many ways, prior research on the priorities and basic expectations of black Americans was flawed. For one, the studies failed to establish controls for social class. They did not properly address the influence of heterogeneity among blacks in their perception of a rank order of discrimination or of what constitutes urgent concerns and priorities. The studies also failed to investigate the possible relationship between these perceptions and a number of independent variables which may be associated with such viewpoints.

Recent examples of studies which help to transcend such flaws include those done by the National Urban League Research Department (August 1980),[23] the *Black Enterprise* readership survey[24] (August 1980), and the work reported by Kenneth B. Clark and Mamie Phipps Clark in *Ebony*, (November 1980).[25] In brief, the National Urban League's initial Black Pulse findings indicate that unemployment is clearly the number one problem in the black community. Inflation ranks a distant third, with three times as many blacks reporting that joblessness rather than inflation is the most serious problem. Nevertheless, blacks acknowledge that inflation is still having a devastating impact on their economic condition. Also, it appears that the black unemployment crisis affects black youth and black household heads. The actual unemployment rate for black household heads during the last quarter of 1979 was 24 per cent, or three times the U.S. Labor Department jobless rate. In addition, the overwhelming majority of blacks today, regardless of economic status, feel that racial discrimination continues to be widespread. Further, the Black Pulse survey found that most blacks are becoming increasingly impatient with what they feel is an eroding commitment toward racial equality. Finally, maintaining strong kinship ties continues to be of significance in the black community. This Black Pulse household survey was conducted in central cities, suburbs, and rural areas between October, 1979 and January, 1980. Interviews were conducted with about 3000 black heads of households.[26]

The *Black Enterprise* readership survey, consisting of 2000 respondents, was a predominantly male sample, with education and income measures being higher than the black population in general. One of the findings of this predominantly male, middle class sample is that the National Urban League, NAACP, and SCLC are no longer viewed as bastions of civil rights. Another observation is that most blacks reported feeling inadequately represented by government but still shy away from forming an independent black political party. Most of those surveyed believe the election of black mayors in major cities has resulted in better government. Nearly half of *Black Enterprise* readers polled think job opportunities for blacks have not improved in the last decade, and it is mainly younger blacks who are most likely to feel that they have benefitted from new job opportunities in the last ten years. Further, those in the readership survey oppose busing just for integration, but support it if it means quality education for black children. The middle-class readership reports being very much aware of the problem of police brutality in their community. The readers also feel that white women are the primary beneficiaries of affirmative action programs, leaving fewer jobs for blacks. Nearly three-fourths of the readership believe racism in America is as prevalent today as it was ten years ago. Finally, the readership's belief that whites harbor some form of racism toward blacks is virtually unanimous — and does not vary by income, age, or location.[27]

In another vein, the Clark's study which is a replication of their earlier work, relates to the image blacks have of themselves. This study is the result of a telephone survey of a national sample of 1200 blacks conducted in August, 1980 by Data/Black Public Opinion Polls. The first of three major findings of this study is that, although there is no base for specific comparison, there are indications that blacks are making progress in developing more positive self-images. Secondly, despite the progress of the post-*Brown vs. Board of Education* period, blacks, in general, have not yet developed a consistently positive self-image and racial acceptance. Finally, black college graduates and higher income blacks seem comparatively less burdened with racial self-rejection than less educated blacks in lower income brackets. The authors note that it is also important to recognize that blacks in the Far West seem to have more positive self-concepts than blacks in other sections of the country. This finding is an interesting comparison with the *Black Enterprise* readership survey which notes that blacks in the West find racism to be more of an obstacle to black business than readers in the Northeast.[28]

In order to provide more current information about the attitudes of black Americans, this study was undertaken in late 1976. Data collection and analysis continued through the end of 1980. A major theoretical position taken in this study is that urgent priorities of black Americans are neither unidimensional nor necessarily unidirectional. However, the urgent concerns and priorities can be divided into two classes which have already been identified as macro-community and micro-community issues. It is also theorized that levels of anomie or alienation would not only differ according to the social class dimensions but that they could also influence black Americans' perceptions of macro-and micro-community issues.

Studies on Alienation Among Black Americans

A number of researchers have sought to explain the attitudes and/or behavior of blacks and their deprivation through the theoretical lens of alientation theory and by such polarities as internality versus externality. Among the earlier leaders in the development of alienation theory and its variants in the United States were Leo Srole,[29] Melvin Seeman[30] and Patricia Gurin and Gerald Gurin.[31]

Seeman's conceptual paper on alienation, published in 1959, laid out many of the forms, types and manifestations of alienation as: (1) powerlessness, (2) meaninglessness, (3) normlessness, (4) social isolation, (5) self-estrangement, and some have used the concept of (6) "cultural estrangement." However, a significant amount of the research reported during the 1960's was based upon a Marxian delineation of alienation. Specifically, the central concern was alienation from work or from the workplace itself. In these instances, alienation and its variants were explained in terms of the lack of a sense of personal worth or of intrinsic identity with work primarily because the person was "estranged" from work situations that were not personally rewarding.

When Seeman and other researchers[32] investigated the relationship between alienation from work and such conditions as ethnic hostility, status striving or voting behavior, they discovered an inability of work alienation to explain these conditions. Seeman also sought to measure the attitude of blacks toward themselves and towards whites. He developed a four-item index of black solidarity called "identification with Negroes" which was tested against work alienation and powerlessness. Again, he found that work alienation explained very little of the attitudes of black Americans during the 1960's but that powerlessness was a far more powerful predictor of both "out-group hostility" and "in-group solidarity." Unlike many of the researchers on alienation during that period, there was some attempt in Seeman's work to examine similarities and differences across occupational lines among blacks in his investigations of both work alienation and other variants of alienation, especially powerlessness.

The urban unrest of the 1960's exposed the depths of the desperation of blacks in all social classes. However, most of the studies on alienation among blacks during that period seemed to have concentrated on blacks within the cities, especially blacks in the traditional ghetto, without consideration of the possible problems encountered by blacks who had moved into the suburbs. An underlying assumption of many of these studies was that the black community lacked group differentation despite the rapidly increasing size of the black middle class during the sixties and early seventies, notwithstanding the ideological polarities which characterized forms of black activism. A brief review of selective studies may be instructive on this point.

Some of the earlier studies on alienation or powerlessness among blacks sought to identify the "sources of alienation." The 1963 study by Russell Middleton is a case in point. He examined the incidence of Melvin Seeman's five variants of alienation in a small southern town. He also attempted to ascertain the degree to which these varients (i.e. powerlessness, meaninglessness, normlessness, isolation, and self-estrangement) were distributed according to race and education. In this study of 207 white and 99 blacks, Middleton found that blacks were more highly alienated than whites on each variant with the exception of cultural estrangement. His findings also led him to conclude that although alienation is pervasive in the black community, it is lower for persons with higher education among both races. Middleton also stated that the primary sources of alienation in the black community are the disabling conditions that thwart the attainment of culturally valued objectives of black Americans.[33]

William W. Phillibur addressed the problem of the locus of alienation among persons in low income neighborhoods by examining whether it was a response to society as a whole or those sectors in society viewed as particularly unresponsive to individual needs. In his sample of 506 low-income residents in Cincinnati, 70 percent were black and 74 percent were less than high school graduates. Hence, he was able to control outcomes by both race and education as Middleton did. The four sectors identified for differential manifestation of alienation were: (1) the consumer system, (2) the police system, (3) the political system, and (4) the neighborhood system. Phillibur concluded that his respondents were alienated against the system as a whole as opposed to specific sectors within the system. The neighborhood sector seemed to have been "excluded from the generalized response pattern." He offered as one explanation for the differential orientation to the neighborhood the probability that the interaction in the neighborhood is primary in contrast to a more secondary character of interaction in the system as a whole.[34]

Commenting on alienation among lower-class blacks in 1965, Daniel Gordon observed that the prevalent tendency of social scientists was to stress the transition of blacks from rural to urban life as the principal explanatory factor. While adjustments to urban life posed serious and often debilitating problems for new immigrants, he argued that other variables appeared to be equally salient, if not more so, as contributors to alienation in this group. He offered three additional variables to account for alienation in the black lower class; namely, (1) discrimination, (2) feelings of dependence, and (3) (lack of) mediating organizations.[35] This observation raises several unanswered questions. For instance, are we to assume that discrimination is less pronounced among the middle-and-upper classes than it is among the lower-class black population? Does affiliation with various formal and informal social organizations reduce the feelings of alienation among urban blacks any more than it does among blacks in suburban communities?

In a 1965 study of 1,000 households in Washington, D.C., Charles V. Willie focused attention on one of the additional variables specified by Gordon. Willie's research was concerned with the relationship between education, deprivation and alienation. He concluded that racial segregation and discrimination in school systems, particularly at neighborhood levels, fostered both alienation and deprivation. In effect, high levels of discrimination and of racial segregation were correlated with high degrees of alienation.[36] As did Gordon, Willie emphasized the importance of discrimination as a correlate source of alienation. Like Middleton and Phillibur, alienation was also viewed as a direct consequence of the oppressive forces unleashed by systemic and societal conditions.

In order to provide greater clarity to the question of in what specific ways are these societal factors related to alienation, Sumati Dubey and Morris L. Grant did an extensive review of the literature on alienation and powerlessness in the black community between 1960 and 1970. This analysis led them to conclude that the most persistent correlate of powerlessness, as a proxy of alienation, in these studies was unemployment. They found evidence that unemployment not only leads to a lack of material resources among the disadvantaged, it also lowers self-image and thereby deepens one's sense of estrangement and normlessness.[37]

The theme of "lowered self-image" was also evident in Gerald Hugh Black's study of "Alienation — Black and White — Or the Uncommitted Revisited." Black examined forms of alienation evidenced in Elliot Liebow's "streetcorner men" and reported in his prize-winning book, *Talley's Corner.* He compared these observations with others made in Kenneth Keniston's important study of *The Uncommitted.* Black observed that the subjects in both books suffered from a fragmented self-image and tended to define themselves in negative terms. They used fantasy to escape from the realities of an omnipresent harsh world. In Black's view, alienation among blacks was especially due to the "inability of our nation to change morally."[38]

As more and more blacks moved into previously white suburban communities, a few social scientists began to focus attention on the impact of neighborhoods and different patterns of neighboring on their attitudes, degrees of social participation, ties to the former black community, and problems of adjustment of blacks in these communities. Studies by Bonnie Bullough and Robert A. Wilson are illustrative of this research.

Bonnie Bullough sought to examine differences between suburban blacks, who lived in a predominantly white area, and "ghetto" blacks, who lived in a large central city, on a scale of anomie and powerlessness. Her sample consisted of 104 suburban black and 106 ghetto city blacks. She hypothesized that powerlessness, anomie and a feeling of normlessness are associated with the ghetto and play an important role in holding people to their old residential patterns. She further hypothesized that as blacks moved into suburbia they would divert their attention away from the less segregated institutions of the ghetto. To explore these hypotheses, Bullough employed the Srole Anomie Scale and her own scale which measured orientation to or away from the ghetto.[39]

Bullough concluded that: (1) ghetto residents felt that they had less control over their lives (powerlessness) than did blacks who had moved to suburbia, (2) ghetto residents scored higher on the anomie scale than did suburban blacks, (3) in general, residents of the ghetto had stronger feelings of powerlessness and alienation than did blacks in the suburbs, and (4) "orientation to the ghetto" is related significantly to a greater expectation for control and to lower scores on the anomie scale.[40]

One of the questions raised by this study was whether or not neighborhoods have a specific property that is conducive to lowering alienation or to stimulating different patterns of social participation. Partial responses to these questions were provided in two studies conducted by Robert A. Wilson. In a study of 645 household heads in three inner city neighborhoods, Wilson employed an anomie scale that addressed both a neighborhood and an individual level. The three inner city neighborhoods were called "the ghetto," "the Northeast," and the "West Side." He found support for Lander's postulate that "as an area reaches maximal heterogeneity, the level of anomie will be maximal" and, therefore, in a racially stabilizing ghetto the anomie level should be less than in a racially changing area. This finding was considerably more prevalent among blacks than among whites, according to Wilson. He also claimed that, of these three neighborhoods, the ghetto displayed the least amount of anomie, "even though it had the highest incidence of social pathology." There was also a high incidence of anomie among whites living in the ghetto when compared to whites who lived in the Northeast and in the West Side. He concluded that a high level of anomie was not a universal characteristic of those blacks who lived in urban black ghettos.[41]

In a somewhat earlier paper, Wilson had explored the "utility of the neighborhood as a social system" by focusing attention on anomie and militancy. These were a condition and an attitude that had come to be identified with black Americans as a consequence of the Civil Rights Movement and the turbulence of the 1960's. He selected 483 households from three inner city neighborhoods in an East Coast town of 83,000 residents. The ghetto neighborhood, referred to above, was the oldest neighborhood in the city. The Northeast was 85 percent black and the West Side was 60 percent black and both were described as neighborhoods in transition from white working class to predominantly black lower class. After testing his subjects on the anomie scale, he found that the mean anomie score was significantly lower among ghetto residents than in the neighborhoods in transition. He also found that the militancy level was higher in the Northeast area, the neighborhood with the highest concentration of blacks. Equally significant was his observation that the more recent migrants to the neighborhood, regardless of the number of blacks in them, scored higher on the anomie scale than those who had lived in the area ten years or longer. Hence, social system properties, or factors internal to each neighborhood, seem to account for variance in anomie and militancy scores.[42]

Each type of study mentioned in this section (i.e. those which focused on sources of alienation, correlates of alienation, and neighborhood conditions) suggests that much more research is needed. As stated earlier on, the alienation studies concentrated on the presence of this condition in a single and presumably homogeneous segment of the black population - the disadvantaged black underclass who resided in the traditional black ghetto. Even that assumption was erroneous since blacks who reside in a black ghetto may also show a high degree of social differentation and diversity with respect to political ideology. Even though class distinctions have become more apparent among blacks with the increasing size of the black middle-and-upper class, it may be argued that blacks of all classes continue to feel the effects of a virulent racism which permeate the American social, economic and political fabric. Further, the conditions designated as "grievances" in the *U.S. Riot Commission Report* of 1968[43] are widespread phenomena in the 1980's.

Many argue that the polarization between the races which the Commission envisaged as a great possibility, unless their recommendations were implemented, is stark reality in many aspects of our daily life today.

Hence another purpose of this study is to address questions raised in this review of literature.

Research Design

The universe from which the sample was selected includes the metropolitan areas of Atlanta, Georgia; Boston, Massachusetts; Cleveland, Ohio; Houston, Texas; and Los Angeles, California. The selection of these metropolitan areas will yield a fairly good geographic balance for a national black sample. Perhaps the area least represented, with a fairly significant black presence are metropolitan areas in the Pacific Northwest, such as Portland, Oregon or Seattle, Washington. Despite this shortcoming, the authors feel as if a significant segment of the American black population has been sampled in this work.[44]

Of the metropolitan areas sampled, metropolitan Atlanta has a black population of 25 percent, the City of Atlanta has a black population of 60 percent. Metropolitan Boston has a black population of 6 percent, while the City of Boston has a black population of 22 percent. Metropolitan Cleveland has a black population of 18 percent, while the City of Cleveland has a black population of 45 percent. Metropolitan Houston has a black population of 18 percent, while the city of Houston has a black population of 24 percent. Metropolitan Los Angeles has a black population of 13 percent, while the City of Los Angeles has a black population of 18 percent (Table 1).

In each of these metropolitan areas, the greater proportion of black households are located in the urban area. As noted earlier, suburban sample selection is of concern also in that a research focus is on urban-suburban comparison across several measures. The urban-suburban sampling ratio is

Table 1

Blacks in Sample Areas

City	Metropolitan Area		City Area	
	#	%	#	%
Atlanta	498,821	25	282,912	60
Boston	160,434	6	126,229	22
Cleveland	345,632	18	251,347	45
Houston	528,513	18	440,257	24
Los Angeles	944,009	13	505,208	18

Source: 1980 - U.S. Department of Commerce - Census Bureau, Boston Office.

Table 2

Metropolitan Areas Sample Selection.

	Planned		Actual	
	Urban	Suburban	Urban	Suburban
Atlanta	150	50	178	50
Boston	180	60	221	75
Cleveland	150	50	56	50
Houston	150	50	183	65
Los Angeles	150	50	39	28
Total	780	260/1040	677	268/945

such as to yield a ratio of approximately three urban households for each suburban household.

In metropolitan Boston, 296* black households participated in the study. Of this number, 221 were urban and 75 were suburban. In metropolitan Atlanta, 228 black households participated; 178 were urban, and 50 were suburban. Metropolitan Cleveland yielded 106 interviews, 56 of which were urban and 50 suburban. In metropolitan Houston, 248 interviews were successfully conducted, of which 183 were urban and 65 suburban. In metropolitan Los Angeles, 39 urban interviews were conducted and 28 suburban interviews were conducted (Table 2).

In Boston, the sampling goal was to yield 180 urban and 60 suburban interviews. In the other four metropolitan areas, the goal was to end up with 150 urban interviews and 50 suburban interviews. Table 2 reflects the planned sampling yield in each metropolitan area and the actual sampling yield. As can be determined from Table 2, the actual sampling outcome in aggregate closely approximates the planned 3:1 urban to suburban ratio. The primary problem areas in terms of data collection were urban Cleveland, urban Los Angeles, and suburban Los Angeles.

Data Collection

Data were collected through the use of an interview schedule consisting of 126 items dealing specifically with the stated hypotheses and background information in such matters as socioeconomic characteristics and place of residence. Specifically, the interview scheduled contains: (1) space for socioeconomic background characteristics and residential area, (2) items regarding social participation,** (3) the micro-community level issues, (4) the macro-community level issues, (5) health related items, (6) an anomie scale, (7) an alienation scale, (8) a powerlessness scale, (9) a social isolation scale, (10) an orientation to the future scale, and (11) a scale measuring distrust of the power structure. Each interview took approximately 50 minutes to conduct.

In each site a field supervisor assisted the co-investigators in training

---

*See "Methodological Note" at end in Appendix for more detail on male-female case weight factor as it relates to sample size in each city.

**The social participation items, consisting of eleven questions were not used in Boston. These items were developed as a result of the pilot study in Boston, and implemented in the four other cities. After Boston, it was also decided to drop the normlessness scale due to overlap with the anomie scale.

10-15 black interviewers over a two-day period. The field supervisors were then responsible for overall supervision and quality control maintenance among the interviewers.[45] Once the field work was completed, interviews with cover sheets were sent to the Solomon Fuller Institute, Cambridge, Massachusetts, where coding, keypunching, computer programming, computer runs, data anaylsis and storage was carried out.[46]

Research in the Black Community

Despite the greater sophistication of survey research methods, there seems to be a growing reluctance on the part of the public to participate in surveys as well as an increasingly critical attitude about the quality of surveys. Experts in the area generally agree that survey research is in some difficulty, that the difficulties may be increasing, and that the problems vary in incidence among government, private, and academic researchers.[47] Problems generally associated with surveys are exacerbated with surveys among metropolitan black households.

Joan Costello notes in relation to the research function:

> Research, in itself, is neither exploitation nor salvation. It is a search for answers to questions through disciplined inquiry, and it is therefore a necessary activity for a society which faces increasingly complex problems.[48]

Historically, however, research which has been carried out by respected scholars and translated into social policy has cast the black population in a negative image.[49] One possible reason is because access to research funding by black researchers has been limited, and the capacity of black researchers, administrators, and politicians to implement more positive findings based upon research work that has been done is limited.

Research provides an important knowledge base necessary for a society or subgroup to understand its functioning. As one examines the types of research that have been conducted and the population groups sampled, one can gain insight into the power relations extant in the society. A working proposition that may be relevant at this point is that research work which is high risk in terms of its potential effect on the subject population tends to have a sample population composed of socially, politically, and economically vulnerable groups.[50]

A set of generalized concerns expressed by black communities in relation to research includes:

(1) The volume of social research outdistances changes in service. If one were to translate available research findings into social policy and practice today, it would take several years to close the gap between knowledge and action.

(2) Since funding is scarce, available funds should be allocated not to research but to programs of vital economic, social, medical, and educational action.

(3) Research efforts should be directed to the study of racism and white institutions which have caused or contributed to the problems of black people in America.

(4) Those who want to study blacks should use their knowledge to influence the power structure.

(5) Blacks have accepted research on their defects just as they have accepted many other things they were powerless to oppose. Blacks need to focus on strengths and competencies, and they must influence the research community to adopt such a focus.[51]

With these concerns, it thus becomes increasingly difficult for black and white researchers to conduct studies in black communities. In Boston, the black community developed a Community Research Review Committee[52] in 1970, to review research using black subjects or focusing on issues of importance to blacks in the Boston area. This committee consisted of a mixture of academics, service agency personnel, and community residents. They were relatively successful as a review mechanism in the Boston area, and have generated interest in other cities in such an organized body to review research affecting the black population.

Research in black communities has thus become an issue of importance to diverse interests. It seems that this issue will be with the research community for the indefinite future. Seemingly then, research in black communities will become more of a negotiated process than has been the case in the past. The problems encountered by the researchers in the study reported here, point to the fact that carrying out research in black communities will be a problem for white *and* black researchers.[53]

The types of problems encountered in this study included the impact of the gasoline shortage on data collection in metropolitan Los Angeles, beginning in May, 1979, the generally hostile reception by most urban Cleveland households to the interviewers,[54] the need to re-do falsified questionnaires in Boston, and the impact of unusually severe weather conditions in the Houston area during 1979-80.

In each city, there were areas viewed as particularly dangerous which made it difficult to assign field interviewers even with a buddy system as an added measure of security. In general, it was noted that young black males were the least successful field interviewers in that they were least likely to be admitted into a home to conduct an interview. The most successful interviewers in general were middle-aged persons, particularly women. An exception to these generalizations was in Atlanta where the bulk of the households interviewing was conducted by a young black male graduate student. The Atlanta fieldwork was done during the January, 1979-June, 1979 period, and thus the level of paranoia and hysteria associated with the death of several black children was insignificant.[55]

Another hindrance to data collection was with the informed consent forms. These forms are necessary in any survey using human subjects in order to inform them of the study purposes and for their protection. Their use arose out of past abuse, by social, medical, and biological researchers in studies involving human subjects. Blacks, and other minorities, have historically suffered at the hands of unethical researchers; thus, the informed consent form was developed to serve a useful function in relation to the protection of human subjects. However, many potential respondents in our study, who would otherwise have agreed to participate, refused to do so when they were asked to sign the consent form. Seemingly, they could not reconcile the guarantee of anonymity with the necessity to sign an informed consent form. This problem again was particularly damaging to study efforts in urban Cleveland, urban Los Angeles, and suburban Los Angeles.

Notes

1. Blackwell, James E., Sharpley, Robert and Hart, Philip S., *Health Needs of Urban Blacks.* Cambridge, Mass.: Solomon Fuller Institute, 1978, p. 3.
2. Gordon, Milton, *Assimilation in Urban Life.* New York: Oxford University Press, 1964.
3. DuBois, W.E.B., *Souls of Black Folk.* Chicago: A.C. McClure, 1908.
4. A recent Harris poll indicates that black leaders feel more strongly about the issue of school desegregation than does the black population in general. For the black population in general, jobs are the main concern. For black leaders, school desegregation is the main concern.
5. Blackwell, et al., *Op. Cit.* in terms of futurism from a popular culture standpoint, blacks are close to invisible. This seems to reflect in popular culture a pessimistic view of the future of blacks.
6. Black Americans as a group disproportionately suffer from hypertension. (Cf. *Ibid.*).

7.   Cf. Poussaint, Alvin, *Why Blacks Kill Blacks*. New York: Emerson Hall, 1972, and "Black on Black Crime," *EBONY* (Special Issue, August 1979).

8.   Blackwell, James E., *The Black Community: Diversity and Unity*. New York: Harper & Row (originally published by Dodd, Mead & Company), 1975, Chapter 10. See also Cruse, Harold, *The Crisis of the Negro Intellectual*. New York: William Morrow,1967.

9.   Blackwell, et al., *Op. Cit.*, p. 4. For use of the macro-and-micro-concepts in an organizational and community analysis framework, see also Hart, Philip S., *Problems in Organizational Renewal*, Unpublished Ph.D. Dissertation, Michigan State University, Department of Sociology, 1974. This dissertation was cited by C. Sower in "An Experimental Sociology of Institutional Renewal," *Rural Sociology*. 41:1 (Spring 1976) as a major component in the sociology of institutional change.

10. Yette, Samuel F., *The Choice: The Issue of Black Survival in America*. New York. G.P. Putnam and Sons, 1971, p. 31.

11. Blackwell, et al., *Op. Cit.* 1978.

12. Alienation consists of measures of anomie, powerlessness and social isolation as defined by scales in this research.

13. The Solomon Fuller Institute, Cambridge, Massachusetts, a non-profit research and education organization, was the recipient of the research grants. The Center for Minority Group Mental Health Programs, National Institute of Mental Health, was the granting agency. The initial study, conducted in Boston, was grant number MH27815, entitled "Health Needs of Urban Blacks and Policy Implications." The second study entitled "Health Needs, Priorities, and Alienation Among Blacks," was grant number MH 32239-01. This grant allowed the research team to conduct field work in Atlanta, Cleveland, Houston and Los Angeles.

14. Blackwell, et al., *Op. Cit*, p. 6

15. Myrdal, Gunnar, *An American Dilemma*. New York: Harper & Row, 1944.

16. *Ibid.*, pp. 60-61.

17. Logan, Rayford, *What The Negro Wants*. Chapel Hill, N.C.: North Carolina University Press, 1944.

18. *Ibid.*, Passim.

19. Blackwell, et al., *Op. Cit.*, p. 7.

20. Banks, W.S.M., "Rank Order of Sensitivity to Discrimination," *American Sociological Review* 15(1950), pp. 294-303.

21. Edmunds, Edwin R., "The Mydalian Thesis: Rank Order of Discrimination," *Phylon 15* (1954), 247-303.

22. Ebony, *Op. Cit.*, 1979.

23. National Urban League, *The Black Pulse Survey Report*. Washington, D.C.: Research Department, National Urban League, 1980.

24. Black Enterprise Magazine, *Black Americans Speak Out: A Black Enterprise Survey*. New York: Earl C. Graves Publishing Company, 1980.

25. Clark, Kenneth C. and Clark, Mami, "What Black Americans Think of Themselves," *Ebony*. Chicago: Johnson Publishing Company, November 1980.

26. National Urban League, *Op. Cit.*

27. Black Enterprise Magazine, *Op. Cit.*

28. Clark And Clark, *Op. Cit.*

29. Srole, Leo, "Social Integration and Certain Correlates: An Exploratory Study," *American Sociological Review* 21:5 (1956), pp. 709-716.

30. Cf. Seeman, Melvin, "On the Meaning of Alienation," *American Sociological Review*

24(1959), pp. 783-791; _____, "On The Personal Consequences of Aliena-
tion in Work," *American Sociological Review* 32 (1967), pp. 273-285;
_____, "Powerlessness and Knowledge: A Comparative Study of Alienation
and Learning," *Sociometry* 39(1967), 106-125; _____, "Alienation and
Engagement," in Angus Campbell and P.E. Converse (eds.). *The Human Meaning of
Social Change.* Ann Arbor: University of Michigan Press, 1971: _____.
"Some Themes in the Alienation Perspective: A Commentary on Toch," *Journal of Com-
munity Psychology* 7(1979), pp. 12-17, _____," *The Urban Alienation:
Some Dubious Theses From Marx to Marcuse,*" *Journal of Personality and Social
Psychology* 19:2 (1971), pp. 135-143.

31. Gurin, Patricia and Gurin, Gerald, "Internal-External Control in the Motivational
Dynamics of Negro Youth," *Journal of Social Issues* 26(1969), pp. 29-55.

32. Cf. Seeman, *Op. Cit.,* and Nettler, Gwynn. "A Measure of Alienation," *American
Sociological Review* 22:6 (1957), pp. 670-677, and _____, "Anti-Social
Sentiment and Criminality," *American Sociological Review* 24: 2 (1959), pp. 202-208,
and Dean, D., "Alienation: Its Meaning and Measurement," *American Sociological
Review* 26 (October 1961), pp. 753-758.

33. Middleton, Russell, "Alienation, Race and Education," *American Sociological Review* 28
(December 1963), pp. 973-977.

34. Phillibur, William, "Patterns of Alienation in Inner City Ghettos," *Human Relations* 39
(April 1977), pp. 303-310.

35. Gordon, D., "A Note on Negro Alienation," *American Journal of Sociology* 70 (January
1965), pp. 477-478.

36. Willie, Charles Vert, "Education, Deprivation and Alienation," *Journal of Negro Education* 34 (Summer 1965), pp. 209-219.

37. Dubey, S.N. and Grant, M.L., "Powerlessness Among Disadvantaged Blacks,"
Casework 51 (May 1970), pp. 285-290.

38. Black. Gerald H., "Alienation-Black and White, or the Uncommitted Revisited," *Journal
of Social Issues* 251 (August 1969), pp. 129-141.

39. Bullough, Bonnie, "Alienation in the Ghetto," *American Journal of Sociology* 72
(March1967), pp. 469-478.

40. *Ibid.*

41. Wilson, Robert A. "Anomie and Militancy Among Urban Negroes: A Study of
Neighborhood and Individual Effects," *Sociological Quarterly* 12:369-386.

42. _____, "Anomie in the Ghetto: A Study of Neighborhood Type, Race and
Anomie," *American Journal of Sociology* 77 (July 1971), pp. 66-88.

43. Kerner, Otto, *Report of the National Advisory Commission on Civil Disorders.* New
York: The New York Times, Bantam Books, 1968.

44. Among the statistical areas that the U.S. Census Bureau collects and publishes data are
four census regions consisting of Northeast, South, North Central, and West. The
metropolitan areas included in this study are representative of these census regions.

45. The field supervisor for Boston was Robert Sharpley, Solomon Fuller Institute in Cambridge; in Atlanta, Wiley Bolden of Georgia State University was the field supervisor. In
Cleveland, Butler Jones of Cleveland State University, served in this role. James Kelsaw of
the University of Houston was the field supervisor in that city. In Los Angeles, Belinda
Tucker, Center for Afro-American Studies at UCLA, was the field supervisor.

46. Computer programming technical asistance was provided by Michael Forte, Harvard
University and the Educational Development Center, Newton, Massachusetts.

47. Bailar, Barbara A. and Lanphier, C. Michael, *Development of Survey Methods to Assess Survey Practices.* Washington, D.C.: American Statistical Association, 1978, 1.1.

48. Costello, Joan, "Research in the Black Community," University of Chicago, *Journal of Education* (Special Edition, 1973), p. 497.

49. Cf. Grimshaw, Allen (ed). *Racial Violence in the United States.* Chicago: Aldine Publishing Company., 1969.

50. Cf. Mitford, Jessica, "Experiments Behind Bars: Doctors, Drug Companies, and Prisoners," *Atlantic Monthly* (March 1972), pp. 64-73, and America, Richard, "Public Research and Racism; The Case of the Racist Researchers," *The Black Law Journal* October 1971), pp. 77-85.

51. Costello, *Op. Cit.*

52. The Community Research Review Committee reviewed the pilot study proposal prior to the fieldwork. The CRRC approved of the project. The CRRC began as a spinoff from the Community-University Center (Joint Center) for Inner City Change, a Ford Foundation and NIMH funded project.

53. Much of the foregoing discussion is from Philip S. Hart, "Community Research Review Committee: An Historical and Contemporary Perspective on Research in Black Communities," paper presented to the Association for the Study of Afro-American Life and History, New York City, October, 1973.

54. In fact, one of our middle-aged female field interviewers in urban Cleveland reported that she was chased off the property by a gun-wielding black adult male. This case obviously was extreme, but it represents the general hostility accorded our field interviewers in urban Cleveland.

55. As of June 1981, twenty-eight young blacks had been murdered in Atlanta over a relatively short period of time. It is assumed by Atlanta authorities that the child-killings began in May 1979. Undoubtedly, field surveys begun in Atlanta *after* May 1979 have met serious difficulties in gaining entrance to homes for the purpose of securing an interview due to the expected paranoia that resulted from these murders.

CHAPTER 2

A Profile of Five Cities

As suggested in Chapter I, the cities selected for this study were chosen for very special reasons. They represent essentially different regions of the country and the areas of the nation in which a substantial proportion of the black population resides. Although each city is distinctive or unique in some of its special features, collectively, Atlanta, Boston, Cleveland, Houston and Los Angeles have a great deal in common. For instance, each has a significant numerical proportion of blacks in its metropolitan area. Although blacks in these metropolitan areas tend to be concentrated within more or less self-contained sub-communities within the city limits, especially within the older, central city areas, an increasing number of blacks have moved into their adjacent or nearby suburban communities.

Like white migrants to the city, whether from other cities and towns or from nearby rural communities, blacks were pulled into these cities by the promise, hope and aspiration for economic prosperity, educational opportunities, cultural enrichment and, perhaps, a better quality of life. Similarly, for those blacks who moved into suburban communities, the motivations were in part conditions and factors not necessarily indistinct from those motivations found among white migrants to suburbs. Both groups undoubtedly moved to new residential areas in search of better housing provided in suburban communities, or school systems with facilities and educational programs perceived capable of meeting the needs of their children, or by some external evidence of status attainment.

However, blacks and whites may differ widely on the degree to which such factors as escape from the racial strife and turmoil of cities, or to circumvent busing for school desegregation played in the decision to re-locate to a particular suburban community. Greater agreement may be observed among the two groups on the salience of the "safety issue" (escape from city

23

crime) for reaching a decision to move to suburbia. This study does not address these issues with the specificity required to make definitive judgments concerning such motivations. Hence, assumptions about commonalities or discontinuities between blacks on the emotionally laden issues of busing, avoidance of racial strife, and crime are based entirely upon what the black participants in the study reported and empirical evidence drawn from related literature.

During the 1960's, however, each of the five cities was the scene of some form of racial confrontation, interracial strife and social turbulence. Neither emerged from that period of widespread unrest and upheaval without having undergone important social changes which ultimately affected the pattern of race relations within the metropolitan community. For instance, Los Angeles had its Watts. Cleveland had its "shoot-outs." Boston had its central city riots. All were scenes of often hostile, tumultuous encounters between blacks, the police, and other representatives of the "white power structure," and defenders of the special interests of the dominant white population. Yet, each city was the recipient of significant infusions of federal dollars to develop new "Great Society" programs or to strengthen existing social and economic strategies designed to improve the education, economic, political and health status of black residents.

This chapter presents a brief introduction to the changing status of blacks in each of the five cities studied. While not intended to represent a definitive characterization of the historical and social experiences of blacks, each profile serves the heuristic function of establishing a context in which the study was conducted.

Blacks in Atlanta

The City of Atlanta has undergone dramatic transformations within the past two decades. Race-baiting politicians, who swept into power on promises to perpetuate segregation and white supremacy, are gone. That brand of politics has been consistently repudiated by the citizenry in most elections since 1968. The overt manifestations of racism and discrimination do not appear to be as blatant as they once were prior to and during the two decades of civil rights activism. Atlanta now labels itself "the city, too busy to hate."

Atlanta is a city characterized by a high degree of political activism among blacks, an immense variety of educational and cultural opportunities, and rapid commercial and industrial development. Atlanta is the home of Nobel Prize Winner and famed civil rights leader, Dr. Martin Luther King. It is the home of civil rights activist, Julian Bond, the first black elected to the State House of Representatives in the twentieth century. It is the residence of Andrew Young, the first black elected to the U.S. House of Representatives from a Southern State in the twentieth century and former U.S. Ambassador to the United Nations.* It is the headquarters of the Voter Registration Project and of the Southern Christian Leadership Conference.

Atlanta boasts a large number of colleges and universities. These include: the Atlanta University complex: (Spelman College, Morehouse College, Clark College, Morris Brown College, Interdenominational Theological Seminary and Atlanta University), Emory University, Georgia Institute of Technology (Georgia Tech), Atlanta Junior College, and others.

The city prides itself on its rapid industrial commercial and business growth and expansion. The industrial growth is evident in the expansion of Peachtree Plaza, the downtown commercial and business center, which includes high rise hotels, the Omni, an immense variety of business establishments and large banks both within the plaza and the major downtown area. The city counts several prominent blacks in its list of successful business entrepreneurs — bankers, insurance company, newspaper, and construction firm owners, engineers, and travel agents.

The city has numerous impressive residential areas with commodious houses, landscaped lawns, spacious lots, and clean streets. Yet, all these things — the industrial development, renewal of the downtown section, the existence of educational and cultural opportunities and handsome houses of the middle-and-well-to-do classes — mask the presence of a number of enormously disturbing problems that the city presently faces.

Perhaps, the most public of all of Atlanta's problems is the extraordinarily high prevalence of violent crime in the city. For instance, within a period of some fifteen months between 1979 – 81, 28 young blacks disappeared from city streets or their homes and were murdered. The incidence of violent crime was so high in 1979 that State troopers were brought into the city to relieve city police officers from traffic duties so that more of them could be assigned to the job of fighting serious crime in the city. Relations between the police department of Atlanta and the citizenry are not, however, cordial, according to many. The crisis precipitated by the disappearance and murder of the 28 young blacks has encouraged a resurgence of improved relations, and inter-racial cooperation and com-

---

*In November 1981, Young defeated a white candidate for Mayor of Atlanta, subsequently succeeding another black person, Maynard Jackson.

munication between the elected officials and citizens.

Atlanta has a black mayor and a number of black elected and appointed officials. The outgoing mayor, Maynard Jackson, who comes from one of the city's elite families within the black community, has often identified Atlanta's major sources of crime as unemployment, uncontrolled inflation, lack of effective gun controls, and the immense drug traffic. In addition to the mayor, the commissioner of public safety is black. In fact, a black male has served in this position since 1974 when public pressure forced the incumbent white commissioner to resign.

According to 1978 data, Atlanta's racial composition has shifted from a predominantly white population to one that is over 60 percent black. The total population is estimated at 460,000. Fifty-four percent of Atlanta's population is female. Slightly more than one-third (34 percent) of the population is under 25 years of age and a little more than one-fifth (22 percent) is 55 years of age or older.[1]

In addition to crime, Atlanta faces problems which affect a significant cross section of its residents. Perceptions of these problems, as well as what conditions that may be identified as problems, may vary across a number of dimensions elucidated in this analysis.

Blacks in Boston

Prior to the anti-busing crisis that erupted in Boston during the mid-seventies, many Americans outside Boston regarded Boston as the most liberal and egalitarian city in the United States. It's reputation derived in great part from the presence of 67 colleges and universities, including Harvard and the Massachusetts Institute of Technology (M.I.T.), the historic role which Boston played in the American Revolution and in the antislavery movement, and the participation of many of its white citizens in civil rights causes outside the city itself. Most non-Bostonians had no real conception of the deep-seated racial antagonisms and ethnic separation which governed day-to-day relationships in Boston. Most non-Bostonians were unaware of the existence of two Bostons: on the one hand, it is the city of education, the repository of revolutionary history; on the other hand, it is a city characterized by racial isolation, neighborhood segregation, class distinctions and divisions, neglect and poverty, institutionalized discrimination, political exploitation, abuse of political power, and fear.

In January, 1981, *Marketing and Media Decisions* proclaimed Boston to be "reemerging as a world class city" and that Boston, once widely admired as the "hub of the universe" and "the Athens of America" after falling on hard times, was bounding back to a position of respect.[2] Explicit in this viewpoint were certain specific features of the public's perception of Boston: (1) its physical charm, (2) educational facilities, (3) industrial redevelopment, (4) world renowned health and hospital facilities, and (5) its cultural attributes.

Boston's "physical charm" is expressed in its distinctive architectural style, historic landmarks such as Faneuil Hall, Beacon Hill, the Old North Church, Bunker Hill Monument, the physical beauty of the Boston Commons, grave sites of leaders of the American Revolution, and the harbor and lakes of the city. Others think of the distinctive architecture expressed in its various triple decker houses, townhouses and mixtures of single-and-double- family homes.

Education in metropolitan Boston is "big business." There are approximately sixty-seven colleges and universities in the Greater Boston Area. Among these institutions are Harvard Univeristy, the Massachusetts Institute of Technology, Boston University, Boston College, The University of Massachusetts at Boston, Northeastern University, Simmons College, Tufts University, and Emerson College. According to one estimate, there are approximately 300,000 college and university students in metropolitan Boston. Therefore, it is estimated that one of every six people in the Greater Boston Area is a college student.[3] It is also believed that some 200,000 of these students spend $280 million per year over and beyond their tuition, room and board fees and that they are responsible for an additional $200 million in out-of-state financial aid. In addition, the institutions they attend attract about $480,000,000 in research funds to the city and state.[4] These institutions employ thousands of workers who live in Boston and nearby towns. Educational institutions also contribute to the economic growth of the city through their building programs and cultural activities.

A majority of students in Boston are never exposed to the "other Boston." The college student's world is restricted to the university environment, which is largely white, and to the cultural community. Entertainment pursuits often lead them to conclude that "Boston is the most liveable city" in the United States. Perhaps, it is so, at least from the perspective of some white Bostonians and temporary residents.

Government and business officials claim that Boston is in a period of economic and industrial rejuvenation. This economic growth is in direct contrast to the dismal picture of economic life pervasive during the early and mid-seventies when a vast number of engineering firms were victims of NASA cutbacks and the recession of that period. In the late seventies, the rejuvenation was spurred on by the movement of a number of electronics firms into the Boston area. Among these were Wang Laboratories, Digital Equipment Corporation, Data General and many other computer firms. Because of the expansiveness of their operations, these companies have generated thousands of jobs for residents of metropolitan Boston, including some neighborhoods in the black community. Industrial parks were constructed which, in turn, fostered economic growth and development in these areas. In addition, large-scale economic benefits are currently derived from the John Hancock and Prudential Insurance companies in Boston.

Another major component of the city's economic base is the medical-health care industry. Among the facilities which comprise this industry are the New England Medical Center, Boston City Hospital, Massachusetts General Hospital, Beth Israel, Boston University Medical Center, Peter Bent Brigham, Deaconess, Children's, Tufts University Hospital, Lahey Clinic, and the Massachusetts Eye and Ear Hospital. These medical centers are known throughout the world for the leadership roles that they have played in health care, medical advances and in spearheading trends in the development of medical technology. In addition, there are 22 neighborhood health centers distributed strategically in various Boston communities.[5] The continuous construction of health facilities is another contributing factor toward the economic roles performed by the health care industry in Boston.

Boston is widely known for its cultural richness represented by such institutions as the Boston Symphony, the Boston Pops, which was associated for more than 50 years with the name of Arthur Fiedler, the Museum of Fine Arts, and others.

There is, however, another world found among the 599,062 residents of the city. The second Boston is comprised of rigidly constructed and controlled, tightly knit neighborhoods in which life is almost totally dictated by a distorted *gemeinschaft*, a sense of territoriality and fierce loyalty to the residential community. These neighborhoods are like turfs that may be absolutely off-limits to "those who do not belong." These "sub-communities" have names like South Boston, Charlestown, East Boston, North End, West Roxbury, South End, Dorchester (North and South), Roxbury and Mattapan. In most communities, which are over 90 percent white, strangers are not welcomed, especially if they are minorities. Fear and suspicion of "outsiders" prevails in most Boston communities regardless of racial and ethnic composition. Consequently, it is extremely difficult for individual residents to establish extra-community networks because they are bound by an ethic of loyalty to their own locale. This situation spawns

racial isolation, separation, animosities, strife and misunderstandings, in-
transigence with regard to outreach activities of an inter-racial nature, fears
about themselves or of their interaction with people from "the outside," and
a ubiquitous fear of crime.

The estimated 1980 population of Boston was 599,062. According to
data released by the U.S. Census Bureau, the white population diminished
by one-fourth between 1970 and 1980. In 1970, the white population was
524,709. The black population then was 104,707. By 1980, however, the
white population had declined by 25 percent or to 393,937, but the black
population had increased slightly to more than one-fifth (21 percent) or to
126,229. In 1980, Boston's population was 70 percent white, 22 percent
black and 8 percent Hispanic/others. A decade earlier, the population was
82 percent white, 16 percent black and 2 percent Hispanic.[6]

Although many whites and blacks continue to move outside the city to
the neighboring suburbs, approximately 93 percent of black Bostonians live
in one of five contiguous sections of the city; Fenway/Kenmore, South
End, Roxbury, Dorchester and Mattapan. The remaining 7 percent of
blacks in metropolitan Boston are distributed in such nearby towns as
Newton, Brookline, Natick and Needham.[7] In none of the nearby towns
which ring Boston is the black population any greater than 3 percent of
total population. In many of them, the black population comprises less than
1 percent or there are no blacks living in the towns at all.*

For instance, according to the Boston Redevelopment Authority
Household Survey, there are absolutely no black residents in such Boston
neighborhoods as East Boston, Charlestown, and South Boston. Blacks
comprise one percent of the neighborhood communities of Roslindale,
Back Bay/Beacon Hill and Central. On the other hand, in the areas of the
city in which blacks are in the majority, such as Mattapan and Roxbury,
the white population of these neighborhoods is 11 and 8 percent, respectively.[8] The suburban towns of Newton and Brookline, from which the
suburban sample for this study was drawn, have a black population of
about 1 percent each. In each case, this percentage translates into a population figure of about 1,200 black persons.

That other side of Boston, from the perspective of many black
residents and visitors, is a city whose raw racism has been exposed by efforts to create a desegregated school system out of a system considered by

---

*Cambridge is a notable exception to this generalization. However, if one examines the racial
composition of suburbs located 15 miles or farther from Boston, the proportion of blacks is
considerably higher than that found in closer suburbs (e.g. Brockton (5.2 percent), Sharon (2.7
percent) and Stoughton (2.4 percent).

the courts as deliberately segregated. The manisfestations of that racism are evident in the lack of freedom of movement of blacks from one part of the city to another. For example, a black college professor, newly arrived in the city, was attempting to find her way from her campus back to her residence in the South End. Suddenly, she was stopped in her car by police in two patrol cars and was asked, "Do you know where you are?" Her reply was negative but that she was attempting to read her map to ascertain her location. The police officers informed her that she was in South Boston and that since it was not safe for blacks; they "would escort her out of the neighborhood."

The inability to take advantage of recreational activities is another example of the lack of freedom to move from one place to another. Many blacks report reluctance to attend baseball games at Fenway Park (the home of the Boston Red Sox, a team that does not have a commendable reputation for racial integration) or basketball games played by the Boston Celtics in the Boston Garden and, to a lesser degree, football games played by the New England Patriots in Foxboro Stadium because of fear of racially motivated physical assaults and verbal abuse.

Unprovoked physical attacks against black visitors to historic Bunker Hill Monument have now made that site all but off-limits to blacks unless they are part of a guided Grey Line Tour. Random attacks against blacks walking across the City Hall Plaza have made many blacks leary of groups of two or more white youths walking near them. Random attacks against individual blacks and inter-racial groups of Navy men assigned to the Charlestown Navy Yard, and a sniper attack that paralyzed an innocent black youth playing a football game on a Fall afternoon, have convinced many that wanton, senseless attacks, though often episodic in nature, are symptomatic of a deeply rooted racism in the city. Consequently, an untold number of black individuals have turned down jobs in Boston because they do not perceive it as a "liveable city for blacks."

Blacks in Metropolitan Cleveland

For most of this century, Cleveland was regarded by black Americans as one of the most liberal cities in the United States. This reputation was built upon a positive racial climate, job opportunities for blacks in the city, the political and social integration of blacks into the community life, and a certain amount of residential integration on the east side of the city. As a result of this perception, when the great exodus of blacks from the South began circa 1915, blacks flocked to Cleveland from such southern and border states as Kentucky, West Virginia, Tennessee, Alabama, Mississippi, Arkansas and, to a lesser degree, from the Carolinas.

Blacks found jobs in the steel mills, manufacturing firms, rubber-production, and in the auto industry. Many opened their own businesses, particularly in the service areas, to fulfill the needs of a growing black community. They went to such high schools as East, East Technical, John Hay, John Adams, Glenville and Collingwood — all on the east Side — since blacks were never welcomed on the western side of the Cuyahoga River. Many went to one of the colleges in metropolitan Cleveland, to Ohio State University, to one of the many private colleges in Ohio, or to a black college. Many became professionals, entrepreneurs, and highly skilled employees. Hence, a clearly defined social stratification system emerged within the black community of Cleveland.

At first, blacks concentrated in the areas south of Cleveland's main thoroughfare, Euclid Avenue, which stretches from downtown Public Square east to 116th Street. Eventually, ethnic succession was completed in these neighborhoods. Between World War I and World War II, blacks migrated to the Glenville area in which a substantial proportion of the Jewish population was concentrated. From these two sections, blacks began to follow the paths of Jews into Mt. Pleasant, Wade Park, East Cleveland, Cleveland Heights, Shaker Heights and other suburban communities, particularly during and immediately after World War II. They also "invaded" Hough. As the white ethnic population succumbed to blockbusting and panic selling, the Hough area became a black ghetto by the mid-1960's. Hough and some sections of East Cleveland were the sites of major urban conflagrations and "shoot-outs" during the turbulent 1960's.

Over 90 percent of all blacks in metropolitan Cleveland live east of the Cuyahogo River which divides the city into its east and west sections. The east side is not only home to the overwhelming majority of blacks, it is also the section more heavily populated by Jews, Italians, and white Anglo-Saxon Protestants. West Cleveland is populated by middle-European white groups such as persons from Poland, the Slovakian and Balkan nations. These latter groups have traditionally been less receptive to the idea of residential integration with blacks.

The east side of Cleveland is the business, commercial and industrial center of the city. It is the locus of Cleveland's most historic and cultural landmarks, and most widely known educational institutions. This section has the historical Cleveland Museum of Art, Severance Hall — home of the

Cleveland Symphony Orchestra — both of which are situated next door to Case Western Reserve University and are sandwiched between an ever-expanding black neighborhood and Cleveland's Little Italy. Cleveland State University is on Cleveland's most famous street or avenue — Euclid Avenue — which is only a few minutes ride to the downtown section. The Cleveland Browns and Indians play in the municipal stadium situated on the east side of Lake Erie.

It is a grand old city, once known for its many tree-lined, spacious streets, comfortable houses, and cleanliness. This image was replaced by that of a city in near bankruptcy, fiscal and residential deterioration, a river that is so polluted from the refuge of the steel mills and manufacturing firms that "it can be burned," violent confrontations between blacks and the police force, and other urban problems. Yet, this city was among the first major cities in the nation to choose a black person as a mayor when Carl Stokes was elected to that position in 1967. It is the city that sent Louis Stokes to Congress, and it is a city in which blacks continue to play a major role in political and educational institutions.

In 1960, Cleveland was the eight largest city in the United States. Since that time, it has steadily lost its population to its adjacent and nearby suburbs. In 1970, the white population stood at 458,048; however, by 1980, the white population had declined to 307,284 at a loss of 33 percent. The 1970 black population was 287,841; by 1980, even the black population had dropped by 13 percent to 251,347. According to the U.S. Census Bureau, the 1980 population of 591,594 also included 17,772 Hispanics, and 15,211 classified as "other." Cleveland is one of several cities in the United States that will probably have a black majority by 1990.[9] These data show that two demographic patterns occurred during the seventies. First, immigration of blacks and whites slowed during the decade. Second, and equally significant, a substantial proportion of the black population moved into adjacent and nearby suburbs such as Cleveland Heights, Shaker Heights, Pepper Pike, Garfield Heights, Beachwood and others.

For many blacks who remain in the central city, especially on the east side, there are constant reminders of poverty, neglect, and urban decay. In 1980 black joblessness stood at 19 percent.* Many have become discouraged workers as a result of their futile efforts to find meaningful employment in any capacity. Much of the crime in the city is believed to be acquisitive or associated with the need to find some way, however illegal, to "survive."

---

*According to the Bureau of Labor Statistics, the joblessness rate for blacks and other minorities in metropolitan Cleveland was 19 percent in 1980.

Many persons engage in various sorts of "hustles" to earn sufficient food to feed the family and "to pay the rent." Many are trapped in inadequate housing-accommodations that readily reveal the years of neglect and abuse.

For other blacks in the central city, who may or may not be in poverty and who may not be middle-class urban residents, life is more than a matter of basic survival. Some are the poor and near poor who hope for the fulfillment of the American dream but are conscientious about keeping up their present homes and protecting their neighborhoods. Some are the well-educated and the well-off who are proud of their city and are intent on remaining in it because this "is where they belong."

In many ways, Cleveland is a divided city, not only geographically but also philosophically, and in terms of orientation to govenment, ideology, race and ethnicity. For many blacks, Cleveland is no longer the city that advertises itself as "the best location in the nation." It no longer offers unparalleled economic and educational opportunities to black people. Its central city school system no longer enjoys the national reputation for academic excellence as such schools as Glenville, John Adams and East Tehnical School enjoyed for generations. There is a major conflict over such issues as busing for school desegregation; however, public school quality began its decline long before busing became a political issue. In politics, allegations of misconduct by city officials and the bitter late 1970's mayoralty campaigns had a profound impact on city life. Racial and class hostilities, suspicion and fears spread with alarming speed in many parts of the city. It is in this context that the interviews were conducted in Cleveland in 1979-1980.

Houston: "The Brass Buckle on the Sunbelt"

To most Americans Houston is, undoubtedly, perceived as an oil-rich boomtown or in terms of its boosters' perceptions: "The Brass Buckle on the Sunbelt"[10]

The boomtown image of Houston stems from its reputation as one of the fastest growing cities in the United States. It also arises from the rapid industrial, commercial and technological expansion that the city has experienced during the past two decades.

The rapid population growth of Houston is immediately evident in basic statistics. In 1960, the city's population was about 958,000. By 1980, it was estimated to be 1.75 million.[11] The Houston Chamber of Commerce estimated a 37.8 percent increase in population between 1970 and 1979 from 1,232,802 to 1,699,000. In 1980, Houston was the fifth largest city in the United States.

This rapid growth in population can be attributed to Houston's sunbelt location, robust economic climate, comparatively low taxes and its "diversity of commerce and industry "which, in turn, facilitate a high rate of employment opportunities for white collar workers.[12] Although some of Houston's population growth resulted from increases in childbirths, a substantial proportion is the direct consequence of the practice of annexation. The city has enormous annexation powers which it uses frequently to incorporate suburban developments almost at will. As a result, the city acquires increasingly larger land areas and expands it tax base.[13]

The population of Houston is comprised primarily of white Anglos, Blacks and Hispanics. Hispanics represent 15.5 percent of the population, blacks comprise 23.8 percent and 60 percent of the population is represented by white anglos and other groups. The white population is decreasing in Houston while increasing at a fast rate in Harris County outside of the inner city 610 Loop (a highway surrounding downtown) and in suburban areas. The process of white population increase out of the city limits is not a recent phenomenon; rather, it was initiated during the WWII period. Most of the city's "area growth has occurred in the western portion of Harris county."[14]

Most blacks in metropolitan Houston live within the limits of Loop 610 — an area that coincides almost precisely with the 1940 city limits of Houston. This area is officially described as Houston's "inner city" and, population density is about 60 persons per residential acre compared to 14.4 persons per residential acre for the city as a whole. In 1976, the population within Loop 610 comprised about 38 percent of the total Houston population, down from 43.2 percent in 1970.[15] According to one estimate, minorities, most of whom live inside the Loop, total about 680,000 persons in Houston — a population that is larger than all but 12 cities of the United States.[16]

Despite the relatively high birth rate among blacks in Houston, the percentage of blacks in the total population is only slightly above its 1950 figure of 21 percent. The percentage in 1980 is below the 1970 figure of 26 percent black in the city's population. During the same period, the absolute number of blacks increased in the city. This fluctuation is explained by the rapid increase in the white and Mexican-American population induced by the annexation of predominantly white suburbs and by the in-migration and natural increases in the Chicano population.[17]

Diversification characterizes the booming economic life of Houston, and it is undoubtedly the central fact in the strength of the city's economy. Within this context, however, the dominant source of economic expansion is in the area of energy. The energy industry includes the manufacturing of petrochemicals and drilling equipment. Houston leads the world in this endeavor. Forty percent of the nation's petrochemicals are produced by the city's petrochemical complex. Twenty-four of the twenty-five largest oil companies have their management functions located in Houston. A significant number of the major U.S. natural gas pipeline companies are also headquartered in Houston.[18]

Further evidence of diversification in Houston's economy comes from trade, service and construction industries, technology and space, and international business. The Port of Houston is the nation's third largest port in the amount of tonnage handled. It is estimated that this port is responsible for approximately one-third of the economy in the Houston area because of the revenue produced and the number of jobs generated.[19] Construction and service industries account for another third of employment. The city's technological strengths are in medicine and in space. The Texas Medical Center is world renown for its research, treatment and educational facilities. The center employs almost 25,000 persons. The Lyndon B. Johnson Space Center is the central unit in America's space technology program, which includes manned-space flights. The diversification of the economy has also had its impact on international business. As a result, international banking has grown rapidly and 38 foreign banks were represented in Houston in 1978.[20]

The profile of a prospering and expanding Houston does not, however, provide a complete picture of life in this city. The non-prosperous derive little benefit from the "boomtown" atmosphere of the commercial and industrial sections or from well-to-do sections of the city, such as Bellaire and far western suburbs.

Central city residents inside Loop 610 have a higher unemployment rate and an annual income below that of the city as a whole. The situation is exacerbated by the outward migration of jobs from Loop 610 and the resulting difficulties in obtaining jobs. For many, housing and the quality of life in some neighborhoods are major problems. The local government often fails to deliver many needed services because of management ineptitude and bureaucratic bungling, both accounting for "the falling apart" characterization of Houston.[21]

Blacks in Los Angeles

Los Angeles is the third largest city in the United States. Its 1980 population was 3,782,752. Of this number, 1,666,683 are classified as white; 505,208 are black; 815,984 are Hispanics (primarily Mexican Americans); and 644,872 are classified as "other." Between 1970 and 1980, the city experienced a loss of white population, largely to neighboring suburbs and to Orange County. Specifically, the white population declined from 2,173,600 in 1970 to its present population of 1,666,683 or a loss of slightly more than a half million whites. However, the city showed a modest gain of approximately 2,000 blacks over its 1970 black population of 503,606. The largest gain in population groups between 1970 and 1980 was in the "other" category since only 138,555 persons were in this classification in 1970.

Although blacks are dispersed in many areas of the city, most blacks are concentrated in the central regions. Comparatively few blacks reside in such communities as Glendale, Alhambra, Bellflower, Torrance, Culver City, Malibu, Hollywood-Wilshire, and Whittier. Blacks, like other migrants in this rapidly growing city, are attracted to Los Angeles because of its location, industrial growth, and job opportunities, as well as its cultural life.

Interwoven as it is with the history of Mexico, early black Los Angeles history can be traced to the Archino General de la Nacin in Mexico City. According to Edgar Goff,* documentation exists in the towns, villages and states of Northwestern Mexico, which shows where descendants of black Moors, recruited from Spain and North Africa, migrated and settled. Eventually, they moved farther north into Southern California when the Spanish throne requested that Father Serra select sites for his mission in the northern province.

The 1790 census for California indicated that 20 percent of the adults were from Villa Sinaloa which is significant since most early black Californians were descendants of Villa Sinaloa. Pio Pico, the last Mexican Governor of California (1845-1846), was a Spanish-speaking black. Pio Pico's family was of mixed ancestry — mulattos, with Negroid characteristics, united with Indian, Spanish and African blends. One interesting aspect of this fragment of black Los Angeles history is that it reveals a close interconnection between blacks and Mexican culture. Numerically, blacks and Hispanics now represent more than one-third (35 percent) of the total population of Los Angeles, according to 1980 census data.

---

*The following historical summary is based upon Edgar Goff, "200 Years of Black California History," *California Eagle*, April, 1979, p. 13.

Beginning with the Great Depression of the 1930's, there was a relatively steady movement of blacks into Los Angeles until the end of World War II. The primary source of the black migrant population was the South. These blacks were lured to the city by better economic opportunities than were available to them in the southern states and by a more favorable climate. As a result of the influx of blacks during the Depression and in the World War II period, a large black community developed in metropolitan Los Angeles. However, the ratio of blacks to the total population of the area is substantially below that of the proportion of blacks in other cities such as Atlanta and Houston.

Blacks in Los Angeles, in time, developed a tradition of active participation in community affairs. Further, a significant professional class arose among the black population that became active in the political, social and economic life of the community. However, there are today large areas of the city, especially south central Los Angeles, in which a sizeable proportion of the black population resides, which are poverty-stricken and isolated from the broader community. Yet, the range of involvement of blacks in the life of the city is impressive among all social classes.

For instance, Thomas Bradley became the first black ever elected Mayor of Los Angeles in 1973. In 1981, his broad-based popularity, the exceptionally high margin of his victory for a third term as mayor, coupled with his low-key but highly effective managerial and leadership style, stimulated widespread speculation that he would become a strong candidate for governor of California in the next general election.

Black Angelenos have also had a long history of service on the City Council and the School Board. They have organized and maintained strong affiliated chapters of the major civil rights organizations, and established grass roots community organizations. One representative of the latter is the Watts Labor Community Action Committee (WLCAC) which has helped in many ways to strengthen the basic infrastructure of the black community.

Although blacks comprise only 18 percent of the population, black business has thrived in Los Angeles. Perhaps, the prime example of black business success is Motown Industries, transplanted from Detroit to Sunset Boulevard in Hollywood. In addition, the black banks, savings and loan associations, and insurance companies perform important services for a growing black community. However, the core of the visible entrepreneurial enterprise system in metropolitan Los Angeles is the entertainment industry. This industry has never developed a reputation for equality of opportunity across racial lines. Black ownership is inconsequential with respect to the ownership of movie studios, major production companies or in the distribution and exhibition of major motion pictures. Further, despite the plethora of acting talent among blacks, native or migrants to the city, only a handful of blacks have ever achieved stardom in Hollywood.

Two black newspapers flourish in the Los Angeles area. The California *Eagle* was founded in 1879, and is published as a tabloid. The Los Angeles *Sentinel* is younger and publicizes itself as the "largest black newspaper in the West."

As in the case of Atlanta, Boston, Cleveland and Houston, there is yet another face of Los Angeles which may not be immediately visible to the casual observer or to those who have lived in isolation from the city itself. There is a face of poverty, urban congestion, the urban poor and of the disillusioned and disenchanted. Fifteen years after the racial explosions in Watts and after millions of dollars allocated for the improvement of the economic and social life of its residents, many of the problems which produced the original conflict remain. Macro-community issues such as economic conditions, income maldistribution, quality of education offered, and political involvement are as crucial today as they were in 1965. Micro-community issues such as street crime, relations with the police, the delivery of social services and conditions of the city streets have not been resolved.

Blacks in Los Angeles, like blacks in the remaining four cities and like blacks and whites throughout the nation, are searching for effective strategies that will enable them to adjust to the myriad ramifications of inflation. Black Angelenos, like whites and blacks in most large cities of the United States are encountering educational problems of enormous significance, only some of which are induced by efforts to bring school systems into compliance with federal mandates or guidelines for school desegregation.

Clearly, these cities do show a number of commonalities. However, subsequent chapters will not only demonstrate such similarities but will also reveal the degree to which their individuality with respect to attitudes and behavior of their black residents emerges.

Notes

1.   Brown, Lee P., "Crime Specific Planning: The Atlanta Experience," *The Police Chief*, (July 1980), pp. 53-59.

2.   *Marketing and Media Decisions*. Boston: January, 1981, pp. 115-131.

3.   *Ibid.*

4.   *Ibid.*

5.   *Ibid.*   .

6.   Cited in John Herbers, "Census Finds More Blacks Living in Suburbs of Nation's Large Cities," *The New York Times*, May 31, 1981, p. 1, 48 and by Robert A. Jordan, "Boston's White Population Down 25%, Blacks Up 21%," *Boston Globe*, April 17, 1981, p. 1.

7.   Blackwell, James E., Robert Sharpley and Philip Hart, *Health Needs of Urban Blacks*. Cambridge, Mass.: Solomon Fuller Institute, 1978, p.16.

8.   Center for Survey Research, *The Racial Composition of Boston's Neighborhoods: The Boston Redevelopment Survey, 1980.* Boston: The Survey Research Center, 1980, (Prepared by Karen Burglass).

9.   Herbers, *Op. Cit.*

10. Burka, Paul, "Why Is Houston Falling Apart?" *Texas Monthly*, (November 1980), p. 189.

11. Houston City Planning Commission, *Houston: Year 2000.* City of Houston: Planning Commission, June 1, 1980, p. 13ff.

12. *Ibid.*

13. *Ibid.*

14. *Ibid.*

15. *Ibid.*

16. *Ibid.*

17. *Ibid.*

18. Cf. Houston Chamber of Commerce, "Houston Facts," January 1, 1979, Texas Employment Commission, *Annual Planning Report, Houston Texas SMSA*, May 1978, p. 24, and Houston Planning Commission, *Op. Cit.*, pp. 111-115.

19. *Ibid.*

20. *Ibid.*

21. *Ibid.*

22. Herbers, *Op. Cit.*

CHAPTER 3

Critical Issues in the Black Community:
A National Profile

This chapter, will examine the issues and concerns identified in this study as most urgent to the five city participants. The analysis is based upon the aggregate responses of participants from Boston, Atlanta, Houston, Cleveland and Los Angeles. Special attention is given to certain demographic characteristics, and a rank order of the priorities or urgent needs specified by the participants in relationship to the demographic characteristics.

Characteristics of the Participants

Of the 945 persons who provided usable data, their residential distribution was as follows: 296 (31.5 percent) from Boston; 248 (26.1 percent) from Houston; 228 (24.1 percent) from Atlanta; 106 (11.2 percent) from Cleveland, and 67 or 7.5 percent of the participants were residents of the Los Angeles area. In all instances, the numbers cited include both suburban and central city residents. However, 72 percent of the participants were urban residents while 28 percent lived in suburban communities within the metropolitan areas of the cities studied. The concentration of blacks in urban areas reported in this study is somewhat below U.S. Census data which show that approximately 81 percent of all black Americans reside in urban communities.*

More than four of every ten participants (43.8 percent) were either

---

*This difference is due to the over sampling of blacks in suburbs for this study. As a result, the percentage of black urban residents was below the national average.

natives of the city or of the state in which they were interviewed. About four of every ten (40.2 percent) were born in the South while 7.7 percent were natives of the Northeast and 4.3 percent were born in the Midwest or in the Northwestern States. Only 3.1 percent were born outside the United States and .09 percent were natives of the Western States.

Residential stability was measured by the question: How long have you lived in this city? The responses indicated a high degree of stability among this group. For instance, almost six of every ten (59.2 percent) had lived in their present cities 16 years or longer. Another 13.5 percent had resided in the same city between 11 and 15 years; still another 13.8 percent had been residents of the same city between six and ten years, and 19.4 percent were there for one to five years. Only 3.2 percent were recent migrants; that is, they had lived in the city less than one year.

However, when these respondents were asked, "How long have you lived at your present address?," intra-city residential stability was also observed. Almost one-half of them (47.4 percent) had lived at the same address five years or less and within this group 11.3 percent had lived at the same address for less than one year. Slightly less than one-fourth (23.1 percent) had resided at the same address between six and ten years and 29.4 percent were residents of the same dwelling for 11 years or longer. Hence, it is quite probable that this group of participants had developed a high degree of attachment to their cities and, perhaps, significant social bonds within their own neighborhoods. However, the power of neighborhood attachment among these respondents cannot be completely discerned by responses to the questions on length of residence within the city or at the present address because no information was obtained as to whether or not those persons who moved frequently did so from one house to another located in the same neighborhood or to a different one.

Sex and Marital Status: More than one half, (55.2 percent), of the participants were female and 44.8 percent were male. Some 45.1 percent were presently married; 13.5 percent were divorced. Another 10.2 percent reported that they were separated but not divorced; 10.1 percent were widowed, and slightly more than one fifth (21.2 percent) were single and never married. It may be noted at this point that, according to the United States Bureau of the Census, the divorce rate among black Americans is rising. Between 1970 and 1980, the divorce rate among black males increased by 144 percent and that for black women rose equally as sharply by 147 percent. Black men and women in 1980 had a combined divorce rate of 203 per 1,000 which more than doubled the 92 divorces per 1,000 among white Americans. As a group, black men showed a divorce rate in 1980 of 151 per

1,000 married black men while black women showed a divorce rate of 257 divorces per 1,000 black women. In 1970, the divorce rate for black men was 62 per 1,000 while that for black women was 104 per 1,000. The 1970 rate for white men was 32 per 1,000 which more than doubled to 74 per 1,000 in 1980. The rate also doubled for white women between 1970 (56 per 1,000) and 1980 (104 per 1,000).[1] Hence, the marital status of participants in this study was not indistinguishable from national patterns. It is important to note, too, that about four-fifths of all respondents had some direct experience with the institution of marriage.

Family Structure and Authority: By a slim percentage margin, a greater proprotion (35.4 percent) of the subjects indicated that the head of the family household was male. Some 31.4 percent indicated that a female headed the household and 23.3 percent stated that the family was egalitarian, headed by both husband and wife. This percentage (31.4) approximates the U.S. Census estimation of 35 percent female-headed families in the black population.[2] When the question of who is the household head was posed without sex identification, 58.7 percent responded that "it is headed by me" but only 9.4 percent stated that the household was headed by his or her spouse and the same percent (23.2) characterized the family as egalitarian. Interestingly, 8.7 percent reported that the head of the family was a family member other than the respondent or the spouse.

Two-parent families were found in over half (52.4 percent) of all households but 47.6 percent were classified as "single-parent" families as distinguished from female or male-headed families. In these instances, the single parent could have been either male or female. The number of one-parent families in this group was substantially greater than the proportion of such families in the nation as a whole. According to a 1979 report of the U.S. Department of Commerce, about one in every five American families with children is a one-parent family. Not only has the number and percentage of these households increased since 1970, but their composition has also changed. Specifically, more fathers are heads of one-parent families than ever before.[3]

Age: One third (33 percent) of the participants were classified as "young;" that is to say that their age range was between 18 and 30. Slightly less than one half (46.3 percent) were called "middle-aged" since they ranged from 31 to 50. Another one-fifth (20.6 percent) were labeled "older persons" since they ranged in age from 51 to 65 or older (in a few instances). However, both the mean and median age computed was 29 years for these participants. If this group appeared to be somewhat older than expected, that fact may be attributed to the exclusion of all persons below the age of 18 from participation in the study. One obvious shortcoming of this decision was the elimination of both single and two-parented teenage families from the study.

Education: The mean number of years of schooling completed by the participants approximated the national average of 12.1 years for black Americans. Only 12 percent reported a schooling level of zero to eleven years but 50.2 percent indicated the completion of high school and/or some post-secondary education such as clerical training, bookkeeping and drafting. This group was classified as the "medium" level in contrast to the previous group of "low" educational attainment. More than a third (37.8 percent) were designated as having achieved a "high level" of education since they had completed either some college training, graduated from college or held a professional degree.

Occupation: Table 3 shows the occupational distribution of the participants. Of the 919 persons who answered the question on present occupation, slightly more than one-fifth (20.9 percent) were employed in service jobs; slightly less than one fifth (19.8 percent) held jobs in the crafts, and almost one-fifth (19.5 percent) were classified as "profesional, self-employed." Another 15.7 percent were employed in clerical positions and only 6.5 percent were in managerial and sales positions. The unemployment rate among this group, which was 11.4 percent, approximated the national unemployment rate of black adults in 1979 which was 11.5 percent, not including the discouraged workers who have given up the struggle to find meaningful employment. Somewhat more than six of every one hundred (6.0 percent) received a pension of some sort or social security benefits.

When pensioners and the unemployed were excluded from this analysis, a different occupational distribution profile emerged. Although more than 31 percent were employed in professional, managerial and sales positions, almost one half (49.4 percent) reported essentially blue-collar and working class occupations in the crafts and service categories. About one-fifth (19 percent) held clerical positions. Despite their educational attainment, the participants in this study, like blacks in general, were all too frequently employed in positions for which remuneration was low compared to the incomes earned by the white population.

Employment: More than three-fifths of the participants were employed in full-time positions (61.3 percent) and less than one in ten (8.0 percent) worked in part-time jobs. The unemployment rate of 11.4 percent was about the rate reported by the Department of Commerce or the Bureau

Table 3. Occupational Distribution by Category, Number and Percent
(National Profile)

Occupational Category	N	Percent	Percent in Category After Removal of Pension & Unemployment	
Professional,				
Self-employment	179	19.5	23.6	
Managerial, Sales	60	6.5	7.9	
Clerical	144	15.7	19.0	
Crafts	182	19.8	24.0	
Service	192	20.9	25.4	
Pension, SS	57	6.2	—	
Unemployment	105	11.4	—	
Total	919	100.0	100	N = 757

of Labor Statistics. The unemployment rate among black adults was 13.1 percent in 1977; 12.4 percent in 1978; 11.5 percent in 1979, and 14.2 percent in 1980.[4] The unemployment rate reported by this group is further evidence that blacks are about twice as likely to be unemployed as are white adults. Another 14.2 percent of the participants indicated that their principal sources of income were pension, retirement and social security benefits.

The employment status of black adults is precarious. When participants were asked how long they had been employed in their current job, over one-third of them responded less than two years (35.6 percent). About one-fifth had been on the same job in each of the categories of 25 months to 5 years, 6 to 10 years and 11 to 15 years, respectively. However, only two-tenths of one percent of this group stated that they had remained in the same job longer than 15 years.

The degree of occupational mobility which may be gleaned from information presented in Table 3 may reflect a tendency to move to positions which provide better conditions, improved wages and salaries, and opportunites for occupational advancement. For some, this mobility pattern stems from the necessity to find new jobs resulting from job loss. In this sense, the occupational behavior of blacks is indistinguishable from that among whites and other Americans. People often change jobs for similar reasons irrespective of the race factor.

Inasmuch as a substantial percentage of the participants were in single-parent families, an effort was made to ascertain the type of child care arrangements made during the working hours. The day care movement was launched during the 1960's and was facilitated significantly by those aspects of Great Society legislation which enabled more mothers to obtain gainful employment. However, evidence shows that black parents of young children are not particularly inclined to use day care facilities while they work. Only one-fifth (21 percent) of all persons who had young children and who worked sent these children to day care centers.

About seventeen percent (17.4) reported that older children were utilized for child care services in the absence of a working single-parent. Another 14.8 percent indicated that grandparents cared for the children while 9.2 percent "hired a babysitter;" 6.5 percent reported that use was made of "other relatives," and almost one-third (31.2 percent) claimed to make "other arrangements" for their children while they worked.

The category "other arrangements" refers to households where children were left neither in a formal day care center, nor in the care of paid sitters and relatives. They were cared for by friends and by persons who operate unlicensed centers not identified as day care centers. Equally important was the observation that, when the percentages for older chidren, grandparents and other relatives were combined, it became apparent that almost two-fifths of these parents drew upon extended family networks or relationships for assistance in the care of children while they pursued their daily occupations. It is also highly probable that utilization of the extended family relationships is made by two-parent families. However, we can only speculate that such families may be more inclined to place their children in formal centers because of their presumed ability to pay for these services in contrast to one-parent workers who may have less income. In some instances though, the income received by one employee may be equal to or greater than that received by two working parents. Hence, the motivation for the utilization pattern becomes even more speculative.

This finding is somewhat consistent with observations made by Robert Hill whose research also demonstrated that black extended families provide significant and vital day care services for working mothers.[5] His study showed that approximately 51 percent of black working mothers "who need day care assistance" use relatives for such services. While 20 percent rely upon non-relatives, only 5 percent depend upon formal day care centers.[6] Although the respondents in Hill's study were four times less likely to rely upon formal day care centers, his assessment of the importance of the extended family for providing child care during the absence of working mothers is especially germane for this analysis.

Household Size: Information about household size was obtained in responses to three questions, namely; (1) How many people are in your immediate household? (2)How many dependent children do you have? and (3) What is the total number of children you have? Of the 918 persons who responded to the first question, 172 or 18.7 percent stated that only one person was in their household. Another 211 or 23 percent stated that their household consisted of only two persons but 535, well over one-half (58.3 percent) reported a household of three or more persons. The mean number of persons in the household was 2.3; the median was 2.6 and the mode was 3 or more.[7] Some 543 individuals reported dependent children, the number of which ranged from one to more than five. However, 605 indicated that they were parents of children, including both dependent and adult children. Over three-fourths reported from one to three children. One-eighth (12.7 percent) reported a total of four children and one tenth (10.4 percent) indicated five or more children. If this distribution holds true for the black population as a whole, the assumption can be made that the black family is decreasing in size and is moving downward toward the national family size average of 2.2 children.[7]

Yearly Income: The annual income received was divided into three categories: (1) low, (0-$6,000), (2)medium, ($7,000-$19,000) and, (3) high, ($20,000-$30,000). Over half of the participants (54 percent) reported their individual incomes in the medium category while slightly more than one-third (36.8 percent) classified themselves as low-income. Less than one-tenth (8.6 percent) reported themselves in the high income category.

In response to the question "How much is your annual family combined income?," a plurality of participants reported incomes in the medium category (43 percent). More than one-fifth (22.7 percent) were still in the low income category. However, one-third of the participants reported combined family incomes of more than $20,000 per year. The disproportionate number of blacks in the high income category is an anomaly. Current research demonstrates that only about 19 percent of all black families have attained combined family income of at most $15,000 or more. Only a fraction of the black families are in the top 5 percent of national income levels.[8] The mean combined family income of $8,391 is only slightly above the 1979 poverty income level of $7,451, and the median family income of $10,579 is approximately the same as the $10,880 cited by the U.S. Census Department for all black families in the United States in 1978 but $1,000 less than the 1980 figure of $11,650. In any event, it is evident that the median family income of these blacks is only about 57 percent of that of white families in the United States. The ever widening gap between black and white families in income received is a primary source of tension, anxiety and disenchantment within the black community. Undoubtedly, this income disparity is a source of individual stress and racial antagonisms in all parts of the nation.

Table 4. Annual Income Distribution by Individuals
and Combined Family Sources.

Yearly Income Categories	Individual		Combined Family Income	
	N	Percent	N	Percent
Low ($0-$6,999)	320	36.8	124	22.7
*Medium ($7,000-$19,999)	476	54.7	237	43.4
High ($20,000-$30,000 +)	75	8.6	185	33.8
Total	871	100.0**	546	99.9**

*In most instances, the mean, median and modal-income is in the range of $10,500-$11,000 annually. This implies that the majority of incomes fall closer to the $7,000 end rather than the $19,999.
**Rounded off percentages

The combined median family income should be examined, too, in terms of the number of dependent children residing in the household. As previously indicated, 543 of the 546 participants who reported a combined family income had dependent children. Even though 52 percent of them reported having two or three children, more than ten percent had four or more dependent children to support on a median family income of less than three-fifths of that of the white population in the United States.

Unemployment: Among those persons who had been unemployed for a substantial period of time (i.e. from ten months to three years), diverse support patterns were reported. Almost two-fifths (39.4 percent) relied upon unemployment compensation for at least a portion of the unemployment period. It is not known, however, how many respondents were either eligible for unemployment compensation or aware of the mechanisms for obtaining it. Over one-third (35.6 percent) received support from their "spouse's earnings." One-sixth (16.6 percent) received support from parents and about one-twelfth were supported by relatives and children.

The support patterns among unemployed blacks revealed in this study are somewhat at variance with the findings noted by Hill with respect to the participation of blacks in cash programs operated by the Federal Government. According to Hill, only 6 percent of all blacks receive unemployment benefits and only 31 percent receive Social Security. His data also showed that, of all unemployed blacks, fully 70 percent never receive unemployment compensation. With respect to this study, the respondents reported that ·39.4 percent relied upon unemployment compensation at least for a part of the time during their period(s) of unemployment. The difference between the two studies approximates 10 percent. However, as Hill noted, the high proportion of blacks who never receive unemployment compensation may reflect peculiar eligibility requirements and "disqualification regulations" which reduce black participation in such benefits.[9] The importance of family networks and extended relationships is exhibited in this support pattern. In fact, one-fourth of the persons who had experienced prolonged unemployment did receive some degree of financial assistance from family members other than one's own spouse. Of the 309 persons who responded to the question of how important were their children's financial contributions, almost one-fifth (18.9 percent) maintained that these contributions were *very* important. Over one tenth (11.3 percent) said they believe that these contributions were of some importance. However, three-fifths indicated that contributions from children were of little or no importance. It is likely that this category included those persons who had dependent children who were unable to make substantive financial contributions to the family while the parent was unemployed. It may also have included teenagers who simply could not find work.

Explanation for unemployment included plant closing, plant relocations, making access to the job extremely difficult, persistent denial of promotion leading to job resignation, and family related reasons or pregnancy. Other factors included reductions in the work force or cutbacks, loss of job due to automation or lack of training and actual inability to find gainful employment. These explanations underscore problems of major proportions for many black urban residents and portend difficulties of substantially greater magnitude in the 1980's. Many of these conditions impact critically upon the black worker in a blue collar job who is not able to commute to a plant that has relocated at distances such that transportation is all but impossible. That situation is further exacerbated by the constant increase in gasoline and automobile operational costs.

Home Ownership: Of the 932 persons who responded to the question on home ownership, 409 or (43.8 percent) stated that they either owned or were purchasing their house or apartment and 64 or 6.9 percent, were living rent-free in their place of residence. The rate of owner occupancy approximates the national average of 42 percent indicated for black families in 1970 while that for renter occupancy is considerably below the 1970 rate of 58 percent. This change may indeed reflect an increasing capacity of blacks to own their dwelling place. However, if an inference can be drawn from the proportion of owner occupancy reported by participants in this study for the black population as a whole, then the only central conclusion that can be justifiably reached is that the ability of blacks to own property has increased only minimally over the past decade or so.

According to a *Black Enterprise* report, some two million blacks moved from the cities to suburban communities between 1960 and 1977. This trend was consistent with the general population shift from cities to suburbs during the same period. Since the number of white city-dwellers who moved to suburbs was so immense, the proportion of blacks among all suburban residents now residing in America's suburbs did not change appreciably during the two decades. In other words, blacks comprise approximately 5 percent of the entire suburban population. Black home ownership in the suburbs is undoubtedly above that for black home ownership in cities.[10]

Health Problems Experienced: Table 5 shows a rank order of the most common health problems experienced by the participants. Among those who had suffered from physical or mental ailments, high blood pressure was the single most prevalent health problem reported. This condition was followed in order by emotional stress, heart disease, diabetes, alcoholism, unwanted pregnancy, cancer and drugs (with the same 1.4 percent) and mental illness.

The relative position of high blood pressure in this ranking is not unexpected since most data on health problems of black Americans show a comparatively high incidence of heart disease. The ranking of "emotional stress" may be indicative of the overall psychological consequences of coping with racial hostility, variants of discrimination in everyday life, and problems which stem from efforts to earn a decent living, and support oneself and family members.

Although alcoholism ranks fifth among the disorders reported here, its incidence is still relatively low. One explanation for this low rate may be found in the research which shows that high educational attainment is a mediating factor against alcoholism among blacks.[11] Hence, a low incidence of alcoholism may not be unexpected since approximately 90 percent

Table 5. The Most Common Health Problems Experienced.

Health Problem by Rank Order	Yes		No	
	N	Percent	N	Percent
1. High Blood Pressure	233	24.6	716	75.4
2. Emotional Stress	86	9.0	864	91.0
3. Heart Disease	84	8.8	866	91.2
4. Diabetes	38	4.0	912	96.0
5. Alcoholism	34	3.5	916	96.5
6. Unwanted Pregnancy	29	3.1	920	96.9
7. Cancer	13	1.4	936	98.6
8. Drugs	13	1.4	936	98.6
9. Mental Illness	11	1.1	939	98.9

of the participants in this study reported at least a high school education or more. On the other hand, such problems as prolonged joblessness and the loss of self-esteem, coupled with a deepening sense of uselessness and personal demoralization may drive some individuals to seek escape by constant use of alcohol. Hence, the problem of alcoholism may become exacerbated by a relentless state of economic deprivation.

The incidence of cancer reported here seems somewhat low in view of 1981 studies published by the American Cancer Society which showed that one of every four black Americans, or 6.5 million persons can expect to be victimized by cancer, and that one in six deaths among black Americans is attributed directly to cancer. According to these data, black males are the most susceptible to cancer and they are far more likely to be afflicted by prostate cancer than by any other form. The National Cancer Institute data also indicate that black women are more likely to develop breast cancer that is far more virulent than the breast cancer found in white women. Precisely why the cancer rate has increased in such alarming proportions within the black community is not clear. Some atttribute it to the types of jobs to which blacks are consigned — jobs that often expose them to more frequent or extended periods of time to carcinogenic substances. Others cite the continuing failure in the delivery of adequate health services to blacks and the comparative lack of information about cancer, its causes, prevention and control.[12]

Rank Order of Most Urgent Concerns

The effort to identify the most pressing problems and the most urgent concerns confronting blacks focused on two questions. The first was, "What are *your* most urgent concerns?" The second was, "What are the most urgent problems facing the black community?" This bifurcation was designed to elicit responses which distinguished self-directed issues from those which affected the larger black population within the individual's community. Responses to these two questions were categorized according to residence, age, sex, education, income, and occupation. Within each of these categories a rank order of concerns was constructed.

An examination of Table 6 reveals a remarkable agreement of urgent concerns among urban and suburban blacks. In both groups, improving the individual's economic conditions ranked first, while the need for better education ranked second.

The priority which the respondents attached to each of the concerns listed in Table 6 may be further illustrated by an examination of the number and percent of first place votes a particular item received. Of the 465 highest priority ranks recorded by urban residents, 233 or 50 percent were given "better economic conditions." Sixty-one or 13 percent of the first in importance ranks went to "better education." Fifty-one (11 percent) went to "crime and drug abuse" as the most urgent concern while thirty-four (8 percent) were recorded for "equal justice" as the most urgent concern. The percentages of first place votes for the remaining items were eight for "better housing," four each for "more political power" and "better public services," and 3 percent for "elimination of police brutality." Among the urban cohort, the "other category" received no first place votes.

A similar pattern was observed among the 222 highest priortiy ranks recorded by the suburban sample. Of this number, 95 or 43 percent were for "better economic conditions" as the most urgent concern. The 13 percent highest priority ranks given by the suburban group to "better education" exactly matched the percentage reported among the urban population. Both "equal justice" and "more political power" received the first place ranking for 11 percent of the suburban sample while the 7 percent rank for "better housing" as maximum in priority matched the percent reported by the urban respondents. Among suburbanites, only 5 percent of the highest rank were for the crime/drug abuse problem. However, there was statistical agreement between the two residential groupings on the percent of preference for "better public services," and elimination of "police brutality" as first in urgency. In each case, 3 percent of all first priority ranks were recorded for those problems.

The urban respondents ranked "better economic conditions" first 3.8 times more often than they ranked "better education" as utmost in importance and 4.6 times more frequently in the first positon than the number of times they accorded first priority to the problem of crime and drug abuse.[13] The suburban respondents reported "better economic conditions" as their first priority 3.3 more frequently than they reported "better education" as a matter of greatest urgency to them. Suburbanites also mentioned "better economic conditions" 3.8 times more frequently than they reported "equal justice" and more "political power" as their most urgent concerns.

The issue of "better economic conditions" encompasses such problems as inadequate jobs and income, unemployment and inflation. While the frequency with which that factor was reported as the individual's most urgent concern may not be unexpected, its magnitude may be somewhat surprising. This is especially so in view of generalized viewpoints that blacks are so much better off today than they were 40 years ago. That assertion is not without merit; yet, black Americans today only repeat the urgency attached to economic issues which Gunnar Myrdal identified and reported in 1944 in *An American Dilemma*. Similarly, according to research findings of the National Urban League's *Black Pulse Survey Report* of August, 1980, there is corroboration for the observations reported in this study. For instance, the Black Pulse Survey findings showed that the "number one problem in the black community" is unemployment, and that three times as many blacks reported that joblessness (34 percent) rather than inflation (11 percent)* was the most urgent or serious problem in the black community.[14] The Black Pulse Survey also revealed the magnitude of harm done by inflation on black households as perceived and reported by participants in the study. For instance, two-thirds (68 percent) of the respondents who were household heads reported that their incomes had not kept pace with the rising cost of living over the previous two-year period. Consequently, about 44 percent said that they now feel "worse off" financially than they were in the past year.[15] One explanation for this sense of economic despair is found in the depression level unemployment rates among black household heads, as well as among black teenagers. According to the National Urban League, blacks in the United States experienced an actual unemployment rate of 24 percent during the last quarter of 1979 which was three times the U.S. jobless rate reported by the U.S. Department of Labor for the nation as a whole.[16]

---

*Joblessness and inflation were components of the overall definition of "economic conditions" employed in this book. When these percentages are combined (45%), the priority attached to these measures of economic concern matches the general findings in this study.

The dissimilarities in priority rankings across residential areas may be explained by differences in occupational attainment, educational achievement, political sophistication and overall quality of life among blacks. Other arguments also have a high degree of plausibility and relevance regarding these distinctions. For instance, suburban blacks may perceive better education as a collective means of strengthening whatever occupational and income gains they may have achieved in order to remain in suburbia. Equal justice may be visualized as a concommitant of greater political power among blacks while police brutality is relegated to a position of low salience because of limited personal encounters with the police. By contrast, urban blacks may take the position that with the acquisition of equal justice, access to better housing will follow and the problem of police brutality will be minimized. This view may account for "better housing" earning a somewhat higher rating than the acquisition of more political power.

The urgency of these issues address structural conditions blacks encounter regardless of residence or the circumstances under which they live from day-to-day. They also highlight systemic problems which are both racial and political in nature. This fact was illustrated by the identification of education, jobs/income (economic conditions), housing, equal justice and power as problems in need of urgent attention more so than others often associated with minority communities such as crime and drug abuse. (Table 6).

Table 6. Most Urgent Concerns of Individuals by Place of Residence.

Rank Order of Concerns	
Urban Residents	Suburban Residents
1. Better Economic Conditions	1. Better Economic Conditions
2. Better Education	2. Better Education
3. Crime and Drug Abuse	3. Equal Justice
4. Equal Justice	4. More Political Power
5. Better Housing	5. Better Housing
6. Political Power	6. Crime and Drug Abuse
7. Better Public Service	7. Better Public Service
8. Police Brutality	8. Other Concerns
9. Other Concerns	9. Police Brutality

Again, this rank order of most urgent problems is not too indistinguishable from the reverse rank order of discrimination revealed by Gunnar Myrdal in his 1944 study, *An American Dilemma*.[17] As discussed in Chapter 2, the kinds of issues which blacks identified, then and now, are more oriented toward the elimination of structural inequalities based upon race as opposed to matters of social intercourse or interaction with the white population.

When the question of *individual concern* was analyzed in terms of a trichotomy of age, a number of striking changes were noted. (Table 7).

Table 7. Most Urgent Concerns of Individuals by Age Groups.

Rank Order of Concerns		
Young (18-30 years)	Middle (31-50 years)	Older Ages (51 and above)
1. Better Economic Conditions	1. Better Economic Conditions	1. Better Economic Conditions
2. Better Education	2. Better Education	2. Crime, Drug Abuse
3. Equal Justice	3. Better Housing	3. Equal Justice
4. More Political Power	4. Equal Justice	4. Better Housing
5. Crime, Drug Abuse	5. Crime, Drug Abuse	5. Better Public Service
6. Better Housing	6. Political Power	6. Political Power
7. Better Public Service	7. Police Brutality	7. Better Education
8. Police Brutality	8. Better Public Service	8. Police Brutality
9. Other Concerns	9. Other Concerns	9. Other Concerns.

Clearly, improving economic conditions is one issue that has complete support among all age groups. (Table 7). Further refinement of the data showed that in the 18-30 year old cohort, the factor of "better economic conditions" was reported first in priority 2.8 times more frequently than "better education" and "equal justice." It was mentioned 4.2 times more often as the most urgent concern than was "more political power" among persons in this age cohort. Among the 196 highest priority ranks recorded in the 18-30 age group, the following percentages represented first place votes for other issues: "crime/drug abuse" (8 percent), "better housing" (5 percent), "better public services" (4 percent), "elimination of police brutality" (3 percent) and "other" concerns (one percent).

Of the 348 highest priority votes cast by persons in the 31 to 50 year old group, the concern for "better economic conditions" was reported as first in priority 3.5 times more frequently than was concern for "better education," and 7.4 times more often in the first position than was "better housing." With respect to the older persons aged 51 and above, concern for "better economic conditions" was perceived as most urgent twice as often than was reported in the first position for the crime and drug abuse problem but 4.4 times as often as was concern for "equal justice." Yet, this group stated that the crime and drug abuse problem was considerably more serious than was the issue of police brutality. Twenty-one percent of highest ranks were for crime but only 1 percent in the age 50 and above cohort reported police brutality as an issue of the highest priority. This distinction may be a manifestation of a higher victimization rate among the elderly in this group as well as their conviction that better law enforcement and stricter law enforcement will curtail the twin problems of crime and drug abuse.

The same emphasis on most urgent concerns was observed when the responses were analyzed in terms of *the sex variable*. Men and women agreed that the issues of most urgent importance to them were better economic conditions and better education. There was slight disagreement on the relative ranking of equal justice, better housing, and crime and drug abuse although each one of these issues ranked high in the overall ordering (Table 8). The issues of police brutality and improving the quality of public service did not rank high in the list of concerns when responses were differentiated according to either age groupings, or by place of residence, or by sex.

Table 8. Most Urgent Concerns of Individuals
According to Sex Differences.

Rank Order of Concerns by Sex	
Male	Female
1. Better Economic Conditions	1. Better Economic Conditions
2. Better Education	2. Better Education
3. Equal Justice	3. Crime, Drug Abuse
4. Better Housing	4. Equal Justice
5. Crime, Drug Abuse	5. Political Power
6. Political Power	6. Better Housing
7. Better Public Service	7. Better Public Service
8. Police Brutality	8. Police Brutality
9. Other Concerns	9. Other Concerns

However, 51 percent of all 311 first place votes reported by men and 45 percent of all 374 first place votes indicated by women went to "better economic conditions" as the most urgent problem facing them. Ten percent of the first place votes cast for the most urgent problem were equally reported by men for "better education" and "equal justice." On the other hand, 15 percent of first urgency votes recorded by women went to "better education" and 11 percent indicated "crime/drug abuse" as the most most urgent problems. The percentages suggested that men were 5.2 times more likely to report "better economic conditions" as the most urgent concerns than they were to report "better education" as a concern of the highest priority. They reported "better economic conditions" as most urgent by essentially the same margin over concern for "equal justice." On the other hand, women reported "better economic conditions" as most important by a ratio of 2.9:1 over that for "better education" and 4.2:1 over highest priority accorded to crime and drug abuse.

Among men, the percent of all first priority concerns to them for the remaining issues were as follows: "better housing" (8), "crime/drug abuse" (7), "more political power" (6), "better public service" (4), "police brutality" and "other" (2 percent each). Among women, the percent of all first priority concerns for other issues were: "equal justice" (8), "more political power" (7), "better housing" (6), "better public services" (4), "police brutality" (3) and "other" (1 percent).

When the *education variable* was introduced and comparisons were made in individual's perceptions of the most urgent concerns across all education levels, noticeable changes in the rank order of the most urgent concerns were discernible. (Table 9). Irrespective of educational attainment levels, the most urgent concern was for the realization of better economic conditions. Further refinement of the data than the rank orders indicated in Table 9 revealed the magnitude of this concern for people of different educational levels. For instance, of all first priority listings reported, 53 percent in the "low" education group, 52 percent of those in the "medium" category and 41 percent of all first priority votes reported by the "high" education group went to "better economic conditions."

Among persons in the "low" education group, the ratio between first priority votes recorded for better economic conditions to that of first place votes cast for better education (11 percent), better public service (11 percent), and crime/drug abuse (11 percent) was 5:1. Political power ranked first in importance 7 percent of the time while 4 percent of all first priority votes went equally to better housing and equal justice. No first place rankings were reported among people with low educational attainment for either police brutality or the "other" category.

In the "medium" educational attainment level, the ratio between the number of times better economic conditions received a first place ranking and the number of times crime/drug abuse was ranked highest in priority was 4.7:1. A similar ratio was reported for first priority rankings between better economic conditions and better education since that ratio was 4.9:1. The issues of crime/drug abuse and of better education both received 11 percent of all highest priority votes cast in the medium educated cohort. First priority percentages for the remaining concerns were 5 percent each for equal justice and more political power, 3 percent for police brutality, 2 percent for better public service and 1 percent for "other."

Within the "high" education group, the ratio between the number of times better economic conditions received the highest priority rankings and that accorded for better education was 2.4:1. However, the 3.3:1 ratio between better economic conditions and equal justice was somewhat higher. In descending order, the first priority percents of all 269 first place rankings recorded by individuals in the high educational attainment category were as follows: 8 percent for more political power, 7 for better housing, 6 for crime/drug abuse, 3 for police brutality, and 2 percent for the "other" category.

Table 9. Most Urgent Concerns of Individuals
According to Level of Education.

Rank Order by Level of Education		
Low (0-11 years)	Medium (12 years plus Post-Sec. Educ.)	High (College and Professional Educ.)
1. Better Economic Cond.	1. Better Economic Cond.	1. Better Economic Cond.
2. Better Education	2. Crime, Drug Abuse	2. Better Education
3. Crime, Drug Abuse	3. Better Education	3. Equal Justice
4. Better Public Service	4. Better Housing	4. Political Power
5. Political Power	5. Equal Justice	5. Better Housing
6. Equal Justice	6. Political Power	6. Crime, Drug Abuse
7. Better Housing	7. Police Brutality	7. Better Public Service
8. Police Brutality	8. Better Public Service	8. Police Brutality
9. Other Concerns	9. Other Concerns	9. Other Concerns

A high degree of correspondence in the rank order of these concerns was observed when place of residence and educational attainment were examined (Table 6 and Table 9). Urban residents were in high agreement with individuals in the low education group as to how these issues were ranked. The same was true for the high education group and suburban residents. While this agreement may be coincidental, it may also be due to the presence of a significantly higher proportion of highly educated blacks in the suburban communities. Urban residents with low educational attainment appeared to express a compelling need for improved economic and educational conditions, more effective ways to deal with the problems of crime and drug abuse, and the need for a meaningful delivery of public services. With these problems solved, they will then be better prepared to fight for equal justice or have the wherewithal to obtain better housing, and implement strategies for combatting police brutality.

When *the income variable* was introduced into the analysis, unanimity still prevailed with the highest priority given to improving economic conditions. This same ranking persisted when occupational categories were employed as the basis for comparative rankings. In both instances, there seemed to be virtual agreement on the relative high ranking of such concerns as crime, drug abuse, better education and equal justice. (Tables 10 and 11). Low income, unemployed, and persons in low status occupations tended to give higher priority to these four concerns than is generally the case with other groupings identified in these two tables. These groups were also in greater agreement in their rankings than they were with persons in suburbia, with high education and high status occupations. *Yet, all agreed the most urgent issue facing individuals, regardless of place of residence, age, income status, educational attainment or occupational status was improving the economic condition of black Americans.*

Table 10. Rank Order of Urgent Concerns of Individuals by Income

| | Income Categories | |
Low (0-$6,999/yr.)	Medium ($7,000-$19,999)	High ($20,000-Above)
1. Better Economic Cond.	1. Better Economic Cond.	1. Better Economic Cond.
2. Crime, Drug Abuse	2. Better Education	2. Equal Justice
3. Better Education	3. Equal Justice	3. Political Power
4. Equal Justice	4. Better Housing	4. Better Education
5. Better Housing	5. Crime, Drug Abuse	5. Other Concerns
6. Political Power	6. Political Power	6. Better Housing
7. Better Public Service	7. Better Public Service	7. Better Public Service
8. Police Brutality	8. Police Brutality	8. Police Brutality
9. Other Concerns	9. Other Concerns	9. Other Concerns

Table 11. Individual's Most Urgent Concerns by Occupational Category

Occupational Categories

Pensions, SS	Unemployed	High Status	Low Status
1. Better Eco. Cond.	1. Better Eco. Cond.	1. Better Eco. Cond.	1. Better Eco. Cond.
2. Crime, Drug Abuse	2. Crime, Drug Abuse	2. Equal Justice	2. Better Education
3. Better Education	3. Equal Justice	3. Better Education	3. Crime, Drug Abuse
4. Better Housing	4. Better Housing	4. Political Power	4. Equal Justice
5. Political Power	5. Political Power	5. Better Housing	5. Better Housing
6. Better Pub. Serv.	6. Better Education	6. Crime, Drug Abuse	6. Political Power
7. Other Concerns	7. Better Public Serv.	7. Police Brutality	7. Better Public Serv.
8. Equal Justice	8. Police Brutality	8. Better Pub. Serv.	8. Police Brutality
9. Police Brutality	9. Other Concerns	9. Other Concerns	9. Other Concerns

Further data analysis showed that 46 percent of the 218 highest priority votes cast among persons in the low income group, 52 percent of the 356 first priority votes reported for the "medium" income group and 40 percent of the first priority in the "high" income group were reported for better economic conditions. Within the low income category, a ratio of 3.3:1 was observed between the number of first place rankings reported for better economic conditions and the number indicated for crime/drug abuse. Similarly a 3.6:1 ratio was observed between the number of first place votes cast for better economic conditions and the number reported for better education, which received 13 percent of all first priority votes cast by low income individuals.

Among the "medium" income group, a 4:1 ratio was observed between the number of first priority rankings reported for better economic conditions and better education. On the other hand, the 6.4:1 ratio between the economic factor and equal justice was significantly different and showed the enormity of the concern for improvement in economic well being over concern for other issues. These distinctions were not as great, though nonetheless quite important, among persons who reported higher levels of income. Within this group, the ratio between highest priority rankings reported for better economic conditions and equal justice was 2.9:1. On the other hand, a 3.6:1 ratio was observed between highest priority rankings recorded for better economic conditions and more political power, and better education. Each of the latter two concerns received 11 percent of highest priority rankings among the high income individuals.

Although better economic conditions received the highest priority ranking across all *occupational categories*, differences were observed in the relative weight assigned to that concern. For instance, it received 30 percent of the 43 first priority votes cast among persons whose principal income was derived from pensions and Social Security and 39 percent of the 49 highest ranking reoprted by the unemployed. On the other hand, better economic conditions received 53 of the 382 first place rankings listed by persons in the "low status" occupations and 43 percent of the 196 indicated among "high status" occupation individuals. Within-group differentials are also crucial in order to illuminate the nature of these distinctions.

Among pensioners and Social Security recipients, 26 percent of the highest rankings were reported for the problem of crime/drug abuse and 14 percent of the top priority rankings were reported for better education. The ratio between better economic conditions (43 percent) and crime/drug abuse rankings was only 1.2:1 whereas that between better economic conditions and better education was 2.2:1.

Unemployed persons ranked crime/drug abuse as highest in priority 18 percent of the times and better housing received 10 percent of all first place rankings in this group. However, the ratios between the various first, second and third place rankings among the highest priority votes were different from all others. The ratio between the highest rankings reported for better economic conditions (39 percent) and crime/drug abuse in this group was 2.1:1. The ratio between better economic conditions and better housing was 3.8:1.

Among the high status occupations, 14 percent of the individuals ranked equal justice as highest priority compared to the 43 percent who ranked better economic conditions as the highest concern. The ratio between these two rankings was 3.1:1. Twelve percent of their first place rankings went to better education. Therefore, the ratio between the highest rankings recorded for better economic conditions and better housing was 3.5:1.

Within the low status occupations, 14 percent of the highest priority rankings were reported for better education and 8 percent for crime/drug abuse. The ratio, however, between better economic conditions (53 percent) as first priority, and better education was 3.7:1 while the ratio better economic conditions and highest concern for the problem of crime and drug abuse was 6.6:1.

The most striking aspect of the rank orderings is the persistence of the low ranking accorded to police brutality, especially in view of the strong feeling in each of the five cities that blacks and police are mortal enemies. Across income groups, police brutality received only 3 percent of first place rankings. In general, a complex belief system regarding blacks and the police has emerged in the past two decades. At the center of this system is the conviction that the police, especailly the white police, are racially hostile to blacks. Therefore, they are creatures of their own racial bias which governs their attitudes and treatment of black persons and minority groups in general. Given the pervasiveness of this viewpoint, the low ranking of concern over police brutality may be somewhat surprising at first glance. On the other hand, this apparent discrepancy may simply mean that "survival problems," equality of educational and political opportunity, and others are more fundamental in daily living. It is not that police brutality is unimportant; it is simply *less* important than other concerns.

Problems Facing the Black Community

To differentiate urgent individualized or personal concerns from those of the community in which the respondents lived, each person was asked; "What do you feel are the most urgent concerns facing black people in your community?" As in the case of the individual ranking, a rank order of these concerns was constructed for each of several demographic variables.

Regardless of the demographic variable employed in measuring the degree of urgency, it is apparent that the most serious issue facing the black community is the problem of how to improve economic conditions. Second highest priority is assigned to improving the quality of education for black youths. In close approximation to this issue is the concern evident over the twin problems of crime and drug abuse in the black community. The persistence of these issues as matters of great urgency across demographic variables is not unexpected. It is significant that all blacks in this study express a profound awareness of the gravity of these three problems and of the necessity for a concerted action to find solutions to economic deprivation, educational disparities, crime victimization and the consequences of drug abuse.

Residential Patterns: The dominance of the need to improve the economic life and educational program in black communities was evident in their high rank order among both urban and suburban residents. As indicated in Table 12, these issues ranked first and second, respectively. One also observed a high degree of compatibility between what the individual perceived as a personal concern with perceptions of most urgent problems facing the black community among urban residents. The rank order provided in both instances was indistinguishable (Tables 6 and 12). The rankings in the suburban cohorts were almost parallel except for the exchange of positions between "better housing" and "elimination of crime and drug abuse" (Tables 6 and 12). The downgrading of the housing issue among suburban residents was not unexpected, when compared to its higher rank for individual suburbanites, since they were more likely to be residing in reasonably good housing themselves. However, their views about the seriousness of the housing problems were undoubtedly shaped by previous experience, present-day contacts and observations, and what they may have read about the black community.

Table 12. Problems Facing the Black Community by Residence and Rank Order.

Urban - Rank Order	Suburban - Rank Order
1. Better Economic Conditions	1. Better Economic Conditions
2. Better Education	2. Better Education
3. Crime, Drug Abuse	3. More Political Power
4. Equal Justice	4. Equal Justice
5. Better Housing	5. Crime, Drug Abuse
6. More Political Power	6. Better Housing
7. Better Public Service	7. Better Public Service
8. Police Brutality	8. Other Concerns
9. Other Concerns	9. Police Brutality

Among urban residents, the respondents endorsed better economic conditions as the most urgent problem facing the black community by a 5.4:1 margin over the need for better education which ranked second. Of the 472 votes for the highest priority ranking, 261 or 55 percent were cast for better economic conditions while 48 or 10 percent were reported for better education. Forty first place votes, (8 percent) were cast for the problem of crime/drug abuse, which ranked third in overall importance. The ratio between better economic conditions and the crime problem was 6.5:1. Hence, urban blacks were more than six times likely to say that better economic conditions had the highest ranking as a black community problem than they were to view the crime/drug abuse problem as the most serious problem within black communities. Although equal justice was endorsed as highest in priority by the same percent (8) as was crime/drug abuse, that concern received slightly fewer (37) first place votes.

Within the black suburban cohort, the ratio between better economic conditions and better education was 2.7:1 while the ratio observed between better economic conditions and the third most urgent concern, more political power, which received 13 percent highest priority votes, was 3:1. The remaining concerns received less than 10 percent each of all highest priority votes recorded among suburbanites. In descending order, these percentages were: equal justice (9), crime/drug abuse (8), better housing (6), better public services (4), "other" (3), and police brutality (2).

Again, urban residents perceive structural inequities as needing the most urgent attention. The primacy of economic conditions, education, equal justice and housing indicates that blacks continue to feel that far too many blacks are still excluded from the most rudimentary opportunities to create a better life in the American society. Structural inequities are manifestations of systematic malfunctioning antithetical to democratic ideals. Similarly, the high ranking of the crime/drug abuse problem is indicative of malfunctioning in the black community as a sub-system; however, the proximity of this problem to that of equal justice suggests that, at least from the viewpoint of the participants in this study, these problems are clearly intertwined. Some individuals hold the American society culpable for these problems, especially when they claim that inequities are induced by intractable conditions within the social structure (e.g. abject poverty, prejudice, job discrimination, racism and alienation). Others maintain that these problems are not externally created; rather, the black community can blame itself for not controlling crime and drug abuse among its members.[18]

Both arguments can be defended up to a point. Clearly, economic deprivation, persistent and prolonged poverty, lack of educational skills and related resources, combined with encounters with racism, create enormous stresses and strains among some individuals. Again, it may be difficult for many Americans, especially those who have never known poverty or experienced severe economic problems, to adequately comprehend the massive social and psychological problems that may be induced by economic deprivation. These problems may be enormous and costly. Unemployment, for instance, may not only mean hunger, uncertainty about obtaining the next meal, let alone nutritional requirements, it may also generate crime committed to meet basic sustenance needs, loss of self-esteem and raise innumerable questions among some individuals about their sense of personal value. If unemployed, economically deprived and low income persons feel that society has failed them, and if the well-educated believe that racial discrimination affects them, it is not unreasonable to assert that both groups are likely to develop and manifest a sense of alienation. Depending upon the personal resilience of the individual, the coping strategies developed to deal with such conditions as a low sense of personal efficacy, and psychological and social control factors, involvement in either crime, drug abuse or both may be an anticipated outcome of system failures. Some of these persons may become committed to the underground economy as a mechanism for survival in what they have defined as a racist and unjust society.

For them, this is a society in which middle-class businessmen and corporate executives annually receive billions of dollars in "corporate welfare" such as in governmental loans and federal subsidies. Many of them do not hesitate to remind the interviewer or casual conversationalist that society is extremely quick to call for the most severe form of punishment for their petty crimes but is extremely reluctant to permit most white collar criminals to spend one day in jail for engaging in crimes that are considerably more costly on a per offense basis than are the crimes committed by most blacks. For these persons, a double standard of justice operates; no one really cares about them. Hence, they are determined to "get all they can" in the jungle, which is precisely how society is perceived by many in this group. They rationalize that the "big fat cats" rob them everyday; so why not "rip them off" too.

Others, who blame themselves, reject such arguments as indefensible, especially when confronted with the reality that blacks, irrespective of social class, are more likely to be victimized by crimes committed by other blacks.[19] A great majority of black Americans do not accept crime as a categorical necessity. Many do feel that the community itself must seize the leadership in crime prevention or crime deterrence. Importantly, it should be stressed that the misconception about crime-ridden black communities is simply that — a misconception. All black communities are not crime-ridden; although an increasingly larger number are becoming highly vulnerable to crime victimization.[20]

The fear of crime is ubiquitous in all of American society. No community is exempt from it except only in degrees and in terms of the degrees of police and neighbor protection provided in them. But, data from the *Uniform Crime Reports*[21] show that the urban resident is apparently more vulnerable. It is precisely because more blacks live in urban communities than elsewhere, coupled with the consequences of system and institutional discrimination, that they are more likely to be victimized. Therefore, they rank this issue as one of such grave importance facing the black community.

Age: As shown in Table 13, across all age groupings, a consensus prevails with respect to better economic conditions as the most serious problem facing the black community. With the exception of the greater weight given to crime, and drug abuse by persons in the "older" age cohort, a high degree of compatibility was observed among these groups with regard to the concerns they ranked as the three highest in importance. Differentiations in the relative weights assigned to high priority rankings may be best illuminated by an analysis of these rankings by specific age groupings.

Among the young, 42 percent of the 215 highest priority rankings were recorded for better economic conditions, compared to 16 percent for better education. The ratio between these two rankings was 2.6:1. This ratio was decidedly less than the 5.1:1 ratio observed between better economic conditions and the third highest priority ranking of equal justice, more political power and crime/drug abuse. Each of the latter three concerns received 8 percent of the first priority votes. It may be that the young perceive a significant interconnection between the crime problem, the inability of blacks to receive equal justice, and the need for more political power. The next highest priority ranking, police brutality (11 votes) and better housing (10 votes) each received 5 percent of the highest priority rankings. Better public service was accorded the highest priority rating only 4 percent of the time while the "other" category registered only 3 percent of highest rankings.

Over half (54 percent) of 345 first place rankings by persons in the middle age cohort were given to better economic conditions. This factor outdistanced the second priority concern, better education, which received 12 percent of highest priority votes, by a margin of 4.5:1. It superceded in urgency the third place concern, equal justice, with 9 percent highest priority ranking, by a ratio of 6.2:1. All of the remaining issues were viewed as relatively close to each other as measured by the percentages of highest priority rank that each received. These percentages were, in descending order: more political power (7), better housing (6), crime/drug abuse (5), police brutality (2) and "other" (1).

Fifty-one percent of the 146 highest priority ranks reported by persons in the older category went to better economic conditions. This factor outdistanced the second priority ranking, crime/drug abuse, with 16 percent of the first place votes, by a margin of 3.1:1. It was said to be more urgent by a ratio of 6.8:1 over the third priority, equal justice, which had 8 percent of first priority votes. Given the possibly high vulnerability of older persons to be victimized from such offenses as various forms of street crimes (e.g., purse-snatchings and muggings) and breaking and entering, the high priority assigned to the problem of crime and drug abuse within the older population is not unexpected. Neither should it be necessarily unanticipated that the older population would assign a higher priority to the problem of better housing than all other age groups.. Too frequently, the elderly are subjected to substandard housing.[22] Among the older persons, better housing received 7 percent of first priority ranks. This factor was followed in descending order, according to percentage of high priority votes, by more political power (6), better public services (5), better education (4), police brutality (3) and "other" (0).

Table 13. Rank Order of Problems Facing the Black Community by Age Groups.

Rank Order of Age Groups		
Young (18-30)	Middle (31-50)	Older (above 50)
1. Better Eco. Conditions	1. Better Eco. Conditions	1. Better Eco. Conditions
2. Better Education	2. Better Education	2. Crime, Drug Abuse
3. Equal Justice	3. Equal Justice	3. Equal Justice
4. Political Power	4. Political Power	4. Better Housing
5. Crime, Drug Abuse	5. Better Housing	5. Political Power
6. Police Brutality	6. Crime, Drug Abuse	6. Better Public Service
7. Better Housing	7. Better Public Service	7. Better Education
8. Better Public Service	8. Police Brutality	8. Police Brutality
9. Other Concerns	9. Other Concerns	9. Other Concerns

Sex Differences: As shown in Table 14, men and women agreed only that the most urgent problem facing the black community was that of better economic conditions. Among men, 47 percent of the 356 highest priority ranks went to this item, which compared favorably to the 48 percent of 387 highest priority ranks reported by women. On all other items there was discernible disagreement.

Among women, the ratio between first place votes registered for better economic conditions and better education, which ranked second in priority with 14 percent, was 3.4:1. The economic concern outdistanced the third priority of crime/drug abuse, which received 9 percent of the first priority ranks, by a margin of 5.3:1. Better housing, with 35 votes for first priority also received 9 percent of highest priority votes. In descending order by percent of first priority votes, the remaining distributions were as follows: more political power (8), equal justice (6), police brutality (3), better public service (2) and "other" (1).

Men said they believed the most urgent problems facing the black community were better economic conditions, better housing and equal justice. They endorsed better economic conditions as the most urgent problem by a

3.8:1 margin over better housing, which garnered 12 percent of highest priority ranks, and by a 4.8:1 over equal justice, which received 10 percent of first priority votes. Men appeared to be slightly less convinced about their second and third priority ranks than were women, as determined by the percentages of first priority votes each received. Men differed from women in their ordering of all other concerns, too. Note, for instance, the second position accorded by women to better education compared to the fourth place ranking given this item by men in which better education received only 8 percent of highest priority rankings among men and 14 percent among women. Further, men placed the crime/drug abuse problem (with 7 percent of the first place ranks) fifth while women ranked it third in urgency. The remaining rankings among men by percent of highest priority ranks were: more political power (6), better public service (5), police brutality (3) and "other" (1).

Table 14. Sex Differences in the Perception of Most Urgent Problems Facing the Black Community.

Rank Order by Sex	
Male	Female
1. Better Economic Conditions	1. Better Economic Conditions
2. Better Housing	2. Better Education
3. Equal Justice	3. Crime, Drug Abuse
4. Better Education	4. Better Housing
5. Crime, Drug Abuse	5. Political Power
6. Political Power	6. Equal Justice
7. Better Public Service	7. Police Brutality
8. Police Brutality	8. Better Public Service
9. Other Concerns	9. Other Concerns

Education: Table 15 shows the rank order of urgent concerns according to the level of educational attainment. An examination of this table reveals that, irrespective of educational attainment, the respondents reported agreement that the most crucial problems facing the black community are those relating to better economic conditions. In fact, 62 percent of the 77 highest priority ranks registered by the persons categorized as "low" in educational attainment, 56 percent among the 343 in the "medium" level, and 40 percent of the 287 in the high educational level were for better economic conditions.

Within the "low" category, the economic factor outdistanced second place votes cast for more political power, with 9 percent, by a margin of 6.9:1. The ratio between the economic factor and the third ranking priority, equal justice, with six votes and 8 percent, was 8:1. Notably few votes were registered for the remaining issues as of first importance. Significantly, no first place votes were recorded for police brutality as the factor of most urgency facing the black community among the persons categorized as low in educational attainment. Yet, other evidence, such as anecdotal statements made by the respondents and studies conducted under the auspices of the U.S. Commission on Civil Rights[23] suggest that this issue ought to have a higher priority ranking.

Persons with a "medium level" of educational attainment reported crime and drug abuse as the second priority factor. However, the relative weight assigned to this factor, compared to the importance attached to economic conditions, was considerably less. In fact, within this group, better economic conditions outranked crime and drug abuse, (with 10 percent first place ranks), as the most urgent problem by a margin of 5.8:1. It superceded better education, (with 26 votes and 8 percent), by a ratio of 7.4:1.

Among persons with a high level of educational attainment, the ratio between better economic conditions and the second rank reported for better education (.52 votes and 18 percent), was 2.2:1. The ratio between better economic conditions and the third priority, more political power, (with 29 votes and 10 percent), was 4:1.

Little or no differentiation was discerned across educational levels between factors ranked at or near the bottom of the priority listings. The most apparent exception to this observation was the relatively low priority attached to crime and drug abuse by the low education group compared to the higher rank of this factor among higher educational levels. The latter finding appears to confirm other studies which show that highly educated and high status blacks have a high susceptibility to crime victimization.[24]

In general, macro-community issues appear to elicit more frequent identification as urgent problems than do such micro-community issues as delivery of better public services and the police brutality problem. A notable exception to this generalization is the relatively higher rank of urgency attached to better public services among persons categorized as "low" in education. If there is a relationship between residential distribution, income received, occupational level and educational attainment, this ranking should not be unexpected. Often in American society, the poorly educated are regarded as powerless and less capable of influencing authorities to

Table 15. Most Urgent Problems Facing the Black Community by
Level of Educational Attainment.

Rank Order by Educational Levels		
Low (0-11 years) completed	Medium (H.S. + Post Sec.)	High Coll. & Profess. School)
1. Better Eco. Cond.	1. Better Econ. Cond.	1. Better Economic Cond.
2. Political Power	2. Crime, Drug Abuse	2. Better Education
3. Equal Justice	3. Better Education	3. Political Power
4. Better Public Serv.	4. Equal Justice	4. Equal Justice
5. Better Education	5. Better Housing	5. Crime, Drug Abuse
6. Better Housing	6. Political Power	6. Better Housing
7. Crime, Drug Abuse	7. Better Public Service	7. Police Brutality
8. Police Brutality	8. Police Brutality	8. Better Public Service
9. Other Concerns	9. Other Concerns	9. Other Concerns

clean up their streets, pick up garbage more regularly, repair potholes and
street lights or replace outmoded drainage and sewer systems. This situation may account for their higher ranking for more political power and for
equal justice.

Income: Once again, there is complete unanimity across all income
groups that the most urgent problem facing the black community lies in improving economic conditions. This ranking corresponds to that evident
when individuals were asked about problems facing them. If comparisons
are made between problems facing the individual and problems facing the
community by income groups, striking differences emerge, (Tables 10 and
16). Low income persons have agreement on only first and second place
rankings as urgent problems for both themselves and those facing the black
community. In both instances, better economic conditions and the problem
of crime and drug abuse are most urgent. On the other hand, the relative
position of a need for better education suggests disagreement regarding
perceptions of its priority as a community problem. For the low income individual, obtaining a better education was third in importance but the low
income groups rank better education as sixth in importance as an issue facing the black community.

With respect to education, this pattern was reversed among persons in
the middle income groups. When speaking of themselves, a better education was second in urgency while crime and drug was fifth in importance. In
terms of beliefs about problems facing the community, education dropped
to sixth place while crime and drug abuse was elevated to second in importance.

However, the high income cohort now regarded better education as second in urgency in contrast to its third place rank when the question was posed in terms of problems facing them as an individual. While political power and equal justice remained near the top of the priority list in both instances, "other concerns" fell to last place in the priority ranking as issues facing the black community as a whole.

Table 16. Most Urgent Problems Facing the
Black Community by Income Groups

Rank Order by Income Groups		
Low ($0-$6,999)	Middle ($7,000-$19,999)	High ($20,000 - Above)
1. Better Econ. Cond.	1. Better Econ. Cond.	1. Better Econ. Cond.
2. Crime, Drug Abuse	2. Crime, Drug Abuse	3. Better Education
3. Equal Justice	3. Equal Justice	3. Political Power
4. Political Power	4. Political Power	4. Equal Justice
5. Better Housing	5. Better Housing	5. Crime, Drug Abuse
6. Better Education	6. Better Education	6. Better Public Services
7. Police Brutality	7. Better Public Services	7. Better Housing
8. Better Public Services	8. Police Brutality	8. Police Brutality
9. Other Concerns	9. Other Concerns	9. Other Concerns

An examination of Table 16 shows that the low and medium income groups approximate each other in perceptions of problems facing the black community. They were in complete agreement on the five most urgent problems facing the community and near agreement on the seventh and eighth rankings. All groups placed other concerns last in the ranking. (Table 16).

The high income groups agreed with both the medium and the low income groups on most issues perceived as urgent in the community. They agreed on the urgent priority of better economic conditions. They were in near agreement on the relative importance attached to equal justice and political power. But, they appeared to perceive the need for a better education with substantially greater urgency in the black community than did the medium and low income groups. The high income group ranked the problem of crime and drug abuse lower than did low and medium income groups. This difference perhaps reflected a tendency to assess these problems by the conditions that obtain in their own immediate neighborhood environment. However, the actual problem of crime and drug abuse may not be as evident as it is in other communities. (Table 16).

Some of the group preferences suggested in the hierarchical ordering listed in Table 16 became considerably more pronounced with an analysis of descriptive statistics. For instance, more than half of the low income group (57 percent) and the medium income group (56 percent), in contrast to less than one-third (31 percent) of the high income group said that better economic conditions ranked first in urgency within the black community. The relative weights assigned to each of the concerns within each of the income levels were often striking. In the following analysis, special attention is given to the relationships between the first three priorities.

Within the low income level respondents, the ratio between better economic conditions as the highest priority (57 percent) and the crime/drug problem as the most urgent problem (10 percent of all first place ranks) was 5.9:1. However, better economic conditions outdistanced the third ranking priority, equal justice, (with 19 votes and 9 percent), by a margin of 6.2:1. It may be noted that the problem of crime and drug abuse received a single vote more than did the problem of equal justice and only four votes more than did the fourth priority, more political power.

Among the medium income level respondents, the ratio between the percentage of highest priority ranks given to better economic conditions and those accorded crime and drug abuse (9 percent) was 6.4:1. The higher preference shown for better economic conditions in contrast to the third priority, equal justice, (with 29 votes and 8 percent of first priority ranks), was 6.7:1. Once again, second and third place ranks were separated by a single vote (30 to 29) and third and fourth place votes (more political power) were separated by a narrow margin of three votes, (29 to 26), while the distance between the fourth and fifth place ranks was by a margin of three votes or between 26 and 23 votes cast for highest priority rank.

As stated above, slightly less than one-third of the high income level respondents ranked better economic conditions as the most serious problem facing the black community, despite its first place rank among the members of this group. However, 30 or 28 percent of the 106 first place rankings at this income level went to better education as the most serious or urgent problem within the black community. Only 11 votes or 10 percent were recorded for more political power which ranked third. The ratio between the first and second priority rankings was 1.1:1 but the ratio between the first and third priority ranks was 3:1. It may also be noted that the distance between the third, (11 votes), and fourth, (10 votes), priorities was not substantial — a margin of a single vote — in terms of all preferences for the highest priority. Two votes separated the fourth priority rank from the fifth priority, crime and drug abuse, which received only 8 of the 106 votes cast for highest priority problems. However, the ratio between better economic conditions and crime/drug abuse was 4:1.

Occupational Status: In terms of occupational status, four classifications were utilized to assess problems facing the black community. These four groups were: (1) individuals receiving pensions and/or social security benefits; (2) the unemployed; (3) persons in low status occupations, such as blue collar jobs; and (4) persons in high status occupations such as white collar positions, managers and professionals.

As shown in Table 17, individuals on pensions and social security benefits agreed with the unemployed that the two most urgent problems facing the black community were better economic conditions and crime and drug abuse. Similarly, the low status and high status occupational groups also showed complete correspondence in the urgency with which they perceived better economic conditions and better education as serious community problems. Thereafter, the level of congruence in perceptions of community problems fell sharply. Pensioners gave greater priority to such problems as equal justice, better public services, better housing and better education. Their own economic and social conditions within the community undoubtedly influenced these rankings.

On the other hand, the unemployed assigned the next priority to political power, equal justice, better education and better housing, and this hierarchy probably reflected their perception of situations as measured by personal circumstances. By contrast, the low status occupational group appeared somewhat closer to both pensioners and the unemployed in its ranking of crime/drug abuse, better housing, equal justice and political power as the next most urgent problems within the black community. The high status group seemed closer to the unemployed in the relative rankings assigned to equal justice and political power but this group placed the problem of crime and drug abuse below all others. However, it ranked the problem of police brutality as somewhat more urgent in the community than did all other occupational groups (Table 17).

Important distinctions between and within groups were revealed with respect to the relative weights assigned to each priority when descriptive statistics on occupational categories were analyzed. For instance, although all groups ranked better economic conditions highest in priority among problems facing the black community, preference for this item as first priority was not uniform across all occupational groups. Only in low status (55 percent) and unemployed (50 percent) occupational groups did better economic conditions receive 50 percent or more of all first priority votes case.

Table 17. Most Urgent Problems Facing the
Black Community by Occupational Status

Rank Order by Occupational Groups

Pension, SS	Unemployed	High Status	Low Status
1. Better Econ. Cond.	1. Better Econ. Cond.	1. Better Econ. Cond.	1. Better Econ. Cond.
2. Crime, Drug Abuse	2. Crime, Drug Abuse	2. Better Education	2. Better Education
3. Equal Justice	3. Political Power	3. Equal Justice	3. Crime, Drug Abuse
4. Better Pub. Services	4. Equal Justice	4. Political Power	4. Better Housing
5. Better Housing	5. Better Education	5. Better Housing	5. Equal Justice
6. Better Education	6. Better Housing	6. Crime, Drug Abuse	6. Political Power
7. Political Power	7. Better Pub. Services	7. Police Brutality	7. Better Pub. Services
8. Other Concerns	8. Other Concerns	8. Better Pub. Services	8. Police Brutality
9. Police Brutality	9. Police Brutality	9. Other Concerns	9. Other Concerns

Of the 47 highest priority ranks cast by persons supported by *pensions and Social Security,* 22 or 47 percent of them were registered for better economic conditions. The ratio between this factor and the 23 percent first priority votes cast for the second highest rank, crime and drug abuse, was 2:1. By contrast, the pensioners and Social Security recipients reported only 5 or 11 percent of their most serious problem for the third category, equal justice. The ratio between the first and third priorities was, therefore, 4.4:1. The range of highest priority votes registered for the remaining items was from zero (0) for police brutality to three (3) for better public services.

Fifty percent of the highest priority votes cast by the *unemployed* identified better economic conditions as highest priority among black community problems. This factor outdistanced the second ranking item, crime/drug abuse, which received six (13 percent) of the 48 highest priority votes, by a ratio of 4:1. Better economic conditions out-ranked more political power, third in overall priority among this group with a mere five votes and 3 percent, by a margin of 4.8:1. The range of first priority ranks reported for the remaining items was from zero (0) for police brutality and "other" to four (4) each for both equal justice and better education.

With the *low status* occupations, such as blue collar workers, maintenance persons, and waitresses, 217 or 56 percent of the 391 highest priority votes cast showed a distinct preference for better economic conditions as the most important problem facing the black community. The ratio between this factor and the second priority listed, better education, was 4.8:1. Better education received 45 (or 12 percent) highest priority votes. The better economic conditions factor outdistanced the third ranked priority, crime/drug abuse, by a margin of 8:1. The crime/drug abuse problem garnered only 27 votes or 3 percent of all highest priority listings. However, it should also be noted that this problem received only two votes more than did both equal justice and better housing which received 25 highest priority votes each.

Within the *high status occupations*, such as professional and managerial workers and white-collar employees, less than one-half (42 percent of 212) of the highest priority ranks were assigned to better economic conditions. However, this factor was 2.9:1 more likely to be mentioned as highest in priority than was better education, which ranked second, and 3.5 times more often than equal justice which ranked third. Again, it should be noted that only a single vote separated the third (25 votes) and the fourth (24 votes) priorities with respect to the highest priority ranks.

Hence, it appears that the higher the occupational level, the more likely were respondents to emphasize macro-community issues as the most serious problems that the black community faces. Persons on fixed incomes, or unemployed, or who were employed in low status occupations seemed somewhat more inclined to identify micro-community issues as highest in priority. Perceptions and categorizations of the severity and urgency of problems in some ways appeared to reflect one's position in the social structure as well as the general degree of educational, income and occupational success that people share. However, it is evident, according to what these respondents reported, black Americans are far more concerned about their economic well being than they are about any other issue.

Summary and Implications

Black Americans are confronted with a number of serious problems in the 1980's. Many of these problems are structural in nature; some are community-specific and some cut across the entire social, political and economic spectrum of the American society. On some problems, individuals sense that they have the power to affect change and the ultimate resolution of them while on others, a strong belief is prevalent in the black community that their fate is, unfortunately, in the hands of others, especially within a white power structure that is not sensitive to their needs and urgent concerns.

Unemployment among blacks is persistently twice that of the white population and black teenage unemployment has reached disastrous levels in most American cities. As previously noted, black teenage unemployment rates reach as high as 66 percent in some large cities.

The unemployment rates among black Americans continue to soar to unprecedented levels. According to U.S. Labor Department data released in November 1981, the unemployment rate among black Americans stood at 15.5 percent while that for white Americans was 6.9 percent. The overall national unemployment rate of 8 percent was the highest it had been in six years, and there were more jobless Americans in November 1981 than had been unemployed since the waning days of the Great Depression in 1939. According to the U.S. Labor Department, the black teenage unemployment rate, was officially acknowledged as 51 percent in August 1981.

In other words, one of every two black teenagers and one of every six black adult workers was out of work. If all the discouraged workers were included in these estimations, the proportion of jobless blacks would be substantially higher.[25]

Even when governmental work programs are made available to relieve the problems for hard core, unemployed inner-city blacks, the white power structure often diverts these jobs to white youths from suburban communities. Hence, the combined factors of racism, nepotism and influence conspire to deepen the problem among black youths. As a result, all across the nation, many young blacks have no experience with organized work, and no opportunities in the labor force to earn an income.

The black adult employed are also highly vulnerable to current economic woes and to displacement created by high technology and automation. As physical plants relocate to either distant suburban communities or to new regions of the country, blacks find it virtually impossible to relocate with these jobs. Those with limited education suffer the most. And, those who receive pensions and retirement benefits soon discover that double digit inflation has taken an irreversible toll on their capacity to purchase needed goods and services.

Unmistakably, many black Americans do perceive racism and discrimination as major impediments to job attainment and upward mobility on the job. According to the National Urban League's Black Pulse Survey, a large majority of black Americans believe that racial discrimination is widespread. This belief holds irrespective of social class, if economic status is regarded as a proxy for social class. The findings in the Black Pulse Survey showed that approximately 70 percent of blacks who reported annual incomes in excess of $20,000, compared with 61 percent of blacks with incomes of less than $6,000 feel that there is "a great deal" of discrimination today.[26] These findings are supportive of conclusions drawn from data presented in Chapter V of this study which suggest that the increasing effects of discrimination and racism, irrespective of economic status and social class, help to account for alienation in the black population.

The Black Pulse Survey also supports conclusions in various chapters of this study which suggest that many blacks feel that the once apparent commitment to racial equality is rapidly eroding. According to the Black Pulse Survey, blacks are dissatisfied with the "current push for equality." They feel that efforts to assure racial equality are too slow. Significantly, the middle-income blacks, presumed by so many experts to have benefitted most by the Civil Rights Movement of the 1960's, feel that the pace for equality has eroded. Eighty-three percent of all middle-come blacks in that study, (with incomes in excess of $20,000/year), compared to 72 percent of low income blacks (with incomes under $6,000/year) were dissatisfied with the "push for equality." These findings contrast significantly with data reported in a 1970 Lou Harris poll commissioned by the National Urban League in 1970. In that study, only 47 percent of all blacks believed that the drive toward racial equality was "too slow" while 41 percent stated a belief that it was "just right."[27]

By the same token, a prevailing sentiment today is that the few gains that some have made would not have been achieved had it not been for the implementation of affirmative action policies, or the fear of official reprisals were some semblances of these policies not implemented. That alone is insufficient since any number of employers have demonstrated a higher level of ingenuity in the construction of barriers to equal employment opportunity. Yet, black Americans continue to have faith in the capacity of the Federal Government and high educational attainment to eradicate racial barriers to employment opportunity.

However, when one observes the relative low ranking of "better education" among the persons who have not completed a high school education and among the unemployed, low income and older persons, that faith is called into serious question. Some of these persons, especially the impressionable youths, may be acutely aware of the limited occupational and income gains achieved by their parents despite respectable educational attainment. Some may be brutalized daily by a school system in which they are constantly reminded that they are uneducable, untrainable and that the opportunities for advancement are controlled by groups that care little about their welfare. Consequently, they rationalize their conspiracy in their own ultimate fate of rootlessness, disillusionment and normlessness.

On balance, however, respondents report that the issue of better education ranks high as both a personal priority and as an urgent concern within the black community. As indicated by responses to open-ended questions, some of which are reported in Chapter VII, the participants in this study expressed a profound concern over a number of educationally relevant issues. For instance, they frequently referred to the utmost importance of quality education. Primarily because of their desire for the best education that public school systems can offer, there was support for busing as a tool for school desegregation. A recurring theme among many respondents from city to city was that the public school system had failed their children. Some claimed that schools had abdicated their responsibilities to teach, motivate and stimulate. Some asserted that many teachers are not particularly interested in teaching minority children and that disinterest when communicated to pupils creates such horrendous disciplinary problems that learning becomes almost impossible.

Consequently, many persons expressed grave concern over the future of the current generation of black pupils in public schools — that is, will they be adequately prepared not only for college but to fulfill other roles in adult life. The primacy of this concern for better education was underscored by a dominant theme that education remains the essential springboard to upward mobility, economic empowerment and a better overall quality of life. Although these sentiments were more prevalent among the better educated and the employed, they also occurred among other groups. Yet, as black minorities in a white dominated society, there is a sense of shared fate with blacks of other classes — the employed and better educated — that their collective destiny is inextricably tied to equality of educational opportunity.

All have serious questions about the fairness of the justice system and sense that blacks cannot expect to receive the same responses from the justice system as white Americans. Despite the reality that the approximately 5,000 black elected officials in 1980 were substantially greater in number than at any other time in the nation's history, more political power for blacks is needed.

In the first place, these black elected officials represent only 1 percent of all elected officials in the United States. About 146 of them are mayors, most in small towns except in cities such as Los Angeles, Detroit, Atlanta, Birmingham, Newark, Gary, Indiana and Hartford, Connecticut. Only 17 are in the Congress of the United States, all of whom are in the House of Representatives. There are no black state governors and at the time this study commenced there were only two black lieutenant governors, both of whom have since been replaced with white males.

In most state legislatures, the paucity of representation is such as to render the black elected officials relatively powerless as a single bloc. As a result, they must become exceptionally skilled at the art of coalition politics in order to have reasonable assurances that their efforts to support the identified needs of their own political constituency will be realized even in some small way. Other than that, and with only a small voice to prick the conscience of sensitive white legislators, they become primarily symbolic in their value to the black community.

This situation need not exist, however, because black Americans can partially control this outcome by registering and exercising the right to vote, and by involving themselves in substantially larger numbers and with a force of presence in all aspects of the political process. Just as black voters have influenced outcomes in presidential elections, so have they often been a decisive factor in local and statewide elections. For instance, an analysis of voting patterns in the 1981 gubernatorial election in Virginia showed that black voters played a vital role in the election of a Democrat, Charles Robb, as governor of the state for the first time in about fifteen years. *The New York Times* attributed the large turnout of black voters on candidate Robb's behalf to the interjection of racism in the election by a prominent supporter of the Republican Party.[28] In general, however, participation of blacks in the political processes is still wanting even though it has been enhanced immeasurably by the enforcement of the Voting Rights Act of 1965.

The pitifulness of black involvement is evident in the national election of 1980 when only 60 percent of eligible blacks were registered to vote and only 51 percent actually voted. There is overwhelming evidence that the votes of black citizens played a profound role in the past in electing public officials. Hence, the need not only for more political power but more sophistication in how to use the vote to the advantage of black people is mandated by current realities.

Much has been said about the problems of crime and drug abuse and the quality of housing. However, it should be reiterated that without good jobs paying equal wages, it is unlikely that larger proportions of blacks will have sufficient income to be able to acquire loans for the purchasing of a better quality of house. Without rent control programs and tenant pressures on absentee landlords to maintain dwellings adequately, many blacks are condemned to less than desirable housing. In all instances, the enforcement of the Omnibus Housing Act of 1968 and stronger enforcement powers to foster compliance remain an absolute necessity.

Like Americans of all races, black Americans are deeply troubled by the perplexing problem of crime, drug abuse and rising police brutality. The relatively low priority attached to police brutality in the rank order of concerns may be quite deceptive. Crime is especially widespread in central city ghettos; it is increasing in the most affluent communities and in the apparently sanguine and quiet rural areas of the United States. As will be amplified in Chapter VII, black city dwellers are concerned by street crime, unprovoked and indiscriminate violence, especially by the young against each other and against the elderly. But they are also perturbed by a growing police violence against the black population that is so widespread that it appears beyond the capacity or apparent willingness of many police departments to control. In fact, some blacks have expressed a belief that police violence against blacks and other minorities is sanctioned consciously or by failure to take preventive measures against it by some local police departments.

A U.S. Justice Department report in 1981 indicated that a staggering 45 percent of all police homicides committed against Americans were against blacks who comprise just under 12 percent of the nation's population.[29] Further, the Community Relations Service of the U.S. Justice Department reported in 1980 that 249 complaints about the use of "excessive force" by police officers received in 1980 represented a 92.8 percent increase over the number reported in Fiscal Year 1979.[30] And, the U.S. Commission on Civil Rights reported in 1981 that the volume of complaints against excessive and deadly force used by police officers against blacks and other minorities steadily increased over the past several years.[31]

Some of the problems of police brutality, police violence and excessive force may be attributed to unwarranted and indiscriminate use of their awesome powers, their bias and generalized fear of minorities, improper selection of persons for the police force, inadequate training, inattention to the necessity for good community relations between those who have the responsibility of protecting citizens and the citizens themselves, and the unwillingness of some department officials to punish police officers for their own misconduct. These are serious problems and they will be addressed again in Chapter VII.

The most urgent concerns identified in this chapter affect the black population in a great variety of ways. Although it may be that many of these problems are also faced by the white community, the focus of this study did not attempt to address such issues. Its focus was exclusively on the black population. The data presented in this chapter, as well as in subsequent chapters, should be viewed in the context of present-day situations and in comparisons to earlier studies, such as Mydal's 1944, *American Dilemma,* as well as other research findings, where presented. These data will help to explain the degree of alienation presently experienced by a significant portion of the black population. They also help to explain the high degree of distrust of the power structure among black Americans in cities and suburbs as well as shed light on factors which influence their orientation toward the future.

Notes

1.   U.S. Department of Commerce, *Study of One-Parent Families in the United States.* Washington, D.C.: U.S. Government Printing Office, August, 1980.
2.   Reported in *The New York Times*, November 5, 1981, p. A-14.
3.   U.S. Department of Commerce, *The Social and Economic Status of the Black Population in the United States: An Historical View, 1790-1978.* Washington, D.C.: Bureau of Census, Current Population Reports, Special Studies Series P-23, No. 80, 1978, p. 32. Also see, Andrew Brimmer, "The Economic Status of Negroes," *The American Scholar,* (Autumn, 1969), p. 635.
4.   Blackwell, James E., *Mainstreaming Outsiders: The Production of Black Professionals.* Bayside, New York: General Hall, Inc., 1981, p. 26.
5.   Hill, Robert B., *Economic Policies and Black Progress: Myths and Realities.* Washington, D.C.: National Urban League Research Department, 1981, p. 37.
6.   *Ibid.*, p. 38.
7.   According to the U.S. Census Bureau, the national average of households for blacks during the last reporting year was 3.27 persons. This number compared to 2.89 for the white population. See: *The Social and Economic Status of the Black Population in the United States: An Historical View, 1790-1978.* Supra., p. 102.
8.   *Ibid.*
9.   *Op. Cit.*, pp. 51-52.
10.   "Suburban Inequality," *Black Enterprise,* (November, 1981), p. 19.
11.   Blackwell, James E., *The Black Community: Diversity and Unity.* New York: Harper & Row, 1975, Chapter IX.
12.   Cf. "Fewer Blacks Found to Survive Cancer for Five Years than Whites," *New York Times,* October 27, 1980; *The Boston Globe,* October 26, 1980, and Jack Slater, "The Terrible Rise of Cancer Among Blacks," *Ebony,* November, 1979), pp. 131-136.
13.   Citing a number of recent studies of crime by geographic region and by residential patterns, *Time Magazine* reported that four of the cities included in our study ranked in the "deadly dozen" of the most crime-ridden cities in the United States. For example, Los Angeles ranked second in assaults, sixth in rapes, seventh in murder, and tenth in robbery. Houston ranked second in murder, eighth in rape, eleventh in robbery, and twenty-third in assaults. Boston ranked fourth in both assaults and robberies, fifteenth in rape, and twenty-first in murder. Cleveland ranked third in rape, eighth in robbery, ninth in assaults, and fifth in murders. See: "The Curse of Violent Crime," *Time,* March 23, 1981, pp. 1633.
14.   National Urban League, Inc., *Initial Black Pulse Findings.* Washington, D.C.: National Urban League Research Department, August, 1980, pp. 1-2.
15.   *Ibid.*
16.   *Ibid.* and Robert Hill, *Op. Cit.*, p. 17.
17.   Gunnar Myrdal, *An American Dilemma.* New York: Harper & Row, 1944, p.60-61.

18. Among black persons who emphasize greater responsibility of black Americans for their own plight are Walter Williams of George Mason University and Thomas Sowell of the Hoover Institute. On the other hand, Benjamin Hooks of the National Association for the Advancement of Colored People seems more oriented toward system-blame for the economic deprivations experienced by black Americans and for the continuation of racial inequalities.

19. Stark, Randy, *Social Problems*. New York: CRM/Random House, 1975, p.168

20. Blackwell, *The Black Community, Op. Cit.*

21. Cf. *Uniform Crime Reports*. Washington, D.C.: U.S. Government Printing Office, 1980, pp. 200-229.

22. Randy Stark, *Op. Cit.* p.163.

23. U.S. Commission on Civil Rights, *Who is Guarding the Guardians?* Washington, D.C.: U.S. Commission on Civil Rights, 1981, p. vi.

24. *Op. Cit.*, p.164.

25. Cf. "U.S. Unemployment Rate Soars to 8%" *The Boston Globe*. November 7, 1981, p. 1.

26. The National Urban League, *Black Pulse Survey*, Supra., p.2.

27. *Ibid.*

28. *TheNew York Times,* November 6, 5, 1981.

29. Poinsett, Alex, "Police Deadly Force: A National Menace, *Ebony,* (March, 1981), p. 46.

30. U.S. Commission on Civil Rights, *Civil Rights Update.* (December, 1980), p.1.

31. U.S. Commission on Civil Rights, *Who is Guarding the Guardians?," Op, Cit.*

CHAPTER 4

Macro– And Micro–Community and Health Issues: A National Profile

Heterogeneity within the black community is recognized by many sociologists today.[1] Such diversity is not generally accepted by the general public which continues to view black Americans as a monolith and in terms of demeaning stereotypes. This denial of heterogeneity enables believers of stereotypes to think of black Americans as residents of "pathological ghettos," inexorably prone to criminality, or uneducated welfare-chiselers who have never embraced the American work ethic. Adherents to these beliefs are totally out-of-touch with reality. They disregard the immense class differentials among the black population and fail to understand how, even with such internal differentiation, all blacks do feel, in varying degrees, the consequences of racism in American society.

Blacks may, however, show different degrees of concern or have divergent feelings about the urgency of conditions defined as micro-community or macro-community issues, or about their access to health care delivery services. Yet, the power of racism may be so overwhelming that class differences are obliterated in the face of barriers to equality of economic and educational opportunity, justice, political power, or to the general improvement of the quality of life in their respective neighborhoods.

This chapter focuses attention on micro- and macro-community issues, and health concerns. It examines a number of demographic factors which may affect perceptions of the urgency of these issues. Similarly, traditional socio-economic status variables are examined in order to ascertain the impact, if any, which these factors have on this sense of urgency and to determine how class differentials affect such perceptions.

A National Profile of Scale Characteristics

As noted in Chapter I, the following scales were constructed to test the hypotheses: (1) Macro-community concerns, (2) Micro-community concerns, (3) Occupational status, (4) Social participation, (5) Health Access Index, (6) Health Information, (7) Alienation, (8) Anomie, (9) Powerlessness, (10) Social Isolation, (11) Orientation Toward The Future, and (12) Distrust of the power structure. The descriptions of relative position of the respondents on these scales are provided in this section.

Occupation: About 11 percent (11.4 percent) of the participants were unemployed at the time of the interview. Another 6.4 percent were recipients of some form of pensions or social security benefits. A significant majority (56.2 percent) were employed in low status or blue-collar occupations. Slightly more than one-fourth (26.3 percent) were employed in relatively high status or white collar jobs.

Macro-Community Concerns: Macro-community issues or concerns are defined as those conditions in the social structure which transcend a particular neighborhood within the city and which were believed to affect the black community as a whole. Participants' responses to questions pertaining to their own conceptualization of these larger issues (e.g. busing for school desegregation, improvement of the economic condition of black Americans, better quality of education and so forth), were trichotomized as low, medium or moderate, and high concern. Low concern corresponds to the feeling that macro-community issues are not particularly urgent. Slightly more than one-fourth of the respondents (27.7 percent) ranked low on the macro-community scale. The *medium* rank was interpreted as attaching a relatively moderate import to these issues. Slightly less than one-third (30.4 percent) of the respondents received a rank of medium concern. A score of *high* on this scale meant that the individuals saw macro-community issues as issues of the greatest urgency and in need of immediate resolution. Over 40 percent (42 percent) received this ranking on the macro-community scale.

When respondents in the medium and high ranks are combined, it appears that almost three-fourths of the national sample are concerned about macro-community issues. The earlier discussion of urgent concerns according to demographic characteristics showed that some of the macro-community issues (e.g. improving the economic conditions of blacks) ranked either first or exceptionally high in the scale of concerns among participants.

Micro-Community Issues: Micro-community issues are defined as community or neighborhood specific; i.e. they represent concerns believed to be a problem of special importance to the residents of a particular neighborhood. Examples of micro-community concerns include better street lighting, better garbage collection, better police protection and the need of more drug stores in the neighborhood. Since marked distinctions are often drawn across residential and neighborhood lines on the basis of micro-community issues, it is reasonable to expect a different scale distribution from the one found. The overwhelming majority of the participants (70 percent) classified micro-community issues as having "medium" or moderate urgency to them. Only 13.8 percent believed them to be a high urgency while another 15.3 percent categorized micro-community issues as matters of low urgency.

This divergence from expectation reflects a greater urgency for survival needs such as a change in the economic standard of living, equality of educational opportunity and equal justice before the law as opposed to essential quality of life concerns. It may also suggest a strong sense of fatalism about the possibilities for improving the overall quality of life in the neighborhood since so many proposals for better neighborhoods have been abandoned over the years. However, without transformations in the social structure which facilitate gains beyond acquisition of basic sustenance needs for the individual and family, neighborhood-specific issues will of course continue to be of great importance but not as urgent as those factors which address survival in a hostile society.

Social Participation: An index of social participation was constructed in order to discern the: (1) degree to which individuals were integrated into their own neighborhoods, (2) attachment to the institutions and friendship networks of their older or previous neighborhood, (3) patterns of interracial relations, and (4) relationship between their social participation and alienation. Responses to the items resulted in a distribution which classified 5.0 percent as *low* in social participation, 48.0 percent as *medium* or moderate, and 47.0 percent as *high* in social participation.

Health Access Index: The index of access of community health facilities was designed to measure *perceptions* of health care accessibility and to provide a basis for understanding behavior with respect to health issues. One-third (33.4 percent) of the respondents perceived health care access as low; slightly under one-half (49.5 percent) perceived it as a medium and less than one fifth perceived it as high. Inasmuch as the medium ranking is unstable since respondents in this group can shift in either direction, it appears that access to health services is seriously wanting.

Health Information: Many studies have argued that a major impediment to the delivery of health care services in the black community is the lack of information about the services available to community residents. In this study, responses to questions pertaining to information about the existence of health services in a given neighborhood were essentially one of two categories. Over two-thirds (68.2 percent) of the participants reported that they were poorly informed while slightly under one-third (31.8 percent) reported being well informed about available community health care services. Subsequent analyses will demonstrate the often prevalent discontinuity between knowledge and its practical application. For instance, some individuals may have access to health facilities or be knowledgeable about their existence but may never make use of them even when their services are needed.

Alienation and Its Variants: In the following analysis, the relative instability of the *medium* category must be borne in mind. Responses in this category may shift in either direction; i.e., toward high or low alienation. This shift is mathematically determined by the percentage distribution of responses in the *high* and *low* categories. If the percentages are greater in the *high* category, the tilt is from *medium to high*. On the other hand, if the percentages are greater in the *low* ranking, the tilt is from *medium to low*. In both instances, it is assumed that most responses fall in the medium category but the second largest responses may be in either the high or low rankings. Not only is this mathematical determination germane for the alienation scales, it is equally relevant for other scales such as social participation and macro-community issues in which a substantial proportion of the responses were in the medium category.

With respect to alienation and its variants, however, a disregard for the medium ranking permits one to conclude that about the same proportion of blacks report a low sense of anomie as those who measure high on the anomie scale. About equal numbers appear to feel alienated. Twice as many blacks measure high in sense of powerlessness compared to those who measure low in powerlessness. Three times as many blacks score low on social isolation compared to the proportion who score high on this scale. But, if the tilt of the medium toward high dimension were taken into consideration, an even stronger argument could be advanced for the position that feelings of alienation, anomie, powerlessness and social isolation are pervasive among the black population.

Orientation To The Future: The percentage distributions in this scale were 22.8 = low, 67.9 = medium and 9.3 = high (percent). The 22.8 percent participants in the low category were not goal-directed. Neither did they feel that life situations would improve appreciably in the future. In essence, more than a fifth could be characterized as not only disillusioned but loathed to believe that the future promised substantial improvements in their daily lives. By contrast, slightly less than a tenth (9.3 percent) had clearly defined goals and a high degree of optimism about the future. A more refined analysis of the data showed that the more future oriented persons were less likely to be alienated, anomic or to have a strong sense of powerlessness. The opposite was true for the persons with a weakened orientation toward the future.

Distrust of the Power Structure: Attitudes toward the power structure were mixed. Again, the instability of the medium category has to be borne in mind. About one-fifth of the participants reported a high distrust of the power structure, whereas more than two fifths (45.4 percent) indicated a low sense of distrust and more than one-third (34.3 percent) were moderate in their sense of distrust of the power structure. Again, persons with a high distrust of the power structure were more likely to be alienated, anomic and to have a strong sense of powerlessness. The highest sense of distrust was found among black residents of metropolitan Boston. (See Chapter VII).

Discussion of Hypotheses*

Age: The hypothesis that older persons are more likely than younger persons to perceive micro-community issues as a matter of urgent priority was not confirmed. In fact, age did not configurate as a discriminating variable regarding concern for these issues. Age groupings tend to be homogeneous in the degree of priority assigned to micro-community issues.

A closer confirmation of the hypothesis that younger persons are more likely to perceive macro-community issues with greater concern than are older persons was obtained. The slight tendency for younger persons to place greater priority upon macro-community issues may reflect the idealism of youth in contrast to the cynicism and fatalism of older persons who may feel that experience has taught them that they can have little effect on the larger issues which face the black community.

Regarding the relative salience of the age variable for understanding alienation and anomie, the findings are somewhat different than expected. It was hypothesized that younger persons are more likely to rank high on alienation, anomie, powerlessness, or social isolation than are older per-

---

*All statistical relationships can be found in Appendix One.

sons. This hypothesis was not confirmed with regard to alienation. The finding is that the three age groups are "medium" or moderate in alienation. Consequently, age is not the most powerful predictor of alienation. Neither is the hypothesis confirmed with respect to the relationship between age and anomie. On the contrary, older persons in this study are more anomic than are younger persons.

All age groups are in the medium range of powerlessness; therefore, that portion of the hypothesis, as stated, was not confirmed. Neither was support found for the presumed relationship between age and social isolation. The younger age group (persons between 18 and 30) reported lower social isolation than did persons in the older age group (persons above 50 years of age). This finding could be a manifestation of the reality that the American society is a youth-oriented society. It suggests also that this society does indeed offer more social outlets for the young than it does for older persons. Perhaps, younger persons have a larger array of social networks on which to draw and significantly greater spontaneity in taking advantage of those outlets available to them such as nightclubs, single bars, dances and social functions in their own homes.

Sex: The hypothesis that women are more likely than men to perceive both macro and micro-community issues as matters of urgent priority was not confirmed. There is no difference between the sexes in the perception of the urgency of either macro-community or micro-community issues. Both groups are homogeneous with respect to their views on the priority attached to these issues.

Family Status: No support was found for the hypothesis that families headed by men are more likely to view both macro-community and micro-community issues with greater concern that are families headed by women. Nor was confirmation obtained for the hypothesis that single-parent headed families are more likely to view both macro and micro-community issues as matters of urgent priority than are single and never-married individuals. Similarly, no support was evident for the hypothesis that egalitarian families rank higher on macro and micro-community scales than do families headed by a single parent.

In each of the above situations, all groups were undifferentiated in the urgency with which they viewed both macro and micro-community issues. It does not matter whether the family is egalitarian, two-parented or single-parented in the importance attached to the issues that either affect the quality of life in their neighborhoods or which determine their capacity to live and work without fear of hunger, inadequate housing or structural inequality.

The hypothesis that family heads, more than non-family heads, attach greater priority to both macro- and micro-community issues was, on the other hand, only partially confirmed. On macro-community issues, family heads and non-family heads were homogeneous in their regard for these issues. Therefore, that part of the hypothesis was not confirmed. However, with regard to the micro-community issues, family-heads did indeed attach greater importance to micro-community issues that did non-family heads. Confirmation of this portion of the hypothesis undoubtedly reveals a deeper concern by those persons who have the principal responsibilities in the family for the overall welfare of their members. Hence, if streets are not well lighted, if police protection is wanting, if public services are not adequate, if crime is increasing and the perpetrators are not prosecuted, and if other neighborhood needs are insufficiently attended, heads of households do demonstrate far more concern about these conditions than non-family heads, who have only themselves to protect.

It may seen somewhat contradictory to report that the hypothesis that married persons show a greater concern for both macro- and micro-community issues than do single and divorced persons was not confirmed as stated. Again, when the hypothesis was dichotomized, there was no confirmation for the macro-community segment as stated. Nor was there support for the micro-community segment. The specific finding was that divorced, single, never-married and married differed significantly from widowed persons on the macro-community scale. The groups were undifferentiated with respect to macro-community issues. It appears from this analysis that widowed persons show less concern for macro-community issues. This situation may be a result of their age, of their having to live on a fixed income, pension, or social security, and their sense that they have limited influence on the larger issues that affect black people. Therefore, the sense of commitment to altering these large, societal, systemic issues is diminished.

Income: No support was obtained for the hypothesis that the lower a person's income, the more likely is concern for micro-community issues to be of greater priority. On the contrary, this analysis shows that a higher income means a higher priority for micro-community issues. Similarly, a higher combined family income also means a higher priority given to micro-community issues. One explanation for this situation may be that higher income persons who may have been previously victimized by several of the conditions encompassed under micro-community issues, now seek to protect themselves against their recurrence. Further, they may have developed a strong sense of cynicism and fatalism about the delivery of adequate neighborhood services unless community pressure is exerted for that purpose. This relationship may also reflect the ability of high income people to maintain better neighborhood conditions.

Confirmation was found for the hypothesis that the higher a person's annual income, the greater is the priority for *macro-community issues.* Similar support was obtained for the relationship between combined family income and the higher priority given macro-community issues. Hence, higher income persons attach greater priority to both micro- and macro-community issues than do persons in the lower income brackets.

A further test of the relative salience of the income variable for predicting degrees of concern for micro- and macro-community issues was accomplished through an examination of the relationship between unemployment status and types of income with the community scales. No confirmation was obtained for the hypothesis that persons who are unemployed attach greater priority to both macro- and micro-community issues than do persons who are working. The finding obtained was that employed persons are higher in their prioritization of macro-community issues and that this relationship is a highly significant one. Similarly, the employed persons are higher in the priority attached to micro-community issues and this relationship is statistically significant.

A related hypothesis was that persons on fixed incomes are more likely to be concerned about *micro-community* issues that are both unemployed and employed persons. This hypothesis holds true only with regard to the unemployed but it is not confirmed for the employed. One explanation for this finding is that persons on fixed incomes are more likely to be older, long-time residents, widowed and who may have witnessed profound changes in the overall quality of their neighborhoods. They may be more inclined to articulate a need for micro-community improvement purely out of self-interest.

Education: With regard to the salience of education as a predictor of concern for micro-community issues, the findings in this study are consistent with previous observations about socio-economic status variables. It was hypothesized that the lower the number of years of schooling, the more likely is that person to perceive micro-community issues as matters of the highest priority. Precisely the opposite appears to be the case; that is, higher education implies higher importance attached to micro-community issues.

Occupation: Degrees of priority attached to micro- and macro-community issues are also differentiated along the occupational dimension. For example, confirmation was obtained for the hypothesis that the higher the rank on an index of occupational prestige, the greater will be the concern for *macro-community issues.* However, no support was obtained for the hypothesis that the lower the occupational rank, the higher is the concern for micro-community issues. The reverse pattern was observed; that is, the higher the occupationl status, the greater is the concern for *micro-community* issues.

The socio-economic status variables of income, education and occupation produced a high degree of differentiation among the participants with regard to the macro- and micro-community issues. These findings show that the higher the rank on each of these SES variables, the greater the likelihood for the individuals to demonstrate a uniformly higher concern for both micro-community and macro-community issues. This observation holds true when comparisons between the employment categories are made. Employed persons, in general, are more concerned about types of community issues than are the unemployed. What may be operating here as explanatory of an apparent detachment among the unemployed is a deeply embedded sense of futility about any effort to effect change. It may very well be that a significant proportion of persons in the low-status occupations, low income groups, with less schooling, and who are unemployed have become so discouraged by such prolonged disabilities that they have retreated into a world in which survival by any means necessary is their central preoccupation.

Residential Areas: Black suburbanites show a higher concern for both macro-community and for micro-community issues than black urbanites. Confirmation was obtained for the hypothesis that persons in suburbs have a higher concern for macro-community issues than do urban residents. The reverse of the hypothesis is that persons in urban areas are higher in their concern for micro-community issues than are persons in suburbia. Suburbanites show a significantly higher concern for these issues than black urban residents.

Health Information: In order to ascertain the possible existence of a relationship between concern for macro- and micro-community issues, the hypothesis that the greater the health service information flow to service area residents, the lower the tendency to perceive either micro- or macro-community matters of great urgency was advanced. This hypothesis was not confirmed regarding a predicted correlation between health information flow and macro-community concerns. The analysis showed that high macro-community concern is significantly related to low health information flow. There is a significant relationship between concern for micro-community issues and "never used health services."

The central implications of these findings are that for a large number of black communities informing them of what services are available is a problem of great magnitude; many persons do not know about the availability of these services, and probably do not use them even when they are aware of their presense. These findings suggest that the fundamental problem is not essentially one of complacency; rather, macro-community issues simply have a higher priority.

The hypothesis was confirmed with respect to micro-community issues. In order words, this analysis shows that the greater the flow of health services information, the lower is the urgency attached to micro-community issues.

Other Correlates of Macro- and Micro-Community Issues

Inferences have been made that persons with a high degree of concern for macro-community issues have a high degree of concern for micro-community issues. This observation is borne out by the analysis of the data in this research. The strong Pearsonian correlation of .45 between macro-community and micro-community concerns, coupled with its high level of significance, is confirmatory. It is important to keep distinctions of these types of concern in focus. Macro-community issues include such things as economic conditions, a need for higher incomes, concern about high rates of unemployment among the black population, busing for school desegregation, increasing the overall quality of education available to black children, attitudes of law enforcement officials and *delivery* of health services. *Micro-community issues,* on the other hand, include better police protection within the community, improved street lighting, improved transportation facilities, and better *access* to health services. Each set of factors may have its own distinctive relationship to other variables, which, in turn, affect how blacks view their own sense of well being.

Correlates of Macro-Community Issues

The relationship between priority for macro-community and other variables was determined by the significance of the Peasonian correlations ascertained. Of special importance are the correlations between priority for macro-community issues and priority given to micro-community issues, rank on the health information index, rank on the anomie scale, and rank on the social isolation scale.

An inverse relationship exists between high macro-community concern and health services information. In other words, as the urgency for macro-community issues increases there is a corresponding lack of information about health services available in their neighborhood. This finding seems inconsistent with other attributes of individuals who demonstrate a high degree of concern for macro-community issues. It was reported that a high priority to these issues was given by the employed, high status occupations, high income, well-educated and suburbanite population. This is precisely the group expected to have a significant set of information about health services available in communities or areas of the city other than their own immediate community and may be more prone to seek health services in those areas in which their physicians, dentists and psychiatrists are located. The locations may, in fact, be in another section of the city; consequently, these individuals do not pay much attention to whatever health information does flow into their community.

Individuals who claim that macro-community issues are of the highest priority also tend to be more anomic than those who do not. There is an inverse relationship between high priority given to macro-community issues and the degree of social isolation. In effect, persons who have macro-community concerns rank low on the social isolation scales. These individuals are either well-integrated into their communities, into the larger society itself, or they have such significant social networks as to minimize the sense of social isolation. Yet, these very individuals tend to be highly anomic, — a finding which raises serious doubts about the sources of that anomia. One possibility is that the anomia experienced occurs in relationship to the conditions within the larger society itself as opposed to local community peculiarities. Hence, unfulfillment of macro-community needs, structural in character as they are, seems to be manifested in an amomic relation to the larger social system itself.

To summarize, the most important correlates of a high priority given to macro-community concerns appear to be high socio-economic status (as measured by individual annual income, high occupational status, high educational attainment), employment, living in suburban communities, limited information about health services and a high anomic condition. If these variables are then viewed as a configuration of predictor variables, then, they should be regarded as important indicators of who is likely to attach a high degree of significance to macro-community issues. They should also predict who is likely to initiate social protests against public policies which restrict access to the life chances implied in macro-community concerns. It is equally important to note that this concern cuts across all age groups, marital status, type of household, type of family and with both sexes. These groups are homogeneous in their belief that those issues specified as macro-community are of special urgency to them.

Correlates of Micro-Community Issues

As indicated by Pearsonian correlation coefficients, the most signifi-cant correlates of priority given to micro-community issues are a high concern with macro-community issues, the health access index, health information flow, anomie, a sense of powerlessness, a sense of social isolation, and orientation toward the future.

A movement toward increasing concern with micro-community issues is accompanied by a similar change in concern for macro-community issues. In other words, a high priority given to micro-community issues means that a similar weight is assigned to macro-community issues.

While the relationship between micro-community concerns and the feeling of good access to health services is positive, the correlation between micro-community issues and the flow of health services information is negative. The latter variable is regarded as one of macro-community issues and it refers specifically to the delivery of health services. Hence, there was confirmation of the hypothesis that the greater the information flow about health services to area residents, the lower will be the tendency to perceive micro-community issues as a matter of great urgency. Given prior knowledge of the correlations between macro-community issues and health services information, and since the health index refers to health access, the inverse relationship between micro-community concerns and health infor-mation is less surprising. It is more or less apparent from these correlations that the greater the urgency placed on micro-community issues the higher will be the person's rank on the health access index, or the greater will be the feeling that health services are accessible within the community. Yet, the delivery of health services will not be as adequate as desired.

However, concern with micro-community issues is also accompanied by a high state of anomie. The inverse relationship with powerlessness, however weak it appears to be, suggests that persons who are troubled by community-specific issues do not seem to feel powerless to do anything about them. Yet, they tend to be just as anomic as those persons who are concerned with macro-community issues. Similarly, an inverse relationship exists between concern with the community-specific issues and social isola-tion. In other words, as the concern for micro-community issues increases, the feeling of social isolation diminishes. However, the orientation toward the future becomes more positive. In other words, those individuals who demand such things as better police protection or better access to health services and improved street lighting and transportation services are more optimistic about the probability of meeting these needs, and they are less likely to *feel* socially isolated.

When demographic characteristics were cast as predictors of the degree of urgency attached to micro-community issues, it was observed that there was a high degree of consistency in the way these concerns were perceived. Regardless of age, marital status, sex, income distribution, place of residence, household type, family authority structure, or occupational status, the concern for micro-community issues was uniformly high. However, one can speculate that the motivation for this similarity of concern might vary across any one or more of these demographic variables. Differences in motivation may be reflected in degrees of urgency attached to specific issues.

Implications

It should not be surprising, in the context of the structural conditions in which black Americans find themselves and the widespread ramifications of racism in the social system, that there is such a high degree of homogeneity in the way blacks perceive micro- and macro-community issues. Without question, there is heterogeneity among blacks and there is strong disagreement on some issues but the fundamental concerns about survival needs are deeply rooted in social experience. We have stressed that the median family income of these participants was about $300.00 less than the medium family income of $10,850 for the black population as a whole at the time this study was completed. Blacks are paid only 57 percent of the amount paid to white families. The income gap between the races is widening despite the rising educational levels among blacks. Black Americans continue to be concentrated at the lower end of the occupational spectrum. The persistence of racial discrimination helps to explain these inequities.

Even if more black women are located in white collar positions, the fact of the matter is that they tend to be more concentrated in sales and dead-end clerical positions than in higher paying professional and managerial roles. While affirmative action programs have been instrumental in facilitating access to better jobs, and court decisions have made some employees more reluctant to discriminate in the distribution of wages and salaries across racial lines, many find ingenious ways to continue institutionalized discriminatory practice. This situation counterposes the argument among many that blacks can be successfully integrated into the occupational structure on the basis of their merit.

While some persons claim that affirmative action programs and policies are a disaster, if not a public sham, there is little reason to believe that whatever economic and occupational gains blacks made during the civil rights and post-civil rights period of the 1960's and 1970's would have been reaped without these policies. There is more support for the argument that the existence of these regulations, the threat of their implementation, and the publicity given to court decisions in which an aggrieved minority was victorious prevented many individuals from engaging in an overt pattern of racial discrimination. These situations also persuaded some to become a "reluctant conformer" to the American ideal of equality of opportunity when otherwise their tendency would have been to discriminate against blacks.

Regardless of social class and place of residence, blacks demonstrate profound interest in issues of busing for school desegregation and for improving the overall quality of education offered their children. There is a plethora of information about the condition of schools in urban communities, especially in those neighborhoods in which minorities are concentrated, as opposed to educational programs available in suburban communities.[2] The cities included in this study offer little, if any, persuasion against these central findings. Without a doubt, there are equally excellent urban schools. However, a great proportion of the elementary and secondary schools of urban cities fall considerably short of expectations regarding the delivery of educational services to their pupils. These services refer to the quality of the teaching and learning processes, the types of learning facilities available to pupils, the lack of rigor in the academic curriculum, the inattention to fundamental skills of writing and reading, comprehensiveness and understanding of computational procedures. The problems are exacerbated by the attitude of all too many teachers who drive their minority students inexorably toward a self-fulfilling prophesy that these students cannot and will not master rudimentary subject matter. These attitudes result in an inordinately high drop-out and push-out rate of black students from public schools. One apparent consequence is that the sense of despair and alienation festers and worsens.

A direct comparison of monies spent per student in urban vs. non-. urban districts can not be made without factoring in the administration costs associated with patronage and political appointments and other noneducational costs which tend to be greater in urban districts. During

1980-81, Boston per pupil expenditures, for instance, were nearly $1,000 higher than in suburban Brookline or Newton. But the quality of services delivered in Boston was not commensurate with the monies expended.[3]

These disparities across racial lines, deeply rooted in American educational history, have made busing for school desegregation a necessary tool to facilitate equality of educational opportunity. It is not as some critics have charged based on the premise that blacks can only learn when they are sitting next to whites. On the contrary, what is apparent is that the city power structure is consistently more inclined to strengthen the overall quality of the educational programs offered within a school district when a substantial number of enrolled pupils are white. In general, the white power structure is not as concerned with quality education when the school district (system) is predominantly black or of another racial minority.

One highly perturbing aspect of the busing controversy (confirmed in this study) is the undue burden placed on black pupils to assure school desegregation. The prevailing practice is more often for blacks to be bused into white schools than for whites to be bused into schools located in predominantly black neighborhoods. There is deep resentment among blacks and whites about this pattern. Some parents of both races want their children in neighborhood schools. Many blacks object to this unfair burden placed on them and many whites simply do not want black students mixing with their children. Similarly, many black neo-conservatives have joined the chorus of ex-white liberals who sanctioned busing as a viable desegregation tool until some semblance of a metropolitan plan was ordered for their neighborhoods that resulted in their children being bused into predominantly black schools and communities.[4]

Without question, some of these parents are concerned exclusively with the quality of education received by their children in these schools but, indisputably large numbers of parents have indeed moved away from cities to escape contact with black people. Regardless of these positions, an incontrovertable truth is that busing for school desegregation is one of the larger issues of paramount importance to black Americans. What is at stake here is the willingness or the capacity of local governments to allocate necessary financial and human resources, and improve the within-class atmosphere in ways that will strengthen the overall quality of education and the learning environment.

Black Americans are also concerned about all aspects of the criminal justice system. Fear of crime is pervasive and justifiably so since most research shows that blacks of all social classes are more likely to be victimized by crime than are members of the white population.[5] However, the victim of a street crime, a mugging, a purse-snatching or a housebreak does not need sociological studies to either inform or convince him or her how real is the fear of crime victimization for that individual. That fear governs behavior, often controls daily activities, and generates a scrupulous cautiousness in the way people relate to each other, or in what they say to persons with whom they are not personally acquainted.

The fear of crime is matched by a disillusionment with the criminal justice system. The feeling prevails that it is not responsive to the needs of black Americans, and that the criminal justice system is structured to serve the exclusive rights of the white majority. Blacks are acutely aware of the bias that is so widespread among police officials toward them. Blacks know that they are more likely to be suspected of an offense because of these biases. They also know that selective perception and such biases are so endemic in American society that it is not unexpected when one reads or hears about a crime that the perpetrator was black.

Many blacks are in complete agreement with sociological research which shows that black-on-black crime and white-on-black crime are treated less harshly than black-on-white crime. Consequently, when the perpetrator of a crime against blacks is apprehended and brought to trial, there is the strong probability that that person will be treated less severely, in terms of the sentence meted, than if the victim were white. What black Americans articulate with regard to crime and justice is plain and simple — equal application of the law throughout all stages of the criminal justice system.

To accomplish this goal means a concerted effort to extricate police officers from the shackles of their own cultural and racial biases. It requires systematic programs to undo a life-time of negative socialization in such a way that police officials are re-socialized to respect humanity. It means hiring more black officers far beyond the national percentage of 4 percent.[6] It means promoting blacks to the higher echelons of the police hierarchy; detectives, lieutenants, captains and superintendents. It means that the appointment of a much larger number of blacks to judgeships, as well as their election to these offices when that is the normal process of incumbency. It also means both the production of more black lawyers beyond the 2 percent which blacks represent of the nation's 588,000 lawyers, as well as increasing utilization of black lawyers by black people.

Improvements in economic conditions, the income and occupational structure, the quality of education and in the attitudes of the law enforcement agents can generate profoundly positive changes in the sense of well being among black Americans. Also of concern in equal justice before the law are fair jury selection procedures. Blacks, women, the poor, and young people, are less likely to have probability of being tried by a jury of their peers than whites, men, non-poor and middle age persons.

Further discussion of other health issues is necessary in order to expand our understanding of the health implications of macro- and micro-community concerns. We need to know, for example, if there is a relationship between knowledge about health services within an area and the actual utilization of those services. This study hypothesizes that the greater the information flow from health service agencies to residents in the service areas, the more frequent the utilization of health services in those areas. This hypothesis was not confirmed. It appears that information is in fact disseminated by the health service agencies but the area residents are neither hearing nor reading about those services. However, there is a significant relation between the dissemination of health information and the use of health services for accidents. There is also a significant relation between the health access index and "never used" health services. Similarly, the relationship between health access index and use of health services for mental illness is significant.

Clearly, people utilize existing health service facilities for different reasons. The most often cited reason for utilization is for accidents since 17.5 percent of the participants stated that community health centers are used for this purpose. The second most common usage is for acute illness — 14.3 percent indicated that the centers were used in that connection. Even though the relationship between health information flow and use of community health centers for chronic illness is significant, only 6.4 percent of the participants used them in such cases. And only 2.2 percent ever used these centers for assistance with mental health problems. This pattern indicates that not only is utilization of community health centers noticeably low but when individuals do use these services, that the use is for clearly defined purposes which appear to be of an emergency character.

An important question is the degree to which area residents know of the type of health and social services available to them within the local community or in close proximity to their place of residence. Almost three-fifths (59 percent) of these participants stated that they have never heard a radio or television announcement of community health and social services available to them. On the other hand, slightly more than two-fifths (43 percent) indicated that they had seen literature from health centers and less than one-fifth (19 percent) said that they had heard announcements as many as ten times per month, while 15 percent claimed to have heard announcements at least once. It may be that knowledge about health services is a function of how information is, in fact, actually disseminated to potential users. This reality may determine perceptions of what types of services are believed by the participants to be offered in the community centers.

It appears that study participants define community health centers as places in which one can obtain health services during and after pregnancy, for children, for mental health problems, for various types of family problems, drug counseling and aid to the elderly. Of those who have knowledge about community health services, almost one-quarter of them (23.3 percent), characterized their quality as "better than average" to "exceptionally good." This percentage contrasts well with the 27.3 percent who say that the clinic or hospital nearest them is "average" in terms of the quality of services provided.

Four-fifths of the participants (80.8 percent) maintain that they would or could pay for health costs under health insurance coverage. This percentage is below the 87.4 percent of individuals in the total population who claim to carry health insurance.[7] The remaining two-fifths state that their health costs would be paid by their own funds (15.1 percent) or by borrowing money (3.7 percent), or with financial assistance from friends and relatives (2.7 percent).

It is often assumed that black and other minority persons do not see physicians and dentists on a regular basis, that when they do see them, they visit health care specialists more often than not in clinics rather than in private offices. This claim is not supported by our findings. In the first place, 91.2 percent of these participants claim that they have had a physical examination within the past two years. Almost three-fifths of them (59.3 percent) maintain that a regular physical examination is "of some importance" to "very important." Similarly, over one-half (55.5 percent), insist that a regular dental examination is "of some importance" or "very important."

In this group, there is greater tendency to visit physicians and dentists in their private offices than in clinics or hospitals. For instance, 54.6 percent indicate that their last visit to a physician was in the physician's office, and only 12.4 percent sought out physicians in a clinic. By contrast, 69.4 percent stated that their last dental examination was within the past two years and 73.5 percent of those examinations occurred in the office of the dentist. Only 9.2 percent of dental examinations occurred in a community clinic and 8.5 percent were conducted in a hospital setting.

Blacks are more likely to be attended by a physician who is not black than they are by a black physician. In this group, about two-thirds (67.1 percent) indicated that their last physician was not of the same race. This fact may underscore the critical shortage of black physicians in general. It may also be indicative of the problem of maldistribution of black physicians. It should be rememebered that blacks comprise a sizeable population in each of the five cities studied. Yet, the number of black physicians in these cities is disproportionately low. As cited by Dubey and others, another possible explanation for blacks seeking out non-black physicians is that many blacks have indeed internalized the dominant group stereotypes that blacks are less competent and cannot possibly offer the same quality of health services as those offered by white physicians. The city-specific comparisons will be illuminating as to why more non-black physicians tend to the health needs of black individuals even though 16.2 percent of the participants in this study claim to have serious language problems with their physicians.

One measure of access to physicians and health services is the quality of available transportation to make such visits. Only one-third of the participants rated their transportation services as "better than average" to "exceptionally good." About two-thirds claimed that these services were either average or less than acceptable. Given this pattern, the disinclination to take advantage of available health services might not be unanticipated.

The transportation issue is further elucidated by proximity of pharmacies to place of residence. About 53.5 percent of this group assert that the nearest pharmacy is from six blocks to one mile or more from their homes. For only about a third (31.5 percent), the nearest pharmacy is within two blocks and for less than the percent (7 percent) the pharmacy is within a single block of their homes.

Only two social services are believed to be offered within community or neighborhood centers: job counseling and day care services. Over two-thirds (69.9 percent) indicated that job counseling services are available while somewhat less than that percentage (67.7 percent) stated that day care services are available. Finally, it should be evident that the formulation of public policy relative to the conditions of black Americans should take into consideration the expressions of priorities identified in this chapter.

Notes

1. Cf. Blackwell, James E., *The Black Community: Diversity and Unity,* New York; Harper & Row, 1975 - Thomas Pettigrew, *The Sociology of Race Relations.* New York: Free Press, 1980. Charles V. Willie, *The Sociology of Urban Education.* Boston: Lexington

Books, 1980, and Doris Y. Wilkinson, *Black Revolt: Strategies of Protest.* Berkely, California: McCutchon Press, 1969.

2. Cf. Haskins, Jim, (ed.) *Black Manifesto for Education.* New York: William Morrow & Co., 1973; Kenneth C. Clark, *Dark Ghetto,* New York: Harper & Row, 1965; Jonathan Kozol, *Death At An Early Age.;* New York: Houghton-Mifflin, 1967; U.S. Commission on Civil Rights, *Racial Segregation In Public Schools.* Washington, D.C., U.S. Commission on Civil Rights, 1967; Ray C. Rist, "Student Social Class and Teacher Expectations: The Self-Fulfilling Phophesy in Ghetto Education, *"Harvard Educational Review"* 40 (1970), 416-451; U.S. Commission of Civil Rights, *Desegregating The Boston Public Schools: A Crisis In Civic Responsibility,* Washington, D.C., U.S. Commission on Civil Rights, August, 1975; *Report of the National Advisory Commision On Civil Disorders.* New York: New York Times Bantam Books, 1968, and "Black Education: 25 Years After the Brown Decision," *Black Scholar,* 11:1 (Sept. 1979).

3. According to Boston Public School data, Boston's per pupil expenditure was $3,500 in 1980-1981. However, the Boston Municipal Research Bureau claims that the Boston per pupil expenditure is more accurately $5,500. The difference lies in the inclusion of all monies (e.g., municipal, state and federal funds) by the latter.

4. Cf. U.S. Commission on Civil Rights, *Desegregating The Boston Public Schools: A Crisis in Civic Responsibility, 1975.*

5. Stark, Randy, *Social Problems.* New York: CRM/Random House, 1975, Chapter 6 and James E. Blackwell, *Op.Cit.* Chapter 9.

6. This figure was provided by the Massachusetts Afro-American Policemen Association, June, 1980.

7. According to a report of the preliminary findings of the National Health Care Expenditure Study (NHCES), presented at the October 21, 1980 meetings of the American Public Health Association, 12.6 percent of civilian Americans are without health insurance. Percentage distributions by race show 11.7 percent of white civilians and 18 percent of non-whites carry no health insurance. This report also indicated that about 75 percent of all Americans had seen a physician once during the previous year and 40 percent had seen a dentist once during the same period. (CF *National Center for Health Services Research Update,* January 1981, p. 1. and "Many Found to Lack Medical Insurance," *New York Times.* October 22, 1980, A-18.

CHAPTER 5

The Alienation of Black Americans:
A National Profile

Several years ago Alfred McClung Lee, a prominent sociologist, announced his "obituary" for the concept alienation.[1] He attacked the excessive use and mis-application of the term by managerial consultants and "formula-peddling counselors" who tended to define the concept in purely psychiatric ways which implied that the "alienated individuals were" on the borderline of insanity. Arguing that its scientific utility "had died" despite its widespread use by social scientists, Lee raised serious questions about the treatment of this concept. These questions centered around imprecision in interpretation and meaning, both in law and in social science literature.

The legal tradition, Lee pointed out, interprets alienation as the condition of "being separated from one's reason" (or is insane) or it also means that the individual was "estranged" from work and property.[2] In time, it became fashionable for social scientists to interpret alienation in Marxist terms, (i.e. as estrangement from labor or the work place or through social structural perspectives that emphasize strains between society and its members). Lee argued forcefully that interpretations of alienation in the 1960's and early 1970's implied that those persons and groups defined as "alienated" were simply out of step with or rejected the "spokesman's value orientation or conception of social legitimacy."[3] In fact, he asserted that the values and ideas held by the "alienated" might be more satisfying to the group and/or individual thus perceived.

Even a cursory examination of sociological and psychiatric literature supports Lee's position. The popularity of alienation as a conceptual tool and as a device for explaining behavior at odds with societal norms and expectations is evident in the literature of the 1960's and 1970's. Moreover, the tendency among some sociologists is to define conflicting values of

102

minority groups as non-normative and the behavior of persons who cherish such values as pathological. In this way, alienation has been used in a judgmental sense.

The scales constructed for measuring alienation and its variants of normlessness or anomia, powerlessness and social isolation, were based upon the prevailing norms and sentiments of the dominant group society. So prevalent was the use of these scales and definitions that even this research is somewhat guilty of perpetuating the same erroneous myths by partial reliance upon scale items constructed in another historical epoch. It is hoped that the slight modifications in many of these items will permit escape from this tragic pitfall. However, failure to completely control for the influence of cultural variables within the black community and how that might affect interpretations of items normed on the white population might have seriously distorted how one scored on alienation scales. For this reason, it may be argued that the enormous possibility of "tilt" in the medium response category is especially critical in interpretations of findings relative to degrees of alienation among respondents.

In this context, one must be guided by the socio-structural conditions that affect daily life, the sense of well being, and social interaction as well as the impact of racism in perpetuating structural inequities in the American society. Consequently, alienation is viewed both in socio-structural terms and from a conflict perspective. It refers to the degree to which individual members of a group are so disenchanted with societal actions and so disillusioned by socially constructed barriers to the achievement of their legal rights that they have become cynical and uncertain about their capacity to effect systemic change vital for their sense of personal well-being.

Implicit in this socio-structural conceptualization are major questions about the capacity of existing norms of the dominant group system, for instance, to guide and frame the behavior of minorities who may reject these norms. Questions necessarily arise in societies in which structural inequality is so prevalent, prejudice and racism so widespread, and racial separation so deeply embedded about the possible manifestations of alienation.

The consequences of alienation are multiple. For instance, an individual may resign himself to the inevitability of the condition, while another might grow weary of the oppression created by society itself and decide to respond in an aggressive manner. Some members of the outside minority group may seek to break the bonds of group subordination by embracing the values and norms of the dominant groups without working for systemic changes. Still others might seek to transform structural situations in ways that expand the overall opportunity system for the realization of greater rewards by all members of the society. For others, being alienated might be the inspiration for an outpouring of intellectual creativity and productivity.

Conflict arises when the change-oriented goals of the minority group clash with the system-maintenance goals of the dominant group, since the latter is unwilling to share many of its economic, social and political rewards and privileges with those it has defined as less worthy. Hence, conflict will occur when minority groups seek to improve their conditions either through the formalized legal processes of the courts or by means of rebellious and contentious acts. Both are manifestations of alienation since the individuals involved seek to confront lack of autonomy, to exercise more control over their own fate, and to reduce the enormous power differentials between themselves and members of the dominant group. Conflict is likely to continue in varying stages until such time as society comes to terms with these structural inequities that generate alienation.

Degrees of Alienation and Its Variants

Responses on the alienation scales were classified as low, medium and high. On all scales, an overwhelming majority of the responses fell into the "medium" category. However, because of the influence of cultural variables and the force of events which transpired between the formulation of some of the original scale items* and the time in which the interviews were conducted, the likelihood for this finding is not unexpected.[4] Consequently, there is a strong probability of tilt among the medium group toward the high or low position. The persistence of barriers to widespread economic and social progress among all segments of the black community and the continued racism encountered by many of those who have achieved a high degree of success, leads one to suspect that the tilt will be stronger toward the "high" rather than the "low" levels of alienation and its variants.

When the alienation scale responses were trichotomized, 94.9 percent of them were classified as "highly" alienated and 5.1 percent were "low" in alienation. The immense significance of this finding is the large number of blacks all across the nation who expressed at least some degree of alienation within the American society. Almost all of them reported this feeling.

Anomie, powerlessness and social isolation were employed as central variants of alienation. In the case of anomie, defined here as a feeling of

---

*This finding points up the need for the development of a more updated alienation scale.

normlessness, almost two thirds (65.3 percent) of the respondents were classified as "medium" or somewhat anomic. The remaining one third were almost equally divided between a "low" (17.8 percent) and a "high" degree of anomia (16.9 percent). Again, under circumstances such as grave concern for the "hysteria" that seems to be gripping the black community in the wake of the 1980 national election, (it resulted in an administration perceived by many in all segments of the American society as either hostile or less than enthusiastic about continuing social programs designed to benefit blacks and other minorities), the tilt toward "high" anomia might be substantial.

Over three-fourths (76.0 percent) of the respondents were classified in the "medium" or somewhat powerless categories on the powerlessness scale. About one-sixth (16.3 percent) scored "high" on the powerlessness scale while less than one-tenth (7.7 percent) scored "low." As a result, more than nine of every ten blacks showed some degree of concern over their capacity to alter the social structure in ways that would render it more compatible to their goals. Although this sense of powerlessness is pervasive in the black community, it does not mean that blacks have resigned themselves to a powerless state. Quite the contrary, it is precisely this widespread condition that portends major conflicts ahead since the powerless may redefine their strategies in the light of prevailing conditions and seek newer and even more conflictive methods of gaining what they believe to be their inalienable rights.

In terms of social isolation, almost eight of every ten blacks (79.9 percent) were classified as "medium," i.e. somewhat isolated. Only 4.5 percent were in the "high" and 15.6 percent were in the "low" social isolation group. These disparities exist despite the high sense of community solidarity felt by a substantial number of black Americans. This situation is explained by the high degree of *racial isolation* between blacks and whites and high intra-group associations evident in social relationships discussed in Chapter VI. These findings demonstrate that, whatever the nature of inter-racial contacts among blacks and whites is, these are likely to be highly situational, impermanent, and less likely to lead to enduring, intimate inter-racial friendships.

Understanding about alienation may be illuminated by knowledge of an individual's goal orientation relative to the future and of his/her views of the power structure. The "orientation to the future" scale was designed to detect degrees of goal direction and beliefs about the probability that things will get better for blacks in the future. According to this scale, two-thirds of the participants (67.9 percent) were classified as "medium" or somewhat ambiguous about the future. Their goals were ambivalent and less clearly defined than expected. Slightly more than one-fifth (22.8 percent) ranked "low." That is to say, these persons were not goal directed and did not believe that things will get better in the future. They saw no possibilities for change and remained unconvinced about their personal capacity to affect outcomes or to alter their own fate.

When participants were questioned about their trust in the power structure, a significant plurality ranked low in "distrust" of the power structure (45.4 percent). In this instance, the medium category comprised slightly more than one-third (34.4 percent) of the respondents while one-fifth (20.3 percent) were "high" in their distrust of the power structure.

The sense of trust and distrust takes an a new meaning in two of the cities involved in this study, Atlanta and Los Angeles, which have black mayors. The lowest sense of distrust for the power structure was recorded among blacks in Los Angeles where Thomas Bradley serves as mayor. Over two-thirds of the participants in the Los Angeles sample (68.5 percent) registered a "low" sense of distrust. Approximately two-thirds (66.1 percent) of the Atlanta group registered a low sense of distrust of the power structure. Maynard Jackson, also a black American, was in his second term, as mayor of Atlanta.

In Los Angeles and Atlanta, the percentage of participants classified as "medium" or who have a moderate sense of distrust was 29.9 and 28.5, respectively. For the same cities, only 5.4 percent in Atlanta and 1.5 percent in Los Angeles were "high" in their distrust of the power structure.

These data suggest that in these instances blacks had faith in the capacity of a political structure headed by blacks to be fair and expeditious in responding to their needs, and to implement programs from which blacks may reap tangible economic, social and political benefits. These findings may also reflect a high degree of support for a power structure in which substantially larger numbers of blacks may be in prominent managerial and decision-making positions as a result of appointments made by black mayors. Consequently, these persons may themselves be considerably more sensitive to the urgent concerns of the black population.

The responses from Cleveland and Houston are interesting in terms of the low sense of distrust reported by participants in those cities. Cleveland was the first major city to elect a black mayor when Carl Stokes won the mayoralty contest in 1967. Cleveland also had a comparatively longer history of electing blacks to such political offices as membership on the city council and to judgeships than any of the other cities studied. Even though no black was serving as mayor during the period of the study, a black male was chairman of the city council, an almost equally powerful position in the city government. Hence, it was not particularly surprising that almost three-fifths (56.9 percent) of the participants would indicate a low sense of distrust of the power structure or that 39.9 percent were classified as "medium" in distrust, or that only 3.1 percent registered a "high" sense of distrust of the power structure.

In Houston, 62.6 percent indicated a low distrust while 31.3 percent showed a "medium" ranking, and only 6.2 percent expressed a high sense of distrust. These differences may also be explained by the increasingly important roles which blacks are playing in local government as a consequence of federal rulings on voting regulations and the appointment of prominent blacks to key managerial positions by the white mayor of the city.

Blacks in Boston registered the highest sense of distrust in the power structure. Over half (54.4 percent) of the participants indicated "high" distrust in the power structure. Forty point five (40.5) percent fell into the "medium" distrust category and a mere 5.1 percent registered "low" distrust of the power structure. In other words, blacks in Boston were almost 13 times more likely than blacks in Los Angeles and Atlanta, and about 12 times more likely than black residents of Houston and Cleveland to be distrustful of the power structure. The widespread perception among blacks in Boston that Boston is an extremely racist and prejudiced city probably explains these results. The perceptions are fueled by the limited, if not restricted, roles which blacks play in local government, and within the school system which until 1977 did not have a black person elected to the school committee in this century. These beliefs are influenced by the fact that Boston almost never had blacks in high elective position, by entrenched neighborhood segregation, unprovoked physical violence against blacks, and in the impoverishment of a large segment of the black population resulting from exclusion from many white, union-controlled jobs and discriminatory hiring practices.

Correlates of Alienation and its Variants

The alienation scale showed highly significant correlations with anomie, powerlessness and social isolation. It was also significantly but negatively correlated with orientation toward the future. Specially, the correlation between alienation and anomie was .38. Hence, persons who ranked high on the alienation scale also ranked high on the anomie scale. A particularly robust correlation of .78 was noted between alienation and powerlessness. This finding suggests that high alienation individuals also tend to have a deeply rooted sense of powerlessness. Inasmuch as the correlation between alienation and social isolation was quite strong at .60, one can assume that the more alienated the person, the more likely the person is to feel socially isolated. The negative correlation of -.12 with orientation to the future suggests that alienated persons can expect to have a lower sense of self-esteem and/or to have limited faith in the probability that life will get better in the future. Each of these correlations was significant.

Powerlessness: The strongest correlations with powerlessness were obtained for micro-community concerns, social participation, the health index, anomie, social isolation, orientation to the future and with alienation. (As indicated above, the correlation with alienation was a powerful .78).

A negative correlation of -.08 was found with micro-community concerns. The primary inference from this correlation is that persons who have a high sense of powerlessness seem to rank micro-community issues as comparatively low in concern. Although this finding is statistically significant, clearly it is not a particularly robust correlation. Similarly, a negative correlation of -.08 was observed between sense of powerlessness and rank on the health index. As a result, one may conclude that persons with a high sense of powerlessness rank low in the health index or in their belief that services are adequately delivered to the black community.

By contrast, the .40 correlation between a sense of powerlessness and anomie is not only strong statistically, it also demonstrates with substantially greater force that these two alienation variants vary together regardless of direction. Consequently, persons who rank low on the powerlessness scale are also likely to rank low in the anomie scale. The correlation of .20 with social isolation has the same effect. In other words, the higher the sense of social isolation the higher is the sense of powerlessness.

The impact of this sense of powerlessness on the overall sense of well being and on feelings that he or she can affect change is evident in the negative correlation between the sense of powerlessness and orientation to the future. This correlation of -.18 suggests that persons who define themselves as powerless do not feel that life will get better for them and they are likely to be devoid of clearly defined goals themselves.

A sense of powerlessness is also positively correlated with rank on the social participation scale. The correlation of .10 is nonetheless significant while comparatively weak when juxtaposed against anomie and social isolation.

Anomie: Rank on the anomie scale is positively and significantly correlated with rank on the scales of macro-community concerns, micro-community concerns, alienation, powerlessness and social isolation. It is negatively but significantly correlated with rank on the health index, the health information index, and orientation to the future. The correlations with alienation and powerlessness were discussed above. However, among the variants of alienation, the weakest correlation with anomie is that between rank on the anomie scale and social isolation. Anomic persons may indeed be socially isolated but this co-variance is not especially strong.

For that matter, neither is the correlation between anomie and rank on the micro-community concerns scale. Although the Pearsonian correlation of .08 is statistically significant, it is not by any means a powerful marriage. Nevertheless, the correlation indicates that persons who rank high on the anomie scale are also greatly concerned about micro-community issues. The correlation of anomie with macro-community concerns is stronger and substantially more significant. Hence, one can assert with greater confidence that highly anomic persons are also greatly concerned with macro-community issues. Yet, anomic persons tend to have a low orientation to the future and little faith in their capacity to affect change.

The correlation between rank on the anomie scale and rank on the health index, and health information scales are negative. In other words since high anomic individuals rank low on the health index, they believe that the health delivery system is failing them. One can also infer from the negative correlation between anomie and the health information index that high anomic persons feel that they do not receive a sufficient amount of information about health services available to them.

Social Isolation: The correlations between rank on the social isolation scale and ranks on alienation, anomie, and powerlessness scales were presented in preceding paragraphs. However, it should be pointed out that statistically significant correlations were observed between social isolation and macro-community concerns, micro-community concerns and health information scales. The correlation with macro-community concerns is negative. Therefore, a safe assumption is that persons high in social isolation tend to be less concerned about macro-community issues. Similarly, the correlation with micro-community concern is negative. This inverse relationship suggests that a high concern with micro-community issues is accompanied by a low sense of social isolation.

The correlation between rank on the social isolation scale and rank on the health information index is strong, positive and significant. It is, therefore, expected that persons who rank high on social isolation will also assert that they receive an adequate amount of health information from the various sources available in their communities.

Orientation to the Future: In addition to earlier comments about the correlations between rank on the orientation to the future scale and alienation and its variants, statistically significant correlations were observed with two other scales. In more specific terms, rank on this scale was positively correlated with rank on the concern for micro-community issues scale. It was also correlated with rank on the health index. Hence, persons who tend to be optimistic about the future and who have clearly defined goals tend to have a high concern for micro-community issues. They also tend to believe that the delivery of health care services is adequate. Previously discussed correlations suggest that the more future oriented individuals also are less likely to be anomic, powerless and alienated.

Distrust of Power Structure: Significant correlations of rank on the distrust of power structure scale were observed with orientation to the future, concern of macro-community issues, the health information index, rank on the scales of anomie, powerlessness, social isolation and health index. In all of these situations, with the exception of the correlation with powerlessness in which $p < .003$, the level of significance was beyond .000.

These findings show that a high rank on the distrust of the power structure is accompanied by a positive orientation toward the future. Not only do these individuals show a high distrust of the power structure, they also feel that they have the capacity to transform their own situations even if the power structure is not to be trusted. These persons tend to rank high in social isolation but low in their feeling of anomia and in their sense of powerlessness. They are likely to take matters into their own hands rather than trust the unpredictable whims of others in whom they have little confidence.

But, high distrust for the power structure is negatively correlated with a concern for macro-community issues. This finding indicates that high distrust means that individuals have a low concern for macro-community issues. These persons *may* believe that they have some degree of control over the probability of realizing macro-community goals (e.g. better economic conditions, better education, etcetera), and not that they need not become so disillusioned as to feel incapable of improving the collective welfare of black Americans.

The Alienation Hypotheses

In order to more adequately understand the dispersion of alienation and its variants among metropolitan blacks, an effort was made to determine its relationships with socio-economic status, health variables and with macro- and micro-community concerns. In this section, the focus is on findings that results from a test of the several hypotheses generated by this effort.

Age: It was hypothesized that younger persons are more likely to rank high on alienation, anomie, powerlessness or social isolation scales than older persons. This hypothesis was not confirmed for age and alienation. The finding was that the young, the middle-aged and the older age groups all ranked "medium" in alienation. Since each group seems equally but somewhat alienated, age is not a discriminating variable in this regard.

Neither was the hypothesis confirmed for age and anomie. The analysis of the data shows that older persons are higher on the anomic scale than younger persons. The hypothesis was neither confirmed for powerlessness nor for social isolation. Younger, middle and older persons are significantly "medium" in powerlessness. Therefore, age does not appear to have an impact on either alienation, anomia, powerlessness or social isolation in the predicted direction.

Education, Income and Occupational Status: Two hypotheses were offered to test the relationship between the traditional socio-economic variables of education, income and occupational status *and* degree of alienation, anomie, powerlessness and social isolation. One hypothesis advanced asserted that the higher a person's income, level of educational attainment, and rank on a scale of occupational prestige, the lower will be the person's rank on scales of alienation, anomie, powerlessness and social isolation.

The findings in this study confirmed the hypothesis with regard to the relationship between powerlessness, income, education and occupational prestige. With respect to the correlation between income and powerlessness, a respectable chi square was obtained which does indeed suggest that the higher the person's income the lower the person's sense of powerlessness. The relationship between powerlessness and education was even stronger. Hence, the higher the level of educational attainment the lower was the sense of powerlessness.

With respect to anomie, the hypothesis showed a correlation in the predicted direction for both income and education but was not confirmed for the relationship between occupation and anomie. These findings showed that high income persons have a low sense of anomie and that highly educated persons also have a low sense of anomie. However, persons who rank high on the index of occupational prestige do not rank low on the anomie scale.

The correlations between social isolation and socio-economic status variables were somewhat more ambiguous. For instance, the hypothesis was confirmed for that part which predicted high level of educational attainment corresponding with a low sense of social isolation. It was not confirmed for occupational status and was only confirmed for income levels when the combined annual income was employed in the test.

The relationship between alienation and the socio-economic status variables are also unclear. The hypothesis was confirmed for education but not supported for either income or occupation. In fact, the hypothesis was confirmed between education and all variants of alienation. Consequently, it can be inferred that the higher the level of educational attainment the lower will be the sense of alienation, powerlessness, anomie, and social isolation.

The second hypothesis was actually the converse of the first multi-faceted hypothesis on alienation and SES variables. The analysis of the data supported the observation made above with respect to the correlation between alienation and socio-economic status variables.

Health and Alienation: The presumed impact of alienation on health was expressed in items of utilization of health services and information about them. The hypothesis tested stated that the greater the utilization of health services within the community, the lower the persons's rank on a scale of anomie, alienation, powerlessness, or distrust of the power structure. The findings with regard to the separate components of this hypothesis were varied.

For instance, the hypothesis was not confirmed for anomie. Since the X^2 of 8.88 between the health access index and anomie was not within the established level of confidence, the correlation was unacceptable. Neither was it confirmed for powerlessness. The hypothesis was not confirmed for alienation and it was not supported for distrust of the power structure in the predicted direction. What was evident in this regard was that a high distrust of the power structure implies a high health access score.

The findings were equally mixed when the flow of health information was analyzed in terms of alienation, anomie, powerlessness and distrust. The analysis showed that anomie is significantly related to high health information. On the other hand, low health information is significantly related to a feeling of powerlessness. There is also a significant relationship between health information and distrust of the power structure. However, there is no confirmation of a significant relationship between alienation and health information flow.

Alienation and Community Issues: To shed light on the impact of community issues on feelings of alienation, a test was made of the hypothesis that: "The higher a person's rank on a scale of anomie or alienation, the more likely is the person to show a greater concern for micro-community issues. The lower the rank on anomie or alienation scales, the higher will be the concern for macro-community issues." Across all age lines, the hypothesis was unsupported for micro-community issues and anomie, and with alienation. With respect to the relationship with macro-community issues, across all age groupings, the hypothesis was unsupported when used as a measure of alienation. However, when the test of rank on the anomie scale was made in relationship to concern for macro-community issues, the findings showed that all age groups scored in the medium anomie level. They also revealed that among the younger and older age group, medium anomie was correlated with medium concern with macro-community issues. Further, for the middle age group, medium anomie was correlated with high concern for macro-community issues.

Distrust and Alienation: Confirmation was obtained for the hypothesis that the greater the sense of distrust among blacks of the power structure, the greater will be their sense of powerlessness and rank on scales of anomie and alienation. The correlation between distrust of the power structure and powerlessness was significant. It was especially robust with anomie but comparatively weak, however confirmatory, between distrust and alienation.

Alienation and Goal Attainment: Persons who express feeling of high goal attainment rank low on scales of anomie and powerlessness but not on scales of social isolation and alienation. Respectable correlations were observed between high goal attainment, anomie, and powerlessness. However, persons who have a strong sense of group solidarity do have a lower sense of social isolation and a high degree of social participation. While no claim is made that blacks are *more* alienated than whites, since this study did not attempt to measure racial differences in alienation, it seems evident that a significant proportion of blacks *are* alienated. While some of the sources of alienation across racial lines may be similar, as suggested by studies identified in Chapter I, the race variable is nonetheless highly salient. Persistent alienation for both blacks and whites may indeed be rooted in untoward structural conditions, or exacerbated by feelings of isolation from the governmental institutions, or from frustrations induced by inflation and the declining quality of life. However, the feeling of alienation may be heightened when the elements of racism and structural inequality because of racial differences are added to the more generalized explanations. Despite manifest improvements in the objective conditions of blacks in the United States, many blacks perceive racism to be a real, continuous problem. This perception cuts across all class lines; thus, the real argument is not whether or not race or class is important at the present time. Rather, it is the ability of individuals to more effectively cope with both subtle as well as blatant manifestations of racism. Blacks of varying social status positions may conceal feelings of alienation and racism. That does not mean that they do not *feel* such effects.

Notes

1. Lee, Alfred McClung, "An Obituary for Alienation," *Social Problems* 20:1 (Summer, 1972), pp. 121-127.
2. *Ibid,* p. 121
3. *Ibid,* p. 123
4. It is possible that the response to items on the alienation scale would have been more negative had the interviews been conducted after the National Elections of November, 1980. The results of the election have been interpreted by some observers as a shift to the political right and as a manifestation of anti-black sentiments throughout the United States.

CHAPTER 6

Social Participation

Sociologists are particularly interested in discerning patterns and regularities in human life. Identification and specification of patterned behavior not only underscore our understanding of the social world, but also facilitate predictions about behavior with far greater confidence and certainty. This chapter focuses attention upon social participation, i.e. what black people do in their leisure time, with whom and where.

Of special concern are the broader dimensions of social participation, and the patterns and regularities evidenced in social life among metropolitan blacks in the United States. In this connection, several important questions arise. For example, what is the strength of community ties, and institutional bonds in the observed patterns of social participation? Do leisure-time and other social activities reveal a loss of community? To what extent is the form of social participation constrained by residence, isolation and distance, and race? Is social participation influenced by differences in age, sex and residence?

As stated earlier, the black population in the United States is predominantly urban. According to U.S. Census data, more than eight of every ten black Americans reside in metropolitan areas.[1] Yet, the urban environment in which blacks live offers a variety of living and social arrangements. It is characterized by diverse neighboring patterns and forms of social interaction that have been of special interest to sociologists for several years. Ferdinand Toennies spoke of the shift from *Gemeinshchaft* to *Gesellschaft* as people moved from rural more cohesive environments into large impersonal groups.[2] Emile Durkheim's concepts for essentially the same relationships were mechanical versus organic solidarity.[3]

In more recent times, American sociologists have debated the impact of urbanism on social life and have raised questions about social relationships, patterns of interaction, the sense of community, the control of the community over individual behavior, and of the attachment which individuals develop for local communities once they move away from them. Louis Wirth, for instance, concluded that urbanism is accompanied by a shift from primary group relationships to secondary group affiliations and attachment.[4] Herbert Gans spoke of "quasi-primary relationships" in his studies of the urban villagers and of Levittoweners.[5] In the late 1970's, Albert Hunter replicated Donald Foley's 1952 study in which he concluded that urban life was accompanied by a "loss of community."[6] William L. Yancy and Eugene Erickson examined the antecedents of community by focusing on the institutional structures of urban neighborhoods.[7] Hunter also called attention to the relationship between "informal neighborhood" and utilization of local facilities. Finally, in a 1967 study, Morris Janowitz observed a certain attachment that people have to their primary communities even when they move away from them.[8]

Although this study does not attempt to measure the process of urbanism, it does assume that the forms of social participation observed among urban and suburban blacks are a manifest consequence of the restraints and constraints imposed upon them by the conditions and opportunities to interact within their urban environment. Such conditions include residential stability as related to the age of the respondents, recent movement into the city and/or neighborhood, suburbanization and feelings about participation in local community activities, racial isolation, and formal organizations, financial resources, and neighborhood safety. Each of these factors may influence the types of activities people will engage in as well as with whom they associate.

Determinants of Neighboring and Friendship Patterns.

One of the most powerful determinants of neighboring and of friendship patterns is racial identification. In three of the four cities in which social participation was studied, at least seven of every ten respondents stated that they had no close white friends. The exception was Cleveland in which the respondents were far more likely to count 15 or more white persons as close friends. But, in Atlanta, 88 percent indicated the absence of close white neighborhood friends. In Houston and Los Angeles, these figures were 75 and 73 percent, respectively. On this basis, there was clear support for the hypothesis that race is an important determinant of friendship patterns and that black persons are likely to identify close friends from within the black population.

Confirmation was obtained for the hypothesis that place of residence is a predictor of friendship patterns across racial lines. In this instance, urban black residents are more likely to say they have either no white friends or a fewer number of white friends than are suburban residents. Across the country, the data showed that 78 percent of the urban respondents indicated the absence of close white friends within their neighborhood in contrast to 61 percent of the suburban residents. However, suburban residents are more likely to have from one to five white neighborhood friends than their urban counterparts. The suburban - urban percentages were 21 percent and 7 percent, respectively. Similarly, suburban blacks are more likely to count as many as 15 neighborhood white persons as among their close neighborhood friends than are urban blacks.

Young people are twice as likely as older persons to have close friends in the neighborhood when the number of neighborhood residents reaches 15 or more individuals. Eighty-seven percent of the older persons (age 50 or older), 70 percent of the middle age cohort (aged 31 to50), and 66 percent of the younger persons (aged 18 to 30) stated that they had no neighborhood close white friends. Therefore, the hypothesis was confirmed that younger aged persons are more likely to have close white friends in the neighborhoods than are older persons.

No significant difference was observed between men and women with respect to neighborhood friendship patterns across racial lines. What was important was the observation that, for men and women, seven of every ten reported the absence of close white friends in their neighborhoods.

However, educational attainment does make a difference in friendship patterns across racial lines. Confirmation was obtained for the hypothesis that persons with high educational attainment are more likely to have 15 or more close white friends in the neighborhood than are persons with medium or low educational achievement, and that persons with medium or low educational attainment are more likely to indicate the absence of close white neighborhood friends. Ninety-five percent of the persons with low educational attainment, 83 percent of those with medium education and 51 percent of those with high educational attainment indicated that they had no close white friends in the neighborhood.

In much the same manner, friendship patterns are differentiated by various levels of annual income reported by the respondents. Support was found for the hypothesis that the higher the annual income the larger the number of white friends indicated in the neighborhood, and the lower the income the more likely are blacks to report the absence of close white friends within the neighborhood. In general, higher income blacks reported having 15 or more white friends in the neighborhood and only 38 percent of them reported having a total absence of white friends in their residential area. By contrast, 85 percent of the low income blacks and 73 percent of those in the medium category indicated a total absence of white friends in the neighborhood.

These findings depict a high degree of racial isolation in neighborhoods. Whether or not blacks count neighborhood white residents among their close friends is a function of the city in which they live, whether or not they live within the city or in its suburbs, the age of the individuals, their education and the amount of their annual income. The comparatively higher proportion of blacks in Cleveland who count white neighbors as close friends may be explained by Cleveland's long history of residentially integrated communities, especially on its east side in which most of the metropolitan Cleveland interviews were conducted. In those areas of the east side in which blacks resided, and despite the residential succession of blacks in many of these communities over a relatively short period of time, several white residents remain. Even the areas made famous by the urban confrontations of the 1960's and early 1970's, such as Hough-Wade Park, Glenville, Collinwood and Mt. Pleasant, are not all-black neighborhoods. As a result of "Operation Open Housing," which was a significant open housing movement in the sixties and seventies, higher income and well-educated blacks, who could afford the transition, moved into middle-and upper-class communities of Cleveland Heights, Shaker Heights and Pepper Pike and others.[9]

Unlike Cleveland, residential isolation, with very few exceptions, is more total in cities such as Atlanta, Los Angeles, Houston and Boston. For example, because of historic patterns of residential segregation, blacks and whites in Atlanta, were forced to live apart. Within the black community, as was the case in white Atlanta, communities were also often differentiated across class lines. For instance, the well-to-do lived at opposite ends of the same street from the less fortunate. As housing opened up in suburban communities, many of the well-to-do moved into predominantly black sections of these suburbs. Hence, racial isolation within neighborhoods was perpetuated. Wherever it was broken down, it appears to have been the consequence of education, age, and income compatibilities, all of which are salient ingredients in the attraction of people to each other.

Although Boston was not included in the social participation dimensions of the study, the city is characterized by exceptionally high racial isolation and polarization. Over 93 percent of all blacks who reside in metropolitan Boston live in one of three central city communities. Roxbury, Dorchester and Mattapan. The remaining 7 percent of metropolitan Boston blacks are dispersed in such suburban communities as Brookline, Newton, Needham, Natick, and Wellesley. But their percentage in each of these communities or towns is often as low or less than 1 percent of the total population. Because of the racial isolation that many blacks feel in these communities, they have formed Afro-American Cultural Clubs and Concerned Black Citizens organizations to reduce social isolation and to strengthen intra-group bonds. Hence, it is safe to assume that, had the social particiption questions been posed to Boston respondents, the degree of racial isolation would probably have been higher than that found in all other cities.

In general, however, because of discrimination in the sale and rental of housing and structural barriers to economic opportunity, central cities have become single race communities and are places where, more often than not, opportunities for interracial friendships have diminished. Frequently, no efforts are made to establish friendships across racial lines. Lower income, older and less educated black persons remain in the cities but not alone. They are often accompanied by younger, well-educated, higher income whites involved in gentrification as well as by other blacks. The latter individuals either choose to remain in the cities and away from the majority or they are unable to move away because of the discrimination they encounter in their efforts to locate housing elsewhere. In both black groups, a deliberate choice is made to select their close friends from among their black neighbors who also remain within the city because of personal choice or due to barriers of discrimination and low income.

Social Integration in the Home: Whether or not guests in the home are bi-racial is a function of the city in which one lives, place of residence, age and education. For instance, confirmation was obtained for the hypothesis that Northern and West Coast cities (e.g. Cleveland and Los Angeles) would reveal a higher degree of within home social integration than would Southern and Southwest cities (e.g. Atlanta and Houston). In fact, the data show that Los Angeles and Cleveland residents were more likely to report integrated social guests in their homes than were blacks in either Atlanta or Houston. On the whole, respondents say that 60 percent of the social guests in the home are black. However, this tendency to restrict social guests to members of the black population was strongest in Atlanta in which 75 percent reported that their social guests were black from the present neighborhood. In descending order, Atlanta was followed by Houston (59 percent), Cleveland (44 percent) and Los Angeles (40 percent). A similar observation was made with regard to place of residence and age.

Urban blacks are more likely to report that their social guests are black from their present neighborhood. Suburban blacks are more likely to claim racially integrated social guests; however, most of them are blacks from their old neighborhoods.

Younger blacks are more likely to say that they entertain whites in their homes than are older blacks. However, older blacks are more likely to report that they entertain blacks from their present neighborhoods. All age groups are about equal in their tendency to report blacks from the old neighborhood as social guests in their homes.

These patterns do not occur in isolation from other structural components of social relationships such as the level of educational attainment and the amount of annual income received. We might anticipate that the more highly educated and the higher income persons would be more likely to report that they entertain across racial lines because of the increased opportunities to establish inter-racial acquaintances and friends within the workplace and from among participants in formal organizations to which such persons may belong.

The findings in this study support the hypothesis that the more highly educated blacks are more likely to report integrated social guests in their homes than are blacks with less education. Confirmation was also obtained for the position that blacks with lower educational attainment are more likely to have blacks from the old neighborhood as their social guests and that blacks with medium and low educational levels are more likely to have other blacks from the present neighborhood as their social guests.

Similarly, the higher the income blacks receive the more likely they are to say they entertain guests in their homes of both races. Blacks in the low and medium income ranges are more likely to report that they entertain blacks guests from their present neighborhoods.

All of these findings are consistent with previous observations made with respect to racial isolation across residential, urban/suburban, educational and income dimensions. They have a far more significant meaning — one that is in relation to community, institutional attachment, and social bonding.

Meaningful social interaction and enduring social relationships involve a high degree of social reciprocity. Black Americans have often maintained that many of their white friends seem quite willing to accept invitations to their place of residence but that the same white friends almost never reciprocate by inviting them into their homes for social occasions. Questions of status attainment and status loss are often involved in decisions to socialize across racial lines for many white Americans.[10] This phenomenon seems especially apparent among suburbanites who are in the quest for status and who feel compelled to protect whatever status they may have obtained within the community and among their white friends. They not only concern themselves with a specific lifestyle but with the requirements of their status groups. If blacks carry a badge of inferiority and if whites are concerned about the status implications of intimate associations with persons of low status, then, they may very well be less inclined to invite blacks into their own homes unless they can demonstrate that such persons are equal to or superior to them and most of their guests in terms of status attainment.[11]

The general pattern observed in this study is that whites, according to the respondents, as a rule, did not invite blacks into their own homes with any significant frequency.

Blacks in Atlanta were much more likely than blacks in any other city to never have had social contacts within white homes. However, black residents of Cleveland and Houston were more likely to report "frequent" social contacts in the homes of white friends. Although slight variations were found in this pattern from city to city, the hypothesis was confirmed that white friends do not reciprocate by inviting blacks into their homes.

Distinctions in white responses to blacks with respect to social contacts in their homes were hypothesized for place of residence, age, sex, educational level and income category. With the exception of the sex variable which generated no apparent distinctions in white responses to blacks, the results were in the direction predicted. Urban residents were twice as likely to report never having social contacts in the homes of white friends as were suburban residents. By contrast, suburban residents were almost twice as likely to report "occasional" or "frequent" social contacts in the homes of white friends. Over two-thirds (68.1 percent) of the respondents reported "never" "almost never" or "do not have any white friends" for social contacts while less than a third (31.9 percent) reported "occasional" (22.8 percent) or "frequent" (9.1 percent) contacts with white friends within their own homes.

Social contacts in the homes of white friends appear to vary according to age. Older persons are more likely to report "never" having received an invitation to the homes of white friends than are the younger persons. Younger persons, on the other hand, are more likely to report "occasional or frequent" social contact in the homes of white friends. This situation may be explained by increasing rates of desegregation which accentuate greater contact between whites and blacks in the work place and in the marketplace as well as in schools and colleges. It is possible that younger persons of both races have established closer friendship ties which transcend traditional racial barriers.

These findings also show that other factors account for the pattern of social contacts with whites in their own homes. For instance, the data show that blacks from egalitarian families are more likely to report having social contacts within the homes of their white friends than are single-parent families. Further, blacks from households in which "two-parents" are present are also more likely to report such social contacts than are single-parent families. So are the persons who are classified as professional, self-employed, managers or white collar employees. By contrast, the "never" category is comprised primarily of the widowed, older person who subsists on pensions and social security and those who are employed in the blue collar or service types of jobs.

It is not unexpected that confirmation was found for the hypothesis that the higher the level of educational attainment, the more likely are blacks to have social contacts within the home of white friends.

There was also confirmation for the hypothesis that the higher the income level, the more frequent the contact in the homes of white friends.

Persons with high educational attainment are far more likely to report social contacts within the homes of white friends. Persons with low educational attainment are more likely to report "never" having been invited by white freinds into their homes for social occasions. Similarly, persons with high incomes are more likely to report "occasional" or "frequent" social contacts with white friends while persons in the low category are more likely to report "never." The level of social reciprocity is not particularly high among the white friends of blacks.

The sex variable did not generate critical distinctions between the sexes in the degree to which each was invited into the homes of white friends for social occasions.

Home Social Contacts: White Neighbors. Although 52 percent of the respondents who actually have white neighbors, reported that they were "never" (37.8 percent) or "almost never" (14.2 percent) invited into the homes of their white neighbors, some variations among categories of respondents were observed. For instance, black residents in Atlanta were more likely to report a total absence of social integration than were residents of other cities. On the other hand, black residents of Cleveland were more likely to report receiving invitations from their white neighbors for social activities in their homes.

Black suburbanites were twice as likely to report that they have been invited by their white neighbors into their homes for social activities than were blacks who live within the city itself. Even then, the percentages are relatively small; 36 percent for black suburbanites and only 18 percent for urban black residents. However, once again, about one-half of all respondents in each of the residental categories assert that they were not invited into the homes of white neighbors.

Confirmation was obtained for the hypothesis that the young are more likely to be invited into the homes of white neighbors than are older persons.

However, only three in ten young persons indicated frequent social contacts of this type. But, four in ten young, five in ten middle-aged persons, and six in ten older persons reported almost no social relationships within the home of their white neighbors.

Similarly, at least two of the socio-economic status variables showed a strong positive correlation with social contacts within the homes of white neighbors. For instance, the higher the level of educational attainment among black respondents the more likely were they to report being invited into the homes of white neighbors. Persons with low levels of eductional attainment and who report low income levels have no social contacts in their white neighbors' homes. The reluctance by white neighbors to extend themselves to black neighbors is underscored by the data which show that more than half of all income groups among these respondents report almost no such contacts.

Widowers, persons whose income comes largely from pensions and social security, persons who are unemployed or employed in service occupations were more likely to report a total absence of close white friends among their neighbors. In contrast, those persons who reported that they have as many as 15 or more close white friends among their neighbors were the single, never married individuals and persons employed in professional, self-employed jobs, or as managers, sales-persons and clerical workers.

Social Contacts With Blacks: Although black persons were considerably more likely to indicate social interaction with other black persons, the degree of their interaction varied along at least three dimensions. The patterns of social interaction differed according to city of residence, age and educational levels.

With respect to city and residence, the most salient finding was that blacks in Cleveland were more likely than blacks in all other cities to report no social contact with other black persons. Even though the chi square obtained was significant, the 15 percent of persons who responded in this manner was relatively small.

Age, too, is a discriminating variable with regard to social relationships between black persons. Older people were more likely to report an absence of social interaction with other blacks while the younger and middle age groups were more likely to indicate occasional or frequent association. This finding was not unexpected. Conventional wisdom would lead to the same conclusion that the older a person becomes the less likely that person is to engage in external, non-relative oriented patterns of social interaction. This assertion was confirmed by the findings reported in this study.

Persons with lower educational attainment were also more likely to report no social contacts with other blacks. Many respondents with low formal education do not have the money that is required for reciprocal social relationships such as entertainment in homes and clubs. Consequently, they are more likely to watch television at home with other members of their own families. Therefore, social interaction outside the home is less frequent.

Although suburban blacks were more likely to report almost no social contact with other blacks, this finding was not statistically significant. Nor were differentiations observed by sex and income levels. However, almost 30 percent of the suburban blacks reported no social contacts at all with other suburban blacks who lived in the same neighborhood. This finding may provide a clue as to why so many blacks who live in suburban communities claim that other blacks are distant, unfriendly and engage in the same avoidance pattern characteristic of some of their white neighbors. A suburban Boston husband and wife reported that one of the reasons for their decision to move back to the South was the aloofness of other blacks to them. They reported many occasions of encountering other blacks and of attempting to exchange informal greetings only to be met by a "dropping of the head or a shifting of the eyes" to avoid a face-to-face encounter.

The suburban Boston couple feels, as do black suburban residents in Los Angeles, that a great deal of insecurity, ambiguity and uncertainty about their positions in a desegregated community, and imitation of perceived white behavior are factors that help to explain these avoidance patterns. The insecurity is explainable in part by the unfulfilled expectation of having acquired a number of material possessions as evidence of status attainment once one moves into a suburban community. To become friendly with other blacks whom one does not know may lead to expectations of social contacts within each other's homes. In turn, the fear of discovery, of low acquisition of material manifestations of social status becomes an impediment to social interaction.

For many suburban blacks, there is a certain amount of ambiguity about themselves in relation to their new desegregated place of residence.

For some, the new residence means that they *should* have more white friends than black friends or acquaintances. For some, there is a compulsion to demonstrate to whites that they are not the transplanted "authentic ghetto type," complete with suspicion and hostility to whites. So, they tend to over-extend themselves to white persons within their own communities only to confront the reality that social reciprocity is not forthcoming. Consequently, they are compelled either to maintain or to re-establish old social bonds in former urban communities or to develop new patterns in the urban black community, or to become isolated in their new communities.

Among the third group, there may be a tendency to imitate their perceptions of the social behavior of white suburbanites. For instance, this may be viewed as highly selective, formal and informal, within home social activities, aloofness from neighbors, a low sense of neighboring, casual relationships with persons who live in close proximity to them, and within home activities dictated by associations formed in job-related capacities or through memberships in clubs and other formal organizations.

Two other groups are more likely to report integrated social guests in their own homes. These are the persons who live in egalitarian family structures and the single-never married persons. However, households headed either by a male or by a female and the widowed, separated but not divorced persons are more likely to restrict their home social guests to black persons from the present neighborhood.

Social Participation In Clubs, Organizations And Leisure Time Activities

Clubs and Organizations: Information about patterns of participation in clubs, organizations and informal activities within one's own neighborhood or community can be informative about informal networks across racial lines, neighboring, community cohesion and the "sense of community" prevalent among local residents. This issue was addressed in part by studies conducted by such researchers as Herbert Gans[12], Marc Fried[13], Morris Axelrod[14], Eliot Liebow[15], Eugene Litwak[16] and Carol Stack[17].

A majority of these studies were especially concerned with the relative salience of specific types of facilities within neighborhoods for sustaining social cohesion among members and for maintaining neighborhood stability. The focus in this study is not a direct concern with such attributes per se but more so with patterns of interactions among residents with respect to the race variable and the conditions within communities or neighborhoods which give rise to or accentuate observable patterns of social relationships.

Hence, when the question, "When it comes to clubs and organizations in which you participate, they are likely to be which one of the five following possible responses," was posed, respondents answers were quite revealing with respect to study objectives. The large chi square obtained for city differences, for instance, was highly significant. Blacks in Atlanta were more likely to participate in all-black clubs and organizations in their present neighborhood, whether or not the neighborhood was predominantly black or predominantly white. Houston blacks, on the other hand, were more likely to participate in both black and white clubs and organizations in their present neighborhoods than were blacks in other cities. But blacks in Cleveland were more likely to participate in white clubs and organizations in both the old and the present neighborhoods.

The degree to which social bonding or attachment to the old neighborhoods or to which exclusion of blacks from clubs and organizations in neighborhoods occur is evidenced in urban and suburban patterns of responses. For instance, urban blacks were more likely to report involvement in all-black clubs and organizations in their present neighborhoods. Since most urban blacks live in all-black or predominantly black communities, they are not inclined to venture outside these communities for affiliation with clubs and other organizations.

Suburban blacks more often than any other group of blacks report participation in the black clubs and organization of their old neighborhoods. This is a manifestation of their attachment to the friendship cliques formed and nurtured in the old neighborhood prior to moving to suburbia. While such social behavior is indicative of the willingness to travel long distances in order to maintain old social bonds, it may also be expressive of an inability to establish or gain membership into local organizations. While all of these observations may be supported, there is evidence that black suburbanites are more likely to report membership in "black and white" clubs and organizations in their present neighborhood. The latter observation suggests social integration in suburban communities. On the other hand, black suburbanites say they belong to both "all black clubs" and predominantly white clubs and organizations in the suburban communities.

Social integration, in terms of membership in clubs and organizations, appears to be dependent more upon such factors as the level of educational attainment, the amount of annual income and family structure than upon such factors as age or sex.

With regard to level of educational attainment, the data show that the higher the number of years of schooling, the more likely is the person to claim participation in white clubs and organizations in both the old and the present neighborhoods. Similarly, the higher the years of educational attainment, the greater is the likelihood that the person says he/she will participate in black as well as white clubs and organizations in the present neighborhood. On the other hand, medium and low levels of educational attainment are correlated with the reported tendency to participate in "all black" clubs and organizations in the present neighborhood.

It should not be unexpected that low and medium income persons are also more likely to say they participate in all black clubs and organizations in their present neighborhoods. The relationship between these two variables is also strong and statistically significant. The medium and low income persons are also likely to be the same persons whose level of schooling is medium to low. These are undoubtedly the same persons who are confined by their economic circumstances to the central city neighborhoods.

No significant differences were observed in the age of persons or their sex and the nature of their participation in clubs and organizations. However, some differences were observed in reported patterns of club and organization participation according to family structure and type of households. For instance, egalitarian families are more often than not involved in black as well as white clubs and organizations in the present neighborhood. Two-parent families seem to follow egalitarian families with respect to present neighborhoods. They are different, however, in the sense that they are more likely to return to the old neighborhood for affiliation and involvement in the associations of the old neighborhood. In this sense, they tend to retain old community ties and social bonds. This practice may be maintained as a result of an inability to establish informal networks in the new neighborhoods, or because of the superficiality of present-neighborhood associations, or because of a special concern for the friendship cliques of their children. In contrast, single-parent households say they are more likely to participate in clubs and organizations which are "all black" and in their present neighborhoods.

Leisure-time Companions: Unmistakably, racial isolation that is characteristic of other spheres of life continues into leisure time activities. As in various aspects of social participation, response patterns vary by city. Residents of Atlanta are more likely to engage in leisure time activities with black friends who are from their present neighborhood. This pattern is also found to a lesser extent in descending order in Houston, Los Angeles and in Cleveland. Black residents of Cleveland are more likely to participate in leisure time activities with white friends in both the present and in the old neighborhood. It is in Los Angeles and Houston that blacks are more likely to engage in leisure time pursuits with both black and white friends. Again, these findings are statistically significant.

The patterns observed with respect to urban-suburban differences are quite similar to observations made along other dimensions of social participation. Urban residents seem more likely than not to engage in leisure time activities with other black urbanites from their present neighborhood. However, suburban blacks display a certain amount of ambivalence about their relationships and recreational pursuits. For example, while they are more likely to say they engage in such activities with both black and white friends from the present neighborhood, they are also more likely to report that they seek out black friends from the old neighborhood for leisure time pursuits. Not only are these findings also statistically significant, they provide further support for the notion that suburban blacks, while seeking social integration and wishing to establish friendship patterns across racial lines, continue to hold on to their friendship ties and are reluctant to disaffiliate themselves from relationships or to sever those bonds developed in their old neighborhoods.

Although these patterns are not differentiated according to sex of respondent, they are demonstrably influenced by such variables as age, educational level, yearly income, type of household, family authority structure and occupation.

Confirmation was obtained for the hypothesis that age influences leisure time friendship patterns. The findings show that younger persons tend to have both black and white companions from their present neighborhood for their leisure pursuits, while the middle and older aged groups are more likely to say they associate exclusively with black friends from their present neighborhoods for such activities. However, both older and younger persons are more likely to report black leisure time friends from the old neighborhood. As shown in Table 20, these findings are statistically significant.

An even stronger confirmation was obtained for the predictive power of education to influence companion choices for leisure time pursuits. In this study, it was shown that the higher the level of educational attainment the more likely are black persons to select both black and white friends from their present neighborhoods for such activities. On the other hand, the lower the level of education or the number of years of schooling, the more likely are black persons to say they engage in leisure activities exclusively with black friends from the old neighborhood. If the person has only a medium level of schooling, (i.e., a high school diploma or post-secondary education), and is under the age of 30, that person is likely to select only black friends from the present neighborhood for leisure time companionship.

The most salient finding with respect to the possible relationship between level of income and leisure time companionship concerns low and medium income groups. These data show that persons who report low or medium income levels are more likely to say they engage in leisure time activities with black friends from the present neighborhood.

With respect to reported behavior relative to family authority structure and household type, these data show that egalitarian families are more likely to: (1) have leisure time friends who are black in the present neighborhood, (2) have leisure time friends who are black and from the old neighborhood, (3) or have black and white friends as leisure time companions and who are from the present neighborhood; that two-parent families are more likely to engage in their leisure-time pursuits with black friends only who are from the old neighborhood, or with both black and white friends from the present neighborhood; and that one-parent families confine their leisure time partners exclusively to other black persons in the present neighborhoods.

Leisure time companions also differ across occupational lines and employment statuses. The findings in this study show that according to study participants: (1) persons who subsist on pensions and social security restrict their leisure companions to other blacks in the present neighborhood, (2) persons whose occupations are in the crafts category are more likely to have other blacks from the old neighborhood as leisure time partners, (3) unemployed persons select both black and white friends from the present neighborhood for these activities, and (4) persons whose occupations are in the professional, self-employed, managerial and sales categories are more likely to have white friends from either the old or the present neighborhood as leisure time companions.

When asked, "What do you do in your leisure time," answers varied, but there was a remarkable similarity from city to city. Both a teletype operator in Atlanta and a nurse in Houston said: "I go camping whenever I can." A Cleveland suburbanite and a Los Angeles widow said, "I go to church activities." Men in Cleveland, Houston, Los Angeles and Atlanta often cited "spectator sports and playing basketball," whether they were truck drivers, computer analysts, janitors or teachers. More often than not, retired, widowed and blue-collar workers listed "the church" as their most prevalent leisure time activity. In the second category for all groups was "doing things with family members." The respondents gave a high priority to "visiting with friends and relatives," "staying at home, reading or listen-ing to the radio, music or watching television." While several enjoyed "house parties," fewer mentioned "going to the movies," "going out with friends," "bowling, tennis, horse-back riding," and "eating out." Many took walks in the park "until such walks became unsafe." Others picnicked or went fishing. Several were members of fraternal organizations, civic clubs, men's clubs, card clubs, and community groups. These responses in-dicate that people tend to engage in family-centered activities and those leisure-time pursuits that are less expensive to them.

Children: In order to assess the impact of various factors on the social participation of children, two questions were posed. The first question con-cerned where children attended school (i.e, in present neighborhood, out-side present neighborhood, private school that is predominantly black or predominantly white, etcetera). The second question concerned the racial identification of the children's closest friends.

Responses to the first of these two questions shed light on such issues as busing for school desegregation and the shifts in school enrollment from public to private schools from city to city. In the aggregate, over half of the children in the four cities attend school in their present neighborhood. However, when responses are disaggregated according to specific city, clear distinctions between cities in school attendance emerge. For instance, in Atlanta, 64 percent of the black children attend school in their present neighborhood. This figure declines to 50 percent in Los Angeles, to 47 per-cent in Houston and then to 38 percent in Cleveland. However, all of these children are not bused to public school. A significant proportion appear to be enrolled in either an all-black or a predominantly white school. With 13 percent of the respondent's children being bused in its school system, Los Angeles leads all of the four cities along this dimension. However, given the 1981 decision by the California Supreme Court which discontinued busing for school desegregation purposes, that proportion may decline while the proportion in other cities may, in fact, increase.[18] These findings are highly significant.

In terms of urban-suburban differences, the data show that about an equal proportion of the children attend school in their present neighborhood. About 55 percent of suburban children and 51 percent of urban children attend school in their present neighborhood. About an equal proportion also are bused to non-neighborhood schools. These figures are 5.8 percent and 6.2 percent in suburban and urban communities, respec-tively. Another important observation drawn from the data is that suburban black children are one-and a half times more likely to attend either all-black or predominantly white private schools. This finding is not unexpected since not only can suburban residents more often than not afford private school education, there is a certain amount of status attainment associated with enrolling their children in private schools rather than in public institutions.

Persons whose children are enrolled in present neighborhood schools are young (56 percent) and in the middle age bracket of 31-50 (60 percent). On the other hand, persons over the age of 50 are twice as likely as the younger groups not to have school aged children. Consequently, the hypothesis that the younger the parent the more likely is the parent to have children enrolled in present neighborhood schools was confirmed (See Table 20).

Although comparatively few blacks enroll their children in private schools, these findings show a statistical correlation between high level educational attainment and the tendency to enroll children in private school. It should be noted that, despite the statistical significance of this finding, only one in ten blacks who have attained a high level of education actually enroll children in a private school (Table 20).

A further examination of the data shows that no statistically significant correlations were obtained for a relationship between sex of the parent, income levels, and where children attended school. However, it was shown that children of separated-but-not-divorced parents and the children of parents who are either unemployed or employed in clerical positions are more likely to say they enroll their children in schools within their present neighborhoods. The above findings may be suggestive and illuminating in regard to the friendship patterns of children. Again, these patterns differ from city to city as well as across the variables utilized in this analysis.

Black residents of Atlanta are more likely to report that their children's closest friends are black residents of their present neighborhood. This pattern is followed in descending order by Houston, Los Angeles and Cleveland. It is identical to the location of schools attended by their children as reported for these cities. Black Clevelanders are more likely to report that the closest friends of their children are white children in the present neighborhood. But, Clevelanders are also more likely to report that their closest friends are black children from the old neighborhood. These statistically significant findings may reflect both residential integration patterns and the proximity of old neighborhoods to new and often suburban residential areas into which many black Clevelanders moved.

However, when the data are analyzed in terms of the urban-suburban dichotomy, it is observed that the parents of children in both communities report equally that their children's closest friends are black and in the present neighborhood. Here, urban children report as their closest friends other black children from the old neighborhood. This apparent contradiction may be explained by residential shifts within neighborhoods of the urban sector of the metropolitan area as opposed to movement from the city to the suburb. Although statistically weak, the finding is, nonetheless, significant (See Table 20).

Unemployed middle and older aged parents, women, and persons with medium and low levels of educational attainment, with only a low to middle level of income reported that the closest friends of black children are other black children in the present neighborhood. Each of these relationships is statistically significant (Table 20). However, middle and older aged parents and egalitarian families are also more likely to report that their children's closest friends are black from the old neighborhood. Similarly, the higher the level of educational attainment and the higher the person is on an index of occupational status, the more likely are the children's closest friends to be black children from the old neighborhood. These findings are statistically significant (Table 20). On the other hand, egalitarian families are more likely to report that white children in the present neighborhood are the closest friends of their children.

The findings with respect to children seem to support the general conclusions concerning the social participation of their parents. In essence, social interaction appears to be decidedly more intra-racial than inter-racial. There is a tendency for black suburbanites to attempt inter-racial social integration more so than blacks who reside in the central cities of urban communities. However, suburbanites display a high degree of social attachment and maintain strong social bonds as well as informal friendship networks with friends in the old neighborhoods from which they move. Transportation problems and distance factors, which appear to be a barrier to social bonding among other groups, do not appear to inhibit the continuation of social participation patterns of blacks in the old neighborhoods when they relocate to other neighborhoods or communities.

Church Attendance: This observation is dramatically illustrated with regard to church attendance. Earlier on, it was reported that about one-fifth (19.8 percent) of urban residents and about one-fourth (24.2 percent) of suburban blacks were not church-goers. However, it was also reported that slightly less than one-half of the urban blacks (47.9 percent) and only slightly more than one-fourth of suburban blacks attended church in the present neighborhood. In other words, almost twice as many urban blacks attend church in their present neighborhood as do suburban blacks.

However, more suburban blacks (37.8 percent) than urban blacks (24.7 percent) said they attend church in the old neighborhood. It appears that suburban blacks return to urban black churches as a way of maintaining social bonds and institutional attachments. Neither group seemed inclined to attend "integrated" churches. The percentages in this category were 7.6 percents and 10.9 percents for urban and suburban blacks, respectively. These findings are also statistically significant. (See Table 20).

Age is a discriminating variable with regard to both church attendance and racial composition of churches. While only one in three young blacks is likely to be a church-goer, when they do attend church, they are more likely to attend an integrated or a white church than are the middle or older aged blacks. One in five blacks between the ages of 31 and 50 said they are not church-goers. This ratio dropped to one in ten for blacks above the age of 50. However, the older a person is, the more likely is the person to report attendance at an all-black church in the present neighborhood. Three in five of the persons above the age of 50 stated they attended all-black churches in their present neighborhood. The proportion dropped to two in five for the middle aged groups (31-50) and to one in three for the younger persons or those between 18 and 30. All age groups were about equally likely to say they attended black churches in the old neighborhood. The chi square obtained for these findings was statistically significant. (See Table 20).

Men and women differed with respect to church attendance patterns. Forty-five percent of the female and thirty-eight percent of the male respondents reported that they attend a black church in their present neighborhood. However, males were more likely to attend a black church in the old neighborhoods but females were more likely to attend either an integrated church or a predominantly white church. On the whole, men were less likely to be church-goers than women. The degree of statistical significance of these findings is also depicted in Table 20. These findings suggest that, at least in terms of church attendance, men have stronger bonds and institutional ties to the old neighborhood than women. Another implication from these findings is that women are more concerned with establishing new social networks and institutional ties, and within the context of social integration, than men.

Church attendance and the racial composition of the churches attended vary by level of educational attainment and by income. Persons with high levels of education, college and professional school graduates, are less likely to be church-goers. However, when these persons do attend church, they are more likely to attend either an integrated or a predominantly white church than persons who are categorized as either medium or low in educational attainment. By contrast, individuals whose level of schooling is classified as medium or low are not only more likely to report that they are more frequent church-goers, they are twice as likely to attend an all black church in their present neighborhood than are highly educated blacks. However, the highly educated blacks either are not able to or do not wish to break their institutional ties in the old neighborhood since they seem more likely to attend a black church there. It is also possible that some of the variance in church attendance patterns among the highly educated may be explained by the total lack of attachment to the adjacent urban community. They may have moved directly to the suburbs from a distant city.

Similarly, the higher a person's income the less likely is the person to be a church-goer. But, when they do attend church, the high income individuals are more likely to attend a black church in the old neighborhood. On the other hand, low income persons are more likely to say they attend a black church in their present neighborhood.

Persons in different occupational and employment groups also act differently with respect to church attendance behavior. For example, the unemployed, as well as persons employed in managerial and sales positions do not report "frequent" church attendance as do other groups. Persons on pensions and social security are more likely to report attendance at an all black church in their present neighborhood. By contrast, persons in higher status occupational categories, such as the professional, self-employed, managers and sales-persons, are more likely than others to report attendance at either an integrated or a predominantly white church. But many of the professional and self-employed state they attend an all-black church in their old neighborhood.

Other groups that are more likely to report attendance at a black church in the old neighborhood were married persons, and two-parent families. Additional groups which report more frequent attendance at an all-black church in the present neighborhood include households headed by a female, a one-parent family and widowers. Only egalitarian black families report attendance at either an integrated or a predominantly white church more frequently than others.

Differentiations in church attendance behavior according to the city of residence were statistically significant (Table 20). Black residents of Cleveland and of Los Angeles were least likely to say they are church-goers. However, blacks in Cleveland were similar to blacks in Houston in that they were more likely than their counterparts in Atlanta and Los Angeles to report integrated or a predominantly white church attendance. This pattern may be at least partially explained by the higher degree of residential integration in Cleveland and a higher proportion of black Catholics in Houston.

These differences extend to the location of the church attended. For instance, 60 percent of the blacks in Atlanta stated they attend a black church in their present neighborhood. This proportion falls significantly to 38 percent in Houston, to 28 percent in Los Angeles, and then to only 14.4 percent in Cleveland. It is in Cleveland where blacks report higher attendance at a black church in the old neighborhood. Forty-four percent of black Clevelanders said they attend a black church in the old neighborhood. This figure compared to 31 percent in Los Angeles, 29 percent in Houston and only 20 percent in Atlanta. Again, proximity, residential mobility and housing integration patterns seem to influence church attendance patterns.

It should be stressed that religious institutions, such as churches, are essentially neighborhood social structures. They are located for the convenience of parishioners. However, their racial composition may be, in part, indicative of the degree of residential segregation, housing integration, racial isolation and institutional closure in the racial enclaves prevalent in a given city. If the neighborhood is racially segregated, institutional closure, including religious bodies, is likely to be accentuated in such racially isolated enclaves. If, on the other hand, individuals who move away from a specific neighborhood in which these churches are located and into another neighborhood without their church, and if they are not able to establish significant social ties or social cohesion in the new place of residence, a different pattern of church attendance behavior emerges. Such persons are more likely to be drawn back to the old neighborhood in which attachments are stronger, commitment to institutions are less weak and institutional affiliations are more attractive.

In general, forms and patterns of social participation can be explained in essentially the same manner — i.e. in terms of the strength of institutional ties and weakened commitments in new neighborhoods, as well as the degree of racial integration prevalent within communities. Where racial isolation is dominant, cross-racial friendship patterns are both few and weak. There is a definite consciousness of kind which operates in the selection of churches to attend, friends to invite into one's own home, leisure time activities and the friends of one's children. There also appears to be a conscientious effort reported by some black suburbanites to transcend racial barriers in order to reach out to white neighbors. Unfortunately, whites do not appear to reciprocate as frequently and many blacks become alienated from both black and white suburbanites, as well as from blacks in the urban communities. In effect, many well-to-do blacks become prisoners of their own economic success. On the other hand, as racial integration increases, the sense of powerlessness among blacks may decrease. This change may expand access of blacks to power networks, major institutions, sources of capital, facilitate discovery of commonalities of experience and, ultimately, may lead to more enduring cross-racial social participation.

Notes

1. *The Social and Economic Status of the Black Population in the United States: An Historical View, 1790-1978*, Washington, D.C.: U.S. Department of Commerce, Bureau of the Census, Special Studies Series p. 23, No. 80, 1979, p. 14.

2. Cf. Toennies, Ferdinand, *Community and Society (Gemeinaschaft und Gesellschaft*, Tr. Charles P. Loomis, East Lansing: Michigan State University Press, 1957).

3. Durkheim, Emile, *The Division of Labor in Society*. Rr. George Simpson. New York: Free Press, 1949.

4. Wirth, Louis, "Urbanism As A Way of Life," in Paul Hatt and Albert Reiss, Jr., (eds). *Cities and Society*. New York: Free Press, 1957, pp. 46-63.

5. Cf. Gans, Herbert,   *The Urban Villagers*, New York: Free Press, 1962 and _____, *The Levittowners*, New York: Random House-Vintage 1967.

6. Cf. Foley, Donald L., *Neighbors or Urbanites?* Rochester: University of Rochester Press, 1952, and Albert Hunter, "The Loss of Community: An Empirical Test Through Replication," *American Sociological Review* 40: No. 5 (October 1975), pp. 537-552).

7. Yancy, William L. and Eugene Ericksen, "The Antecedents of Community: The Economic and Institutional Structure of Urban Neighborhoods," *American Sociological Review* 44: 2 (April 1979), pp. 253-262.

8. Janowitz, Morris, *The Community Press in An Urban Setting*. Chicago: The University of Chicago Press, 1967.

9. Cf. Blackwell, James E., *The Black Community: Diversity and Unity*. New York: Harper & Row, 1975, Chapter VI, and Juliet Saltman, *Open Housing As A Social Movement*. Lexington, Mass.: D.C. Heath & Co., 1971.

10. Berry, Brian J.L., et al, "Attitudes Toward Integration: The Role of Status in Community Responses to Racial Change," Chapter 9 in Barry Schwartz (ed). *The Changing Face of Suburbs*. Chicago: University of Chicago Press, 1976, pp. 221-264.

11. For further discussion of the role of status in social relationships, Cf. Abrahams, Charles, *Forbidden Neighbors*, New York: Harper & Row, 1955; Hubert M. Blalock, "Status Consciousness; A Dimensional Analysis," *Social Forces* 37:3 (March 1959), pp. 243-258. Eisenstadt, S.N. (ed.) *Max Weberion Charisma and Institution Building*, Chicago: University of Chicago Press, 1968, and Westie, Frank: "Negro White Status Differentials and Social Distance." *American Sociological Review* 17:5 (October 1952), pp. 550-558.

12. Gans, Herbert, *The Urban Villagers: Group and Class in the Life of Italian Americans*. New York: The Free Press, 1962.

13. Fried, Marc, "Grieving for a Lost Home" in Leonard H. Duhl (ed.). *The Urban Condition*, New York: Basic Books, 1963, pp. 151-171.

14. Axelrod, Morris, "Urban Structure and Social Participation," *American Sociological Review* 21 (1956), pp. 14-20.
15. Liebow, Elliot, *Talley's Corner*. Boston, Little Brown & Company, 1967, 36(1971), pp. 258-271.
16. Litwak, Eugene, "Voluntary Associations and Neighboring Cohesion," *American Sociological Review* 36 (1971), pp. 258-271.
17. Stack, Carol B., *All Our Kin*. New York: Harper & Row, 1974.
18. Hallie, Pamela, "Foes of Busing Hail Los Angeles Victory" *The New York Times*, May 13, 1981, p. A-12.

CHAPTER 7

Blacks in Cities and Suburbs: A Comparative Analysis

In previous chapters, specific attention was focused on aggregate national profiles of black Americans, their perceptions of critical issues which confront them, their micro- and macro-community concerns, sense of alienation and social participation. It may be argued that the intensity of these concerns and the prevalence of issues of special importance to black Americans may be a function of the metropolitan community in which they reside. An underlying assumption of this position is that each city is a unique, distinctive entity. As such, the quality of life provided its residents and the life chances experienced by them may influence their perceptions of their social and economic conditions, their sense of well-being and their general attitudes. In turn, these factors may affect certain behavioral patterns. On the other hand, it may be argued that the geographical location in which one resides has limited influence on such patterns and conditions. In this sense, it may not affect the overall perceptions that blacks have of their ability to change their present and future conditions. From this perspective, the problems encountered by black Americans do not differ from city to city; they are more constant than dissimilar. In this chapter, the presentation of comparative data may facilitate understanding of the issues posed by these positions.

General Characteristics

Age: The Boston and Los Angeles respondents tended to be younger than respondents from Atlanta, Cleveland and Houston. Forty-six percent of the Boston respondents and 45 percent of those from Los Angeles gave their age range as 18 to 30. By contrast, the percentages in this age cohort for Atlanta, Cleveland and Houston were 20, 14 and 33, respectively. 61 percent of the Cleveland respondents gave their age range from 31 to 50. Atlanta was the only additional city in which over one-half (58 percent) of the respondents said they were between 31 and 50 years old. The percentages of respondents who reported their ages between 31 and 50 for Boston, Houston and Los Angeles were 36, 45 and 40, respectively. Finally, only in Cleveland did as many as one-fourth (25 percent) of the respondents say they were above 50 years old. Respondents from both Atlanta (22 percent) and Houston (22 percent) approached that proportion. However, in Boston (18 percent) and Los Angeles (15 percent), the percentages of respondents who said they were above the age of 50 years were somewhat lower.

Education: The respondents from the Los Angeles area reported a higher level of education attainment than that observed in the other areas. Ninety-two percent of the Los Angeles area respondents reported a combined medium (48 percent) or high (44 percent) level of educational attainment. Only 8 percent reported a low level of educational attainment or less than high school education. In this study, *medium* refers to high school completion or some post-secondary training but the *high* refers to some college, or a college graduate and/or professional school education.

By contrast, two-thirds (67 percent) of all Atlanta area participants reported an educational attainment at the medium level. However, the remainder of the Atlanta area respondents were almost evenly distributed between low level (18 percent) and high level of educational attainment (15 percent). The Houston respondents approximated those from Los Angeles in their distribution across all educational levels. In Houston, the percentages in the low, medium and high levels were 12, 41 and 47, respectively. In other words, 88 percent of the black Houstonians said they had gained a high level of schooling.

Among the Boston area participants, the largest percent (38) indicated a medium level of education. About one-third (34 percent) reported a high level and slightly more than one-fourth (28 percent) reported a low level of education. By contrast, the percentages among Cleveland area respondents for low, medium and high levels of educational attainment were 3, 37 and 60, respectively. These findings suggest that educational attainment among blacks in metropolitan Boston is skewed from medium toward low while education among blacks in the remaining four city areas is skewed from medium toward high levels.

Employment: The highest rate of full-time employment among all respondents was observed in the Cleveland sample. Among this group, slightly more than three-fourths (76 percent) reported full-time employ-ment. In rank order, according to percent of full-time employment, were Atlanta (71 percent), Houston (63 percent), Boston (51 percent) and Los Angeles (48 percent). By contrast, the highest rate of unemployment observed was among the Boston sample with twenty-five percent in this category. In terms of reported unemployment, Boston was followed in order by Los Angeles (20 percent), Houston (15 percent), Atlanta (11 per-cent) and Cleveland (8 percent). With the exception of Atlanta, the unemployment rate recorded in each of the study areas was substantially above the national unemployment rate of blacks (which fluctuated between 11.5 and 14.2 percent) during the study period.

Another relevant employment-unemployment distinction concerned the distribution of individuals who said they were retired. Among this group, the Los Angeles area respondents indicated the highest percent of blacks who were retired, living on pensions and/or social security benefits. Twenty-six percent of the Los Angeles cohort were in this category. This percent was followed in rank order by Atlanta (15), Boston (13), Houston (12) and Cleveland (3).

Income: Since Boston area participants were less likely to be employed full-time and more likely to be unemployed and/or retired, the finding that these respondents ranked highest in percent of low income individuals was not unanticipated. Fifty-three percent of all Boston area respondents reported an annual income in the low level of $0-$6,000 per year. By con-trast, this figure was 42 percent in Los Angeles, 40 percent in both Atlanta and Houston, and only 12 percent in Cleveland, which also reported the highest percent of full-time employees.

Not unexpectedly, the highest percent (61) in the medium income group of $7,000-$19,000 per year was found among Cleveland area par-ticipants. Cleveland was followed, in order of percent in medium income level, by Atlanta (56), Houston (51), Boston (45) and Los Angeles (43). Similarly, the highest percent (27) of any group in the high income, or above $20,000 per year classification, was observed in the Cleveland area. Los Angeles, which ranked second in this classification with 14 percent blacks who reported high income, was followed in order by Houston (9 percent), Atlanta (4 percent) and Boston (3 percent). The disproportionate number of Cleveland area blacks who said they had a high annual income may be explained by the overrepresentation of suburban middle and upper-class blacks in the Cleveland area sample. The high income distributions observed in the remaining cities did not appear to be outside the level of ex-pectation, especially in view of the high unemployment rates prevalent among blacks in these metropolitan communities.

Marital Status: The largest percent of single/never married respondents was found in the Cleveland area sample in which one-fifth of the respondents designated their marital status as such. In Houston and Los Angeles, slightly less than one-tenth (9 percent each) said they were single/never married. In Boston, one twentieth (5 percent) classified themselves in this way while in Atlanta, slightly less than one fifth (17 percent) stated they were single/never married. The majority (53 percent) of Boston area participants, on the other hand, said they were married. Less than half (46 percent each) among metropolitan Clevelanders and Houstonians, and only two-fifths (40 percent) in the Atlanta area so characterized themselves. However, only one-fourth (25 percent) of the Los Angeles area participants stated that they were presently married.

Yet, the divorced category selected by the Los Angeles areas participants (18 percent) was only slightly above that percent reported by participants from the Atlanta area (17 percent) and the Cleveland area (16 percent). The Los Angeles "divorced" percent was almost double the percent divorced in Boston (10), and well above the divorced percent (13) among blacks in metropolitan Houston.

These differences may be partially explained by the one-third (32 percent) in metropolitan Los Angeles who said they were "separated but not divorced." However, slightly more than one-fourth (26 percent) of Houston area blacks and slightly more than one-fifth (22 percent) of blacks in metropolitan Boston stated that they were separated but not divorced. These figures compared to 11 percent and 7 percent of blacks in this category in Atlanta and Cleveland, respectively. Los Angeles area respondents also indicated a slightly higher proportion of widowed (18 percent) than did those in the Atlanta (15 percent), Cleveland (11 percent), Boston (9 percent) and Houston (7 percent) areas.

Home Ownership: According to data reported by study participants, home ownership among blacks in Atlanta (55 percent), Cleveland (53 percent) and Houston (47 percent) was substantially higher than the 42 percent nationwide among blacks who owned their own homes in 1970. (See Chapter III). The 33 percent rate found among both Boston and Los Angeles area respondents was significantly below the national rate of home ownership for black Americans. Hence, the highest levels of home ownership were in the same cities in which blacks reported higher percents of full-time employment. Conversely, the lower rates of home ownership and the highest rates of persons who resided in rented dwellings were in the metropolitan areas in which blacks showed the lowest rates of full-time employment and the highest rates of unemployment. In terms of rented dwellings, the percent distributions observed were: Boston (64), Los Angeles (58), Houston (42), Cleveland (41) and Atlanta (38). On the other hand, living in rent-free dwellings was distributed as follows: Houston (12 percent), Los Angeles (9 percent), Atlanta (7 percent), Cleveland (6 percent) and Boston (3 percent). Another explanation for these distributions with respect to home ownership among blacks in these metropolitan areas may be that Cleveland, Atlanta and Houston have had a longer history of well-established middle-class black families who valued owning their own homes and were able to purchase real estate.

Macro- and Micro-Community Issues

With respect to overall concern for macro-community issues, striking dissimilarities between the cities were revealed. For instance, 80.5 percent of the Los Angeles area respondents and 77.1 percent of Houston area participants reported a high concern for these issues. By contrast, 78.7 percent of the Boston area respondents expressed a low concern about macro-community issues and none expressed high concern. On the other hand, approximately two-thirds (66.2 percent) of the Houston area and about one-half (50.5 percent) of the Atlanta area respondents stated a high concern for macro-community issues. Very few respondents from the metropolitan communities, Cleveland (0.0 percent), Los Angeles (0.0 percent), Atlanta (1.5 percent) and Houston (1.7 percent), stated a low concern for macro-community issues. These differences were statistically significant. (See Appendix I).

Similarly, the differences between concerns for macro-community issues expressed by urban and suburban residents, as separate entities, were also statistically significant. (See Appendix I). However, suburban residents were more than twice as likely (33.8 percent to 16.5 percent) as urban respondents to say that they viewed macro-community issues with high concern. On the other hand, urban residents (34.0 percent) were far more likely to express a low concern for these issues than were suburban respondents (0.6 percent). Urban residents (32.2 percent) were even more likely to claim a modest or medium concern than were suburban respondents (22.9 percent) for macro-community issues.

Micro-community concerns, those regarded as community-specific, were ranked by Houston and Cleveland area respondents as highest in importance. The high concern percentages were as follows: Cleveland (39.6 percent), Houston (29.5 percent), Los Angeles (14.1 percent), Atlanta

(13.1 percent). Only among the Cleveland area residents, no "low concern" votes were reported for micro-community issues. However, the range of "low concern" votes for these matters ranged from a high of 32.1 percent in the Boston area to 1.3 percent in Houston. The percents of "low concern" for micro-community issues for Atlanta and Los Angeles were 8.5 and 4.2, respectively. Hence, it must be evident that most respondents selected the "medium level" of concern for micro-community issues.

Priorities and Urgent Concerns

It may now be useful to disaggregate data and compare the five cities along two dimensions: (1) most urgent problems faced by individuals, and (2) their perceptions of the most urgent priorities faced by the black community.

As shown in Table 18, whether in cities or suburbs, blacks in each of the five cities said that the most urgent problem they faced centered on how to improve their economic conditions.

In terms of *urban* residents, further refinement of the data showed that the concern for better economic conditions ranked highest for 68 percent of all first place selections made by urban residents in Boston. Other first priority ranks for better economic conditions were: 66 percent of all highest priority ranks in Atlanta, 65 percent in Houston, 60 percent in Los Angeles and 52 percent in Cleveland.

By contrast, among urban residents, the overall second priority (listed in Table 18) received only 12 percent of all first priority ranks in Atlanta, 15 percent in Boston, 19 percent in Cleveland, 15 percent in Houston and 18 percent in Los Angeles.

Among the *suburban* residents, better economic conditions consistently received a larger share of the first priority or most urgent concern ranks. However, the magnitude of that concern varied from city to city, especially with respect to its proximity to or distance from the overall second priority factor. For instance, better economic conditions received only 33 percent of all first priority votes cast in Atlanta suburbs while more political power, the second concern in terms of overall priority, received 18 percent.

By contrast, the percent of first priority votes for better economic conditions varied in other cities from 50 percent in Boston, 50 percent in Cleveland, 48 percent in Houston to 45 percent in Los Angeles. On the other hand, the overall second concerns received percents of first priority votes that ranged from 19 percent in Boston, 17 percent in Cleveland, 17

Table 18. Your Most Urgent Concerns by Metropolitan Areas and Urban/Suburban Residence

Urgent Concerns Rank Order	Atlanta		Boston		Cleveland		Houston		Los Angeles	
	Urban	Suburban	Urban	Suburban	Urban	Suburban	Urban	Suburban	Urban	Suburban
1	BEC	BEC	BEC	BEC	BEC	BEC	BEC	BEC	BEC	BEC
2	BE	PP	EJ	EJ	C/D	BE	BE	BE	BE	BE
3	C/D	EJ	PP	PP	BE	PP	EJ	EJ	(3)PB	EJ(3rd)
4	BH	BH	C/D	C/D	PP	BH	C/D	PP	(3)BH	PB(3rd)
5	EJ	BPS	BE	BH	BH	EJ	BH	C/D	(3)EJ	C/D(3rd)
6	PP	BE	O	BPS	EJ	C/D	BPS	PB	(3)PP	BH(4th)
7	BPS	PB	BH	BE	PB	PB	PB	BH	BPS	PP(4th)
8	PB	C/D	BPS	O	BPS	BPS	PP	BPS	C/D	BPS

Legend: BEC - Better Economic Conditions
BE - Better Education
C/D - Crime/Drug Abuse
BH - Better Housing
BPS - Better Public Service
EJ - Equal Justice
PB - Police Brutality
PP - Political Power
O - Other

percent in Houston, to 16 percent in Los Angeles. (See Table 18 for rank orders).

Another important observation was the relative difference in the value seemingly placed on better educational attainment between blacks in metropolitan Boston and blacks in all of the remaining four cities. Individuals in Boston placed education substantially lower in priority than did blacks in other areas. Measured largely from anecdotal statements, blacks in metropolitan Boston appeared far more cynical about public education than were blacks in other areas. This cynicism was represented by statement that "Schools won't get any better no matter who's in charge." This pessimistic viewpoint may also reflect the negativism which probably increased as a consequence of the protracted conflicts over busing for school desegregation which began to escalate in 1974 with the implementation of the court order.

Problems in Cities and Suburbs

In order to avoid unnecessary repetition of previous discussions on the urgency of various problems which individuals identified, special attention will be devoted to selected problems in this section. Distinctions were made earlier on between perceptions of individual problems from those faced by the black community. However, it may be fruitful in this section to focus attention on either one of these categories without considering the other or to highlight the intersection and interconnections between the two.

Priorities and Issues in Metropolitan Atlanta

Although the economic issues were specified as most important by both urban and suburban blacks in Atlanta, there was also concern over the relationship between blacks and the police. The relatively low rank accorded the issues of concerns with police may have been an artifact of a narrow focus on "police brutality." The concerns that citizens have about their police force may be considerably broader than the concept police brutality. Consequently, the focus on police brutality may not have captured the scope of acrimonious feelings and general concerns that people have about their relationships with the police.

Many black Atlantans do feel that police bias, for instance, interferes with their chances for equal justice. Further, the paucity of blacks in critically important echelons of the criminal justice system minimizes their chances of equal justice. These feelings persist despite the presence of a black commissioner of public safety and one black judge in the city. There are 533 black police officers out of a total police force of 1,270. This number is below the authorized level of 1,317 police officers.

For a substantial part of the late 1970's, the police department was embroiled in a bitter discrimination suit originally filed by black police officers who alleged systematic discrimination. These allegations were countered by charges levied by white police officers who accused the city of reverse discrimination in its hiring and promotion policies which they claimed favored blacks at the expense of whites. As a result of these charges and counter charges, the city found itself trapped in a five year hiring freeze which had the ultimate effect of creating a severe shortage within the police work force.

In 1979-80, during one of the worst crime waves in the city's history, Atlanta was more than two-hundred police officers below the officially sanctioned level. In addition, police officers claimed that they were underpaid and under-equipped. This situation could have influenced their perception and reaction to blacks. The behavior of white police officers could have been affected if they projected hostility against a black mayor and a black commissioner of public safety onto the black population as a whole. This embitterment may not have been manifested in situations clearly defined as police brutality but it may have been evidenced in more routine forms of interpersonal relations and in stricter enforcement of the law in instances that would normally be dismissed as trivial incidents.

The fear of crime is nonetheless real in Atlanta. Immediately prior to the initiation of this study, Atlanta had surpassed Detroit as the "murder capital" of the nation. While, serious crimes increased by 29 percent the first quarter of 1979, the overall rate of crime decreased by 17 percent during the last quarter. The overall rise in crime rate declined during 1980; nevertheless, compared to the first nine months of 1979, the rates of serious crimes (homicides, rape, robbery, aggravated assault, larceny and auto theft) rose by 19 percent.[1] Although most murders and other serious crimes are intraracial, whenever a single inter-racial incident receives broad public and media attention, the erroneous impression is immediately conveyed that white persons are easy prey for the "black criminal element" and the city should be avoided at all cost.

The fear which grips the white population, whether consciously or subconsciously, controls relationship patterns across the color line. This fear is just as real and has a more substantial justification for the black population. Blacks have a greater need to worry about victimization by the lawless. They are far more likely to be preyed upon for either "aggressive or acquisitive purposes."[2] This fear is further compounded as the public comes to feel that the police department is reluctant or unwilling to perform its duty of crime prevention and control, or when one segment comes to regard the police force as indifferent to the problem of crime within its community because of the race factor.

The concern over drug abuse is not without justification. Local enforcement officials maintain that Atlanta is a major distribution center for illegal drugs. It is also asserted that many of the serious crime problems are drug related. Drug trafficking, combined with crimes related to a high rate of unemployment among the black population, can induce fear and panic among any group of people in any city. Such is the case in Atlanta. In effect, the interrelationship between the factors of equal justice, crime, drug abuse and police brutality is poignantly real.

Atlanta does have a program designed to check the spread of crime in the city. According to Commissioner Lee P. Brown, the Anti-Crime Action Plan was initiated and developed by the Department of Public Safety in partial response to the national publicity Atlanta received in 1978 about its rampant crime problem. It is a multi-faceted plan whose many components involve diverse strategies dictated in a large measure by the nature of the offenses and their past frequencies.[3]

The Anti-Crime Action Plan called for concrete steps to be taken in areas where more specific legislation is needed such as the ordinance which authorizes city police officers who live within city limits to take marked patrol cars home after work. The specific purpose of this ordinance is to increase the visibility of police officers throughout the city. In addition, attention is focused upon each of the Part I offenses as characterized by the Uniform Crime Reports.[4]

In many instances, the plan called for better data collection and analysis systems, closer cooperation between residents and public safety officials, and increase in the number of police officers, a more effective and efficient utilization of law enforcement resources in general, and a wide array of specific programs (e.g. SAFE -- Safer Atlanta for Everyone, Atlanta Flying Squad, Crime Stoppers, etc.)[5]

Professional organizations, including the Atlanta Bar Association, and special consultants, such as former U.S. Attorney General Griffin Bell, became active participants in the overall effort to combat crime in the city. The Law Enforcement Assistance Agency (LEAA) funded projects designed to facilitate the overall objective of curbing crime in general.

Strategies to control drug trafficking included an accelerated and more aggressive effort to enforce laws regarding possession of narcotics and for the apprehension of offenders. Plain clothes officers were assigned in larger numbers to attack the problem of "street dope peddlers," prostitution related to drug abuse, and to curtail flagrant solicitation, through the apprehension of "Johns" who seek out prostitutes.

This brief overview of the plan suggests that aggressive and concerted action was taken to reduce the crime rate. The implementation of the Anti-Crime Action Plan has met with some degree of success, despite the notoriety given to the wanton killing of young blacks in Atlanta. For instance, during the fourth quarter of 1979, Atlanta experienced a 17 percent decrease in crime over the same period in 1978 and a 9 percent increase for the 1979 year as a whole.[6]

The need for better economic conditions as suggested by two-thirds of the urban residents reveals the plight of so many poverty-stricken and near poverty level residents. It is also a concern among the upwardly mobile persons who understand that improvements in their daily living can only occur if their overall economic status rises. Many of these individuals undoubtedly regard higher educational attainment as the principal escape from their present condition or as the major resource required to realize better life chances. The relative high rankings accorded to these two factors is not unexpected.

Suburban residents rank the need for better economic conditions as their most urgent concern. Again, this position is not unexpected since there is a tendency for those who have achieved some semblance of the "American Dream" to consciously fight to maintain that standard or improve upon their level of living and to enrich their lives through economic betterment. On the other hand, "better education" drops to a sixth place position in priorities among this group; its second place position is replaced by "the need for more political power." This factor is closely followed by the need for equal justice among suburban residents.

It is somewhat surprising that both urban and suburban blacks give equal rank to the need for "better housing." More than twice as many suburban blacks awarded first place votes to this factor as an urgent concern as did urban residents. That disparity may be explained in this way. Many urban blacks do live in old, well-established neighborhoods with well-constructed dwellings and, in general, a good quality of housing. Suburban blacks may define their need in terms of the acquisition of status symbols — a house in a higher status neighborhood that may cost considerably more to purchase than their present place of residence. Hence, to them "better housing" may have a different meaning than it does for some of the urban residents.

Suburban residents also ranked the need for better public service slightly higher than urban residents. Such concerns as the need for better education, the elimination of police brutality and crime/drug abuse are ranked lower by suburban residents. Explanations for these differences may be apparent from comments made by some of the respondents about these issues. A suburban manager of a downtown department store commented that "a lot of us are not informed about all these issues because we feel that if we sit back everything will be taken care of, which is not true. We have to be more concerned and do something about crime, taxes, and discrimination." A real estate agent asserted that "ending of discrimination would mean better racial relationships among blacks and whites because so many blacks feel as though whites are given first priority in everything." A laborer in the heart of the city observed that "black people now realize that we need our economic rights to be able to make it in this society. And that means jobs." A disabled pensioner was firm in her belief that "our kids are good enough to go to school with white kids and they deserve the opportunity." Importantly, economic issues were paramount; however, the priority given to other issues was dependent upon both personal experience and consciousness about the conditions prevalent in the community itself.

Differences in perceptions of urgent concerns observed when the questions were cast in terms of black community problems as opposed to personal concerns were so minimal that no detailed analysis is warranted here.

Urgent Concerns and Priorities Among Metropolitan Boston Blacks

The rank order of urgent concerns and priorities for blacks in metropolitan Boston is revealing in terms of the present conditions of blacks in the Boston community. The underlying conditions explicit in the rankings noted in this area are almost identical to the kinds of concerns implicit in Gunnar Myrdal's "ranked order of discrimination" reported in his *American Dilemma* in 1944. In this path-finding analysis of institutional discrimination and racial segregation in the United States, Myrdal noted that blacks were more concerned about improving their economic condition, gaining equality before the law and achieving some degree of political power than they were about any other issues.

Almost four decades later, blacks in metropolitan Boston, irrespective of place of residence, are in perfect agreement that the same three factors, better economic conditions, equal justice before the law and more political power, continue to persist as the most urgent priorities and concerns among black people. Quite explicit in this finding is the reality that, despite notable educational and political gains achieved by black Americans during the past four decades, a significant proportion of the black population does not believe that a reasonably good life is within their reach. Too many blacks in metropolitan Boston, like blacks in other parts of the nation, cannot find adequate jobs, are unemployed or under-employed and are paid considerably less then whites are paid whenever they are employed.

Many of the remedies established to reduce occupational and wage discrimination have not had the universal effect that was intended with their establishment. For instance, a factory worker in Boston states that "the employment section in the paper has a little box that reads 'help wanted, equal opportunity employer'. This is not true." The implication is apparent. Many firms that advertise that they are "equal opportunity employers" have no intention of abiding by affirmative action regulations. A cashier indicates that she has lost faith in the willingness and the capacity of the American society to eliminate racial discrimination in jobs when she states that "I don't believe racial discrimination will ever end for blacks." A registered nurse identifies the problem of income distribution when she says that, "I think it (salaries/wages) should be equal. If the black has the degree, he should be paid the same . . . for the job." However, as previously noted, racial differences in wages earned are enormous and the gap between blacks and whites appears to be widening. A secretary does not believe that the economic condition of blacks is likely to be alleviated in any appreciable way because "a capitalist society is based upon inequality."

The urgency of the problem of equal justice before the law is underscored by the increasing belief among many blacks that "it is almost impossible for blacks to get justice" in Boston. Such persons point to highly publicized cases in which whites who allegedly committed crimes against blacks were exonerated even when the evidence was overwhelmingly directed toward a verdict of guilty. They believe that blacks are more likely to be harrassed by the police and to be victimized by the criminal justice system.[7] They are convinced that some judges are far more lenient on white offenders than they are on black offenders. When they read reports of the Spotlight Team of the Boston Globe which suggests that some white judges automatically and customarily sentence black offenders to the maximum security facilities for hardened criminals such as Deer Island and Walpole Prison while white offenders are remanded to the less dehumanizing institutions of Concord and Billerica, their position is reaffirmed.[8]

Although it does not necessarily follow that a black official in the criminal justice system will be either more just or lenient on blacks who appear before them, many blacks believe that to be the case. However, in metropolitan Boston, their chances of appearing before a black judge or magistrate are relatively slim. There are only 12 black judges and magistrates in Boston at different levels of the court system.

Political empowerment is a major issue in metropolitan Boston. Despite their increase from 16 percent of the city population in 1970 to 22 percent in 1980, blacks in metropolitan Boston exercise little significant political power. The chairperson of the Boston school committee, elected in 1977 to the School Committee, as the first black to serve on that body in this century was, until the November 1981 election, the only black elected official in ten years. In addition, there are five black legislators elected from the Boston area to the Massachusetts Legislature. This number included four members of the Massachusetts House of Representatives and one state senator. Almost all of the black elected officials from metroplitan Boston, with the exception of two elected to the school committee in 1981, were elected from districts in which the black and minority population were in the majority. Blacks have not been generally successful in attempts to win city-wide elections. Black political empowerment may be improved in the future since voters approved a measure in 1981 that would permit district representation on the city council and school committee beginning in 1983.

A major factor in the lack of political power among the black population is their comparatively low voter registration. Further, even among black registered voters, the actual number of persons who vote is so few as to render blacks far less effective than would ordinarily be the case. For instance, in the 1979-1980 city elections, only 44 percent of the black population voted. In the 1976 and 1980 national elections, the percent of blacks who voted were 49 and 51 percent, respectively.

Because of the large number of white candidates whom blacks have suspected of racial hostility toward minority groups, blacks have tended to cast their city votes for those persons whose views appeared to be the least injurious to them. As a result, many blacks maintain that some city officials take their votes for granted. Consequently, the benefits that accrue to the black community as a quid pro quo for their loyalty to Democratic candidates are relatively nil. Few blacks hold positions of importance in the city government. Among that pitifuly small number, many are in essentially ceremonial, powerless positions with limited decision-making authority. In fact, Boston's lone black deputy mayor resigned in 1980 in part because of the limited opportunity to make critical decisions with respect to various governmental functions. Some blacks who are placed in positions that customarily imply some degree of power and decision-making authority soon discover that their white assistants, in fact, exert more political clout than they do because of their immense network of friends and relatives within the political system. Consequently, decisions made by black bureaucrats may be undermined or circumvented by the furtive dealings of their white assistants.

The overall failure to become active participants in the political process encourages many white candidates not to take black voters seriously. Limited voter participation is a central manifestation of disenchantment with the white power structure and its refusal to respond to the urgent needs of the black community. During the 1980 elections, many blacks stayed away from the polls because of the belief that "it does not matter who is elected. No white man is going to do very much for the black folks." However, a significant number of black voters did support the black candidate for mayor of the city and enabled him to make a respectable third place finish in the city-wide balloting. One explanation for the strength of this showing is, of course, that a significant number of voters from all races were persuaded by his approach to the city's problems and the kinds of solutions he proposed. Many were like a black shipper for the Boston Edison Company, who believed that "if . . . more blacks were in higher positions, maybe other young blacks would have something to relate to." Consequently, some blacks are like the European immigrants before them and most white ethnic groups in 1981 who seek to retain whatever political power they have gained by bullet voting for candidates from their own group.

Urban and suburban blacks, as individuals, also view the problem of crime and drug abuse as a most urgent priority. Although crime has increased throughout metropolitan Boston in the past decade, the respondents in this study identify this problem as the fourth major problem affecting them as individuals. They are victimized not only by the actuality of crime against them, or members of their families or their friends but by fear of crime. Even though most of the crimes they fear are acquisitive in nature, there is also a prevailing dread of potential violence or aggressive crime committed in connection with acquisitive acts. Specifically, an elderly woman lives with the constant possibility that she might be mugged, brutalized or knocked down by some person who may snatch her purse. A college student fears that he might be assaulted as he returns from a party. A young nurse fears that she might be raped as she returns from her job late at night.

In fact, according to a study conducted under the auspices of *The*

Boston Globe, such fears are not without foundation. Findings in this study showed that in the Boston neighborhoods included in this study the actual number of crimes committed in 1979 were among the highest in the city. For example, 9,787 crimes were committed in Roxbury/North Dorchester, 6,166 in Dorchester, and 5,387 in Mattapan. Relative to the 15 districts included in the study, these three areas ranked third, fifth and sixth, respectively. There were 27 murders, 120 rapes, 1165 aggravated assaults, 2,094 cases of burglary, 2,627 cases of larceny and 2,400 auto thefts committed in Roxbury/North Dorchester alone.[9] Only 16 percent of all of these crimes were actually solved by the Boston Police Department.[10] In the case of murder, 63 percent of the cases were solved in contrast to only 46 percent of the rape cases. The figures for robbery, burglary, larceny and auto theft were 16 percent, 12 percent, 12 percent, and 3 percent.[11]

Crime in Boston, like crime all over the United States, tends to be far more intra-racial than inter-racial. Hence, many blacks are deeply troubled by black-on-black crime. An architect in the sample says that he is disheartened by the extent of black-on-black crime. An insurance agent asserts that "we as blacks do not stick together or work together. We would not have so much crime if we did" (work together to deal with the problem of urban crime among blacks).

The most fundamental aspect of this issue is the failure of the social system to address the basic causes of the crime problem. For the ordinary citizen, the roots of crime and delinquency are found in the nature of urban life for black and poor persons in general. The focus is street crime because that is the only form of criminal behavior that is a familiar occurrence. Many know what it means to be victimized by breaking-and-entering, auto-theft, burglary, robbery, petty theft, muggings and the violence that may accompany such offenses. Some have had personal possessions — televisions, stereo equipment, radios, furniture and money — stolen from them and some have had purses snatched and pockets picked. Many feel that the offenders are persons who resort to theft, larceny, robbery and burglary in order to obtain the finance necessary to support a drug habit. The conditions often associated with such criminal behavior are poverty, unemployment, underemployment, lack of money, hunger, alienation from the social system and normative controls, and inability to cope with the oppressive conditions under which many individuals are forced to live. This breakdown or disintegration of the social norms that govern individual behavior, coupled with the cultural mandate to acquire material possessions as evidence of success, may be a further explanation of deviant criminal acts.

Urban blacks attach greater urgency "to better education" than do suburban blacks. Not only does this reflect a disparity in the quality of education provided by the two respective school systems, this response is also a manifestation of diverse school experiences. Suburban black children and their parents may not be forced to question the quality of education offered, in contrast to urban blacks, since it is assumed that suburban schools do a better job of schooling their children. However, black parents of suburban children, even though reluctant to admit it, are quite concerned about evidence of racism in their schools. This racism may be reflected in attitudes and behavior of classmates, teachers and administrators. Other students may subject black children to racial slurs and prevent them from full participation in school acitvities. Teachers and administrators may lower the expectations of black children because "they are black" or assume that because they are black they automatically need "special attention."

Urban black parents worry about the quality of education, the deteriorating facilities in predominantly black schools, and certain aspects of busing for school desegregation. While some individuals in the Boston sample oppose busing, many see a clear necessity for busing as a tool or instrument to assure better education for black children. One factory worker stated, "I don't believe in forced busing but in better education for all children, white and black." Another factory worker insisted that there is "nothing wrong with the bus; its the school system that needs changing." A warehouse worker argued that "forced busing is needed for quality education for blacks." But, a home economics teacher asserted that "forced busing is really not the answer. Equal opportunites are the problem. If this (sic) condition did not exist, there would be no forced busing." A college student stated that "the better teachers are always in the white area. It is an attempt to keep blacks uneducated if they are not bused for school desegregation." But another type of problem is revealed in the words of a painter who said that, "our black children still find it hard living in a white community where some of the white children at school feel that they own the place and the community."

The quality of urban education in Boston is highly suspect. Consternation arises from persistent reports about low reading and mathematics scores of school age children in comparison to national norms. It emanates from the excessive number of public school student walkouts during the course of the year and the uncertainty in any given year as to whether or not sufficient funds will be available to keep schools open for the required number of days for an academic year. All too frequently, the necessity of delivery of quality education is lost in the political machinations and internecine warfare which perennially erupt between the mayor and city council. Fiscal autonomy for the School Committee (Board) is challenged by the Mayor. The mayor's authority is challenged by the city council. The city council is ignored by the mayor and threatens to revoke his authority. The constant reign of political war is a perversion of the checks and balance system in government through intense personality power struggles of elected officials in general. While the battle of will, resolutions, and litigation ensues, school children suffer. The only aspiration that many pupils have is to "get through the twelfth grade and get out." Indeed, only about 20 percent of Boston public school graduates go on to college. In recent years, no more than three seniors in Boston's schools have been semi-finalists in the National Merit Scholarship Program.

With respect to test performance, Philip Hart observed that two of every three black children in public schools read below average in contrast to only one of every three white children. Achievement results also show that "one-half to three-fourths of black students have below average skills in mathematic concepts, computations and application."[12] Hart also states that:

> At the elementary level (Grades 1-5) only 40 percent of black and other minority students (i.e. Hispanic) are reading average or above compared with 70 percent of white pupils. At the middle-school level (Grades 6-8) two thirds of enrolled black students demonstrated below average reading skills compared with one-third white students, indicating retrogression in reading skills as black children move along to higher grades.[13]

Although advancements in reading and mathematics scores have occurred since 1976, further improvements should be made.

Public schools have not treated their charges well, racial considerations notwithstanding. Too many school children have extensive weaknesses in writing and communication skills, mathematics and simple computations, and in general, are deficient in subject matter normally expected of high school graduates and usually attained in high schools across the nation. Pupils are being shortchanged year after year as the overall quality of education deteriorates.

As shown in Table 19, *suburban* blacks assign greater priority to better housing than do urban blacks. They also give greater urgency to the problem of inadequate public services. Both public services and housing are issues of great concern to metropolitan blacks. The gravity of this concern may also be discerned from a study conducted by Philip Hart in 1977 in the Mattapan section of Boston. Hart noted community concerns about hous-

Table 19. Problems Facing the Black Community by Metropolitan Area and Urban/Suburban Residence

Urgent Concerns Rank Order	Atlanta		Boston		Cleveland		Houston		Los Angeles	
	Urban	Suburban	Urban	Suburban	Urban	Suburban	Urban	Suburban	Urban	Suburban
1	BEC	BEC	BEC	BEC	BEC	BEC	BEC	BEC	BEC	BEC
2	EJ	PP	EJ	EJ	BE	BE	BE	BE	BE	BE
3	BE	BE	PP	PP	C/D	PP	C/D	PP	(3)BH	EJ(3rd)
4	C/D	EJ	BE	BPS	EJ	EJ	EJ	C/D	PP	BPS
5	BH	BH	BPS	BE	PP	C/D	BH	BH	PB	BH
6	PP	BPS	C/D	BH	PB	PB	BPS	EJ	EJ	PB
7	BPS	C/D	BH	O	BH	BPS	PB	PB	BPS	PP
8	PB	PB	O	C/D	BPS	BH	PP	BPS	O	C/D

Legend: BEC - Better Economic Conditions
    BE - Better Education
    C/D - Crime/Drug Abuse
    BH - Better Housing
    BPS - Better Public Service
    EJ - Equal Justice
    PB - Police Brutality
    PP - Political Power
    O - Other

ing deterioration and abandonment, the need for "street and sidewalk repairs", better street lighting, better garbage collection, better police protection and better public transportation as some of the services they needed. In general, these concerns are characterized in this study as micro-community or community-specific issues or concerns.[14]

Urgent Priorities and Issues in Cleveland

Both urban and suburban residents of Cleveland attach a greater priority to improving their own economic conditions than they do to other areas of general concern. Second in priority among urban residents is the problem of crime and drug abuse. Improving education ranks third and political power is fourth in priority for individuals in urban areas. Obtaining better housing is given the same degree of priority or urgency as that assigned to assuring equal justice, which is fourth.

Individual suburban residents on the other hand, assign high priority to improving their education, the acquisition of more political power and better housing, Both groups showed an almost equal concern or attached almost the same priority to the first problems with the exception of the importance given to crime and drug abuse among suburban blacks. The sixth place position of this problem, in comparison to the strong second place priority assigned to crime and drug abuse among the urban blacks is a manifestation of the differential magnitude or the perceived pervasiveness of the crime/drug problems in different sections of the metropolitan area.

When individuals were questioned about the priorities assigned to problems facing the black community as a whole, once again there was agreement that better economic conditions are first in priority among black people. Both urban and suburban blacks are about equal in the urgency attached to better education and the significance of equal justice and better housing. Slight variations are evident between the two groups with respect to the urgency or priority given to such problems as crime and drug abuse, political power, police brutality, and better public services.

The distribution of blacks on the employment and occupational scales does not fully address the magnitude and gravity of the economic problems encountered by blacks in their daily lives. A dental assistant defines the untoward economic condition of blacks on poor jobs, low income and the high price that inflation exacts from blacks with insufficient salaries and wages. A factory worker says that competition (from white people) is not allowing blacks to move up fast enough and that "blacks are afraid that they will lose their jobs so they don't speak up against injustice." A manicurist insists that "blacks must still be better qualified than whites in order to get ahead," and an artist insists that "racism and the ramifications of that condition which are necessary to maintain a capitalistic society for the profit of a few at the expense of the majority in the United States" is at the root of the problem.

Others believe that the unemployment problem is not only the most fundamental component of poor economic conditions of blacks in Cleveland, but that also affects other aspects of family life and social conditions. For instance, a teacher maintains that, "unemployment leads to family instability, crime and drugs." A laborer agrees with that assessment when he says that, "unemployment increases the rate of crime for survival." In his view, people who are unemployed will engage in crime in order to meet basic sustenance needs for themselves and family members. A building contractor is convinced that "black unemployment is the result in large measure to job discrimination" and that "job discrimination is a condition that affects all blacks, regardless of social class." This view is shared by a claims adjuster who argues that "the lack of equitable employment opportunity has a stranglehold on black Americans."

One respondent expressed a deep concern about the problem of teenage unemployment. His perspective testifies to a view shared by most blacks throughout the United States: "they (black teenagers) are the adults of the future. If there is no substantial foundation of work labor laid down when one is young, what experience is there to draw upon as adults?"

As discussed earlier, both urban and suburban blacks assigned a high priority to improving education among blacks in their communities. Undoubtedly, this concern for better education in Cleveland was heightened by the controversy which arose over school desegregation during the mid- and late seventies. It was exacerbated by the near bankruptcy of the city that caused schools to close as well as closings created by teacher strikes during the Kucinich mayoralty.

If the viewpoint expressed by a black factory worker in Cleveland is widely shared, then, blacks in Cleveland maintain that, "if schools were totally segregated, then it is possible for black children to not receive the best education." In agreement, a social worker insists that "forced busing will, in fact, upgrade the education of the black child." A prevailing sentiment appears to be that busing for school integration is the most efficacious guarantee for a better quality of education for black children. It is widely assumed that school systems do not really respond to the educational needs of black children. If white children were to enroll in a formerly black school, then more resources will be devoted to upgrading the overall quality of the educational programs offered primarily because of the white presence in these public schools.

Although crime, drug abuse and police brutality do not have the same level of priority among blacks in this classification, each is nonetheless of special concern to blacks in metropolitan Cleveland. A dental assistant says that her greatest priority is "finding some way to eliminate black-on-black crime." A drug abuse counselor is especially concerned about the inattention of the Board of Education to the problem of drug abuse in the schools and of the city in supporting programs designed to rehabilitate drug addicts and help them provide basic needs for their chidlren. By the same token, a school counselor claims that much crime is the result of "a real lack of money." "People will steal in order to eat." Others express a genuine fear of victimization of personal or property crimes.

Between January and August of 1980, there were 186 murders in Cleveland. Of that number, 127 or 68 percent were black and other minority victims. Fifty-nine or 32 percent were white. Most of these offenses were intra-racial or represented "black-on-black crimes."[15] As we shall also see in Houston, blacks fear unnecessary police violence directed against them. During the 1970's, several incidents occurred in which blacks charged unnecessary shootings by members of the Cleveland police force. The city in 1980 established a recruitment goal of 30 percent minorities on its police force.[16]

Perhaps, one of the reasons that blacks assign a high priority to the acquisition of *more political power* is the belief that their conditions will be better if more blacks are in positions of power, authority and influence throughout the city structure. Whether or not that is the case may be a function of the quantity and quality of resources available to blacks who inherit the mantle of governmental authority in a city. James E. Blackwell and Marie Haug concluded in a Cleveland study of power arrangements in 1970 that frequently when blacks achieve the highest elective positions in a city, very few resources are available to them. In other words, blacks are expected to take a dying city, miraculously transform it into a city of economic and social vibrancy within a short period of time. If they are unsuccessful in this endeavor, then the full range of economic and social ills of the city, accumulated over a large number of years under white hegemony, will be blamed on the newly elected black officials.[17]

Yet, blacks have performed and continue to play signficant roles in the political life of metropolitan Cleveland. According to data reported in the *National Roster of Black Elected Officials* in 1979, 53 of the 177 elected officials in the State of Ohio were from Cleveland and Cuyahoga County. Thirty of the 53 were from Cleveland and 23 were Cuyahoga officials.[18] This group included one U.S. Congressman (Rep. Louis Stokes, brother of Carl Stokes, the city's former Mayor), one state senator, one state representative, one county commissioner, one municipal mayor, 27 municipal council members, ten judges, one State educational officer and 10 members of local school boards. During the period of this study, a black served as President of the Cleveland city council and another as President of the school board.

When respondents addressed housing as a major problem, they raised several other issues. They were concerned about the overall quality of housing, deteriorating conditions in some neighborhoods, inattention to the conditions of houses by absentee landlords, and vacant lots as a "haven for trash and old abandoned cars." Others spoke of the continuing practice of discrimination in housing despite the existence of anti-discriminatory legislation. It is the failure to enforce laws that is at the core of this aspect of the housing problem. Still others were concerned about "the lack of pride among some blacks in their own property" and "disrespect for the private property of other people."

Cleveland leaders organized an environmental enrichment program called "Rapid Recovery" during the seventies. The expressed purpose of this program was to improve the landscape along the rapid transit line. This program was initiated primarily in response to the dismay communicated by different suburban riders to the airport about unseemly conditions they saw along the rapid transit lines. Hence, a cleanup campaign was mounted. Apparently, many minority residents who lived along those tracks had complained repeatedly to the city fathers for assistance in cleaning up trash and weeds but to no avail. But, when the "airport crowd" demanded change, action was taken and only indirectly did the local residents benefit. Occasionally, local neighborhoods also organized clean-up campaigns to "clean and beautify their neighborhoods."

Implicit in the interpretation of housing problems are such micro-community concerns as the quality of life in the neighborhood, the conditions of streets, garbage collection rates, cleanliness of the neighborhood, and the safety of the neighborhood. However, it appeared that greater priority is assigned to macro-community issues.

Priorities and Urgent Concerns in Houston

Both urban and suburban blacks agreed that three factors have the highest priority for them as individuals. In rank order, they are: (1) better economic conditions, (2) better education and (3) equal justice before the law. There is no agreement between urban and suburban residents on the urgency or priority that should be assigned to the remaining five factors. For urban individuals the rank order or urgent concerns is as follows: (4) the elimination of crime and drug abuse, (5) better housing, (6) better public service, (7) police brutality, and (8) more political power.

When the question was shifted to perceptions of most urgent problems facing the black community in Houston, there was agreement across residential lines only on two factors. Better economic conditions and better education ranked first and second among both urban and suburban residents.

Mention has already been made of the tremendous gulf between the races in Houston. The enormity of the disparity in occupational achievement and income cannot be explained by differences in educational attainment alone. The amount of education achieved by blacks in Houston, as a group, is indistinguishable from that received by the population as a whole. The problem lies in differential access to the opportunity structure based upon race and the type of educational training that some individuals have. The *possibilities* for better jobs in the energy, technology and business/management fields conjoined with the overall importance attached to education as the central vehicle for upward mobility account for the urgency attached to the factor of "better education."

If better education is to be attained, there must be equality of opportunity for access at all levels of the educational system. Houston is the site of such higher education complexes as the Texas Medical Center, Rice University, Baylor University, Texas Southern University, and the University of Houston. Black high school and college graudates do not have equal access to these institutions. That is one of the central reasons why the U.S. Justice Department ordered the State of Texas to present an acceptable plan for dismantling its dual system of higher education in compliance with the demands of the Adams vs. Califano case.*

While Texas Southern University is a predominantly black public institution, the remaining public institutions in the Houston area are historically and currently predominantly white. In general, predominantly black public institutions have not received equal resources from state

---

*This point was confirmed in a conversation with Jean Fairfax of the NAACP - Legal Defense Fund, Inc. on November 14, 1981.

legislatures — a fact which affects the overall problem of equality of access and opportunity.

The problems of equal justice before the law, crime and drug abuse and the elimination of police brutality are deeply intertwined in the Houston area. The fear of victimization by crime is pervasive, especially among those persons who have familiarity with the "fifth ward" within Loop 610. Crime is also feared by residents of other areas but not apparently to the same degree. Many residents associate crimes of acquisition (e.g. burglary, theft, larceny) with drug abuse. Crime against the persons are regarded as aggressive responses to economic disabilities, racial oppression, and the tensions or anxieties created by survival uncertainties.

A majority of the respondents, regardless of residence or whether they are speaking of individual or community problems of urgency, feel that blacks do not get fair treatment before the law. They also believe that the police force is a "dangerous enemy of black people" and that "whatever they (the police) do that is wrong against black people, there will be a cover-up." There is "little faith in either the capacity or willingness of police officers to tell the truth about their encounters with civilians," especially minorities in metropolitan Houston.

These perceptions appear to be justified on the basis of overwhelming evidence, both empirical and impressionistic. According to a deadly force study conducted by the Public Interest Advocacy Center, of police activity between 1960 and 1978, a serious question must be raised about indiscriminate use of deadly force against blacks and other minorities in Houston. Minorities comprise in excess of 40 percent of the city's population; yet, they represent only 12.2 percent of the 3,000 member police force. [On a per capita basis, there were fewer black officers in Houston in 1978 than there were in 1950.[19] In 1978, 45 percent of the civilian employees of the police department were minorities who earned under $10,000 per year.[20]]

According to the study, 267 police shootings resulted in 124 fatalities of civilians and 143 were wounded. Police and newspaper reports indicated that of the 267 persons shot by police officers, 43 were unarmed, 36 were allegedly armed with a knife or some other instrument and 169 were allegedly armed with a gun. Of these groups, 58 were fleeing the police in an automobile and 74 were fleeing the police on foot at the time of the shootings. Thirty-six victims were shot by off-duty policemen, and 18 victims were reportedly accidentally or mistakenly shot. Juveniles were involved in 42 of the 267 cases. In only two instances over the eight year period covered by these 267 incidents were warning shots fired.[21]

Between 1970 and 1978, not a single police officer involved in these deadly force incidents was ever indicted by state grand juries. Only in the Randall Webster case (which involved a 17 year-old Shreveport, Louisiana youth who was killed after a high speed chase and it was shown that police had planted a gun on Webster)[22] was there an indictment by a federal grand jury. The sentences were, however, probated.[23] During that period, no Houston police officer was imprisoned for taking the life or wounding a Houston citizen, irrespective of race.[24] These conditions are among those situations which lead many blacks to conclude that there is no such phenomenon as equal justice in Houston and that the need for equality before the law is so imperative.

The Public Interest Advocacy Center also found that many of the 267 incidents involved a chase in which the lives of innocent citizens were needlessly endangered. Most of the 267 incidents involved young Houston police officers who were assigned to "patrol" units and not to specialty units. Many of them were repeatedly involved in the use of deadly force. They also noted that severe crimes of violence, such as murder and aggravated robbery, were not the most frequent offenses allegedly being committed. "Aggravated assault on an officer" seemed to predominate among offenses reported by police. It is in this regard, that the question arises of how much faith or trust can citizens have in the veracity of police officers when the victim is dead and cannot testify in his/her own behalf, or feels sufficiently threatened as to become mortally afraid of testifying against police officers.[25]

In addition to the Webster case in 1977, when there were 44 cases of the use of deadly force by police officers, the case of Joe Campos Torres received national attention. Evidence showed that a "pack of police officers" assisted him in a fatal plunge into Buffalo Bayou. There were numerous accusations of a cover-up engineered by the police department and, indeed, the police department refused to take punitive actions against the officers involved in this case. A national outcry over the miscarriage of justice in this case led to an investigation of the police department by the U.S. Commission on Civil Rights and the convening of a federal grand jury to examine possible violations of the civil rights of Joe Torres.[26]

Despite these findings, police violence against civilians continues in Houston. Between 1977 and the end of June, 1978, there were 125 incidents involving the use of deadly force by Houston police officers. One particularly controversial case involved Reggie Lee Jackson, "a black street hustler" who was killed by the police after, according to police accounts, Jackson pointed a pistol at them at a routine traffic stop. Investigations showed that an unfired gun was found in the victim's hand. Eye witnesses to the incident contradicted the official police version by insisting that Jackson, who pleaded for his life before he was shot, was killed in "cold blood."[27]

Not a single police officer involved in the 125 shootings since 1977 has been indicted by a country grand jury. At no time in the 1970's was a Houston police officer ever indicted by a county grand jury for the shooting of civilians. Following the Webster case, 22 police officers were indicted for civil rights violations but these cases involved police beatings and other police misconduct. The primary difficulties related by the failure to invoke punitive action against police who abuse their authority result from half-hearted investigations by fellow police officers resulting in weak evidence in some cases, and inadequacies in the selection of grand jury members.

The process involves selection by grand jury commissioners who are appointed by judges. This process results in the virtual exclusion of minority members from these juries and with the over-representation of often insensitive elite white persons,[28] firmly committed to protecting and supporting the local police.

The problem is further complicated by the under-representation of blacks in the judicial system. The gravity of the situation is evident in the 1980 election results in which two of the four black candidates for judgeships lost their bid. Harris County, as of November, 1980, has one black appelate level judge, two black district judges and two black justices of the peace.[29]

The paucity of blacks in the judicial system and the failure of black candidates to attain such positions persuade some blacks that their chances for equal justice before the law diminish with each defeat of a black candidate. Notwithstanding, there is still a major problem of crime in Houston. The problem is so severe that the city has been referred to as "another Dodge City."[30] During one weekend in August, 1980, 18 persons in Houston were murdered. Most of these wanton killings occurred in black and Hispanic areas of the city and 75 percent of the victims were either black or Hispanic. Although most of the offenders were relatives, friends, neighbors and acquaintances, some residents allege that the police department and society in general display callous indifference to these violent acts because those involved are not of the right race and not of the right social class to generate anti-violence campaigns.[31] There are other problems — the absence of a gun control law in Texas resulting in a large number of "gun-toting individuals" strutting around the town using the gun as a manifestation of one's machismo; the shortage of police officers evidenced by the ratio of one police officer for every 600 people; and the inability or unwillingness of the power structure to mount a systematic attack against the root causes of the crime problem.

Failure of the city to provide housing of good quality and deliver high quality public serivces is well known by many urban residents through first-hand experience. Automobiles are an almost *sine qua non* for existence but many persons are without personal/private transporation — public transporation fails them. Buses are often not on schedule, may not come at all, and when they do arrive, it is alleged, they are likely to be in less than desirable condition. There are problems in scheduled garbage collection, sewerage treatment and disposal, water distribution, potholes in the street, traffic congestion and inadequate drainage after the slightest downpour of rain.Although some of these problems are what we define as micro-community (neighborhood-specific), many are fairly widespread throughout most parts of the city. [32]

Even though urban residents ranked the need for "more political power" in last position among the factors or concerns identified, there is still a very special interest in political power. Blacks are under-represented in elected political officials in the city of Houston and in Harris County of which Houston is a dominant political unit. Of the 4 members of the United States House of Representatives from the Houston area, only one is black. Of the 24 Houston area state representatives to the Texas Legislature, 5 are black. Three blacks serve on the 14 person City Council and 2 of the 7 persons elected to the school board of the Houston Independent School District (HISD) are black. Within the city, there are 2 Justices of the Peace who are black. As of November, 1980, within Harris County, two blacks served as judges in district courts, one as a judge in a family court, and one as associate justice in the court of civil appeals. One black person also serves as a constable for Harris County. [33]

Although blacks are under-represented in elective political positions in Houston and Harris County, those who do serve in these positions fulfill not only a symbolic function, they also may be able to influence decision-making in ways that improve the life-chances and aspirations of black citizens.

For example, the presence of blacks and Hispanics on the HISD, combined with court-action spurred by lawsuits filed by the National Association for the Advance of Colored People (NAACP), persuaded HISD to move forward toward desegregating its public school system.

A tri-ethnic committee which monitors desegregation efforts was created but its plans are increasingly hampered by declining enrollment of white pupils. The enrollment decline and a transfer policy that has resulted in the movement of "well-advantaged minority students" to integrated schools, has left the lower-income minorities in approximately "100 percent one-race minority schools" in the HISD.[34]

Black members on the HISD School Board are seeking to reduce the burden of transportation to schools for desegregation purposes presently carried disproportionately by blacks and Hispanics and to stabilize enrollment trends in schools undergoing the most pronounced changes in racial composition so that the goal of integrated schools can be attained. Integrated schools seem especially important for blacks because they *believe* that better education is offered in integrated schools than in one-race minority schools.[35]

The acquisition of more political power which enables blacks to influence educational outcomes is but one expectation that the black constituent has of black elected officials. The fate of black Houstonians with regard to political power is intimately intertwined with other structural factors such as jobs, income and housing. As long as blacks do not have access to higher paying jobs, and as long as they are not able to purchase adequate housing in the areas beyond Loop 610, and unless strong coalitions can be forged between blacks and other voting blocs, the numerical representation of blacks in elective positions will be lower than their proportion in the total population. The solution to this problem lies in better economic conditions, better jobs, better education, less residential isolation, and stronger participation of blacks in the political process.

Rank of Priorities and Urgent Issues in Los Angeles

When the respondents were asked, "What are your own urgent concerns or priorities as an individual," better economic conditions received the highest rank. Better economic conditions also received the highest rating when the question was posed in terms of priorities or concerns facing the black community as a whole. Urban and suburban residents also agreed that "better education" was second in priority.

The current economic problems encountered by blacks in the Los Angeles area have reached crisis proportions. The rate of unemployment is staggering and blacks are over represented in the low income categories. Some of the comments made by respondents reveal bitterness and grave concern over the economic plight of blacks in the Los Angeles area. A salesperson, for instance, commented that "there are a number of qualified blacks needing a job, but unable to get them. Why? Every person should have equal opportunity." A postal clerk stated that ". . .if there were more jobs, there would be less blacks on welfare and unemployment lines." A nurse's aide commented that "blacks have little or no chance for training. I don't think that things will get better." A mechanic lamented that, "if blacks are trained and can't get a job, then something is wrong." A college student exemplified the discouraged worker syndrome when he observed that "blacks have it hard. Some of my family members have been looking for a job for a year, can't find one, and are about to give up." Finally, a clerk insisted that "younger whites have higher rates of pay than blacks, and blacks have to play games to get more."

Although there is a relationship between educational level and occupational status as well as with income received, in general, other factors appear to be at work. It is almost impossible to obtain even an entry-level job without a high school diploma; although the lack of education is not the problem here. Less than 8 percent of the respondents had less than a high school education. However, more than 40 percent received less than $7,000 in annual income. Some blacks may be earning less than the minimum wage; some think they are paid less than white workers despite their having the same amount of training or more and substantially more experience.

The gravity of the economic issue for blacks in Los Angeles is further underscored by the distance between that priority and all other issues. The number of persons who rated that matter as the most important priority issue was greater than the combined number of all other issues. Clearly, the economic situation for blacks has worsened. While all Americans feel the devastating impact of inflation on their daily lives, the effects of double digit inflation are worse for the poor, the low income and the unemployed. Inflation takes its heaviest toll where housing costs have escalated beyond imagination, where the transportation system is so ineffective that individuals must often spend hours travelling to and from work; where automobiles are viewed as an absolute imperative despite the skyrocketing price of gasoline, and where food prices are among the highest in the nation.

Better Education is a second in priority among Los Angeles area respondents. Not only is this issue related to the economic conditions of many blacks, it refers to the overall quality of education received by blacks in an essentially segregated public school system.

Perhaps, the most controversial and divisive educational issue that the Los Angeles area faced during the period between 1963 and 1981 was that of school desegregation. In 1963, the NAACP filed a suit to force public school desegregation in Los Angeles. This action precipitated an 18 year legal battle over the allegations of misuse of busing to achieve school desegregation. The composition of the School Board changed frequently on the basis of support or opposition to school busing and desegregation.[36]

During the period of legal entanglements and efforts to prevent school integration from occuring, major demographic changes occurred within the city. Some residential areas became completely or almost completely black and other minority in composition. Other neighborhoods or communities became or remained rigidly white. Consequently, the schools reflected the racial composition of residential areas. Some persons charged that the opponents to school integregation became so obsessed with opposition to court orders to desegregate that they permitted the school system to deteriorate.[37] The luster of having once been regarded as one of the most outstanding public school systems in the nation faded. The quality of education offered in many schools was "marginal at best;" the quality of teaching, many alleged, deteriorated; curriculum planning and other pedagogical issues were neglected. The Los Angeles Unified School District lost 100,000 pupils in the period between 1976-81.[38]

In 1979, opponents to mandatory busing were able to place a proposition before the electorate which prohibited court-ordered busing unless it was demonstrated that school segregation was *intentional*. This measure, called Proposition 1, was approved. More legal battles ensued which involved the NAACP and the American Civil Liberties Union in support of court-ordered busing and the school board, then with a majority who opposed mandatory busing for school integration.[39] As these legal battles were fought, the fact remained that about 300,000 of the 525,000 pupils in the nation's second largest public school system attended largely segregated schools.[40] The modest busing program, which involved about 23,000 of the 525,000 school children or approximately 4 percent, continued.

Although the majority of persons in the Los Angeles sample supported school busing, some did express ambivalence about the program. Supporters agreed generally with a school teacher in the sample who said that, this program was the most effective method of guaranteeing the "same education for blacks as whites in Beverly Hills receive." Their interest was in assuring a high quality of education for black youngsters. The ambivalence emerged in terms of the undue weight or burden that the busing program placed on black children who were compelled to spend a great deal of travel time which left them with little opportunity to become actively involved in extra-curricula activities.

In March, 1981, the California Supreme Court upheld the constitutionality of Proposition 1. Court-ordered busing ceased in April, 1981 and 7,300 of the 23,000 pupils bused previously for school desegregation purposes returned to their neighborhood schools. The legal battles will undoubtedly continue until a decision is rendered by the full membership of the United States Supreme Court.

In the meantime, blacks in Los Angeles continue to worry about the quality of education received by the 200,000 black children in the district. They continue to be concerned about the chances for real educational opportunity and the limitations imposed on equal access by economic disabilities.

Police Brutality. Another major priority issue was that of eliminating police brutality, violence and their unwarranted use of deadly force. The Los Angeles Police Department has been criticized severely for its "wild west mentality," its quickness on the draw and for what many believe to be a reckless disregard for human life, especially the lives of blacks and Latinos. In Gerald M. Caplan's 1980 study, "Evaluation Design for Operational Rollout," he argued that a citizen who confronts the Los Angeles Police "should do so at his or her own peril."[41] This warning came as no surprise to the black community in metropoitan Los Angeles whose relations with the police department have been strained to the limits for the past several years.

Even black law enforcement officers have condemned the Los Angeles Police Department (LAPD) for its excessive use of deadly force against black people. As recently as June, 1980, Gil Branche, president of the National Organization of Black Law Enforcement Executives (NOBLE), accused the LAPD of "police homicide" disproportionate to the severity of the crimes.[42] He and other members of NOBLE stressed a persistent pattern of excessive use of deadly force by police officers in minority communities and that, if allowed to continue unchecked, may trigger even greater violence as citizens begin to defend themselves.[43] In fact, many blacks have fought back by attacking police officers.

Several of the allegations made by black Los Angeles residents concerning police violence against blacks were substantiated in a report released by the Los Angeles Police Commission in June, 1980. According to this study, although the LAPD officers may shoot less frequently than officers in the eight other cities with whom they were compared, they kill more frequently.[44] Highlights of the study were:

1. The other cities included in the study were New York; Portland, Oregon; Detroit; Oakland; Indianapolis; Washington, DC; Kansas Ci-

ty, Missouri; and Birmingham, Alabama. Compared to these cities, Los Angeles ranked first in deaths per shooting, fourth in killings per officers, fifth in both shootings per officer and killings per capita, and sixth in shootings per capita.[45]

2. Although blacks comprised 18 percent of the population, 55 percent of all persons shot and 50 percent of all persons killed by the Los Angeles police between 1974 and 1978 were black. Blacks constituted 36 percent of all persons arrested during that period.[46]

3. Despite a decline in the number of blacks shot by police in 1979, the percentage of blacks of the total number of persons killed by the Los Angeles police increased in 1979. Further, the "percentage of police shootings in predominantly black areas" was consistently above the incidence of violent crimes in these neighborhoods. For example, 33 percent of police shootings occurred in three divisions of the city where blacks predominate, although these same areas accounted for only 26 percent of the city's homicides, forcible rapes and robberies.[47]

4. Compared to Latinos and whites, more blacks who were fired on by police were unarmed. This study showed that 28 percent of the blacks who were fired on were unarmed.[48]

5. Discrimination is apparent in the lowered percentage of police officers who are disciplined for "out of policy" shootings at blacks that the percent disciplined for similar acts against Latinos and whites.[49] Police officers are not likely to be disciplined severely for their violence.

6. The number of police shootings declined from 208 in 1974 to 146 in 1979, and continued to drop during the first quarter of 1980.[50]

Because of the empirical evidence which supported allegations of excessive use of deadly force against blacks and discriminatory behavior by the LAPD with regard to blacks, as well as the fall-out from a number of controversial cases in which police brutality appeared evident, the city took steps to mend relations with the black community. In January 1980, the police commission created "an experimental community relations program" which included a steering committee of black citizens to work with the LAPD on police issues of mutual concern. The commission called for a tightening up of training of police officers relative to the use of deadly force. It issued a number of appurtenant policies designed to establish better communications between the police and the black community and to halt unwarranted and questionable stop, search, and arrest procedures and practices.[51]

Equal Justice and Political Power. The perception among many blacks that justice is not racially equal may be one of the explanations for the priority given to the need for more political power. This demand may appear inconsistent with the high visibility of blacks in political positions in the city, county and state or of blacks from Los Angeles who hold national political offices.

According to the latest available data, two blacks from the Los Angeles area are members of the U.S. House of Representatives; two are California state senators; four are state representatives; one is on the county governing Board. Mayor Thomas Bradley was elected to a third term of office in 1980. The mayor of Compton is black. Seven blacks are on the city council; one black is a city attorney; one black holds the position of city treasurer. There are 15 blacks in positions as municipal judges; 12 serve as judges of the Superior Court and one serves as a judge of the court of appeals. Four blacks are members of local boards of trustees of colleges, and seven are members of local boards of education in various school districts. However, there is only one on the Los Angeles school board. The remaining six are on the boards of the Compton and Inglewood school districts.[52]

The central issue here is the degree to which political empowerment and influence on the decision-making processes exercised by black elected officials is commensurate with the prestige and expectations of the positions they occupy. Many blacks recognize the immense importance and necessity of a black presence in the power structure but they also feel that blacks are not represented in sufficient numbers to guarantee systemic changes of direct benefit to black people. Although they have been participants in coalition politics that result in the election of a mayor of the city, even though they represent only 18 percent of the population, those coalitions disintegrate when the issues appear to bear directly on methods of improving the structural conditions of the black population. An example of this phenonmenon is the election of a majority of anti-busing persons to the school board whose energies seem more often devoted to ending court-ordered busing than to improving the overall quality of the school system.

Housing is another major problem for most residents of Los Angeles and the surrounding communities. It is especially acute for those persons who encounter such formidable economic barriers in their daily lives as low paying jobs, unemployment, and inability to save sufficient money to even make the down payment on a house. It is demoralizing to those persons who know that, even if they have money saved, the interest rates on mortgages are so high and incomes are so low that they may not be regarded as an acceptable loan risk. It was estimated that in 1981 the average cost of a house in the Los Angeles area was about $106,000. The combined costs of houses, mortgage money, closing costs and taxes have put the American dream beyond the hope of all too many young persons.

Within the city of Los Angeles, most blacks reside in the Central, Pacoima, South, Southeast and Southwestern districts. These are the older sections of the city and many sections of these areas have the opposite characteristics and housing is of superior quality. Because of the recognized need to improve the overall quality of many neighborhoods and to provide better services to residents, the city has initiated an extensive "environmental enrichment program." Several of these programs are under the supervision of the Community Re-Development Agency of the City of Los Angeles. Many of the funds for this program have come to the city via community development block grants funded by the U.S. Department of Housing and Urban Development.[53]

The overall program calls for the construction of the first shopping center ever built in Watts, financing of senior citizens apartments, rental assistance payments, refurbishing and sale of housing at low costs, and other revitalization efforts in areas under the redevelopment program jurisdiction. It is apparent that a major effort has been mounted to improve the housing and neighborhood conditions under which a significant portion of blacks and other minorities live. The persistence of housing inadequacies and inequalities in access to better housing make this issue a continuing priority concern among blacks in metropolitan Los Angeles.

Health Problems

As demonstrated in the above analysis of urgent concerns and priorities, the health problems identified among blacks were often similar in the cities and suburbs studied.

For instance, the most prevalent problems found among blacks in metropolitan Atlanta were heart disease (319.94/100,000), cancer (150.92/100,000), cardiovascualr disease (70.50/100,000), homicides (55.89/100,000) and non-motor vehicle accidents (34.74/100,000). In addition to these problems, others were identified by the Fulton County Health Department, of which Atlanta is a part. For instance, the Department reported in 1979 that the infant mortality rate was 19.91/1,000 live births. However, in a study conducted at Grady Memorial Hospital in Atlanta, "premature births" were more frequent among white pateints (20.2 percent) than among black patients (16.2 percent). "Mortality rates, both fetal and neonatal," were also higher among whites than among blacks.[54] The perinatal mortality rate per 1,000 *total* births for white women was 28.4 while that for black women was 26.4 per 2,000.[55] These data suggest that both blacks and whites experience serious health problems in Atlanta.

In Atlanta's Grady Memorial Hospital in 1979, 85 percent of the 6,514 obstetric patients were black. Thirty-five percent of all obstetric patients seen during the year were having their first child but less than 20 percent of all patients stated that they were married at the time of their delivery.The rate of married at delivery was substantially lower among black women (22 percent) compared to white women (60 percent). However, the rate of unwed mothers was high among both races.[56]

According to data furnished by respondents in the Cleveland area sample, the most frequent health problems experienced by this group were high blood pressure (16.6 percent), emotional stress (15.5 percent), diabetes and heart disease (each with 5.8 percent) and drug problems (3.1 percent). Similar problems were reported by the respondents from the Houston area. In this group, 18.6 percent stated that they had suffered from high blood pressure, 6.1 percent from emotional stress, 5.2 percent from heart disease and 2.9 percent had experienced an "unwanted pregnancy."

According to the Houston Department of Public Health, the illegitimacy rate for both black and white females has been climbing steadily for more than two decades. Among white females, the illegitimacy rate was 23.53 per 1,000 live births in 1957. It was 191.58 for black females in that year. By 1979, the rate among white females had increased by more than 500 percent or to 109.97 illegitimate births per 1,000 live births. By comparison, the rate for blacks more than doubled to 459.19 per 1,000 live births.[57] Although these data show a comparatively high rate of recorded illegitimacy among black females, they do not take into account the historically higher incidence of abortion among white females, especially prior to the decision of the U.S. Supreme Court in 1973 which legalized the right of females to have abortions.[58]

The mortality rate among blacks is higher than that among whites during infancy and as adults. The white population in Houston has a death rate of 5.07 per 1,000 population while the rate among blacks in Houston is 6.95 per 1,000 population. In 1979, the white infant mortality rate was 13.19 per 1,000 live births while it was 19.45 for blacks. When compared to the 1960 infant mortality rates for whites, 17.48 and for blacks, 30.17, the 1979 rates show dramatic improvements in prolonging life beyond infancy for both races. The comparatively greater success experienced for black children suggests substantial improvements in pre- and post natal care as a consequence of desegregation of health facilities. Overall, the leading causes of death among blacks in Houston in 1979 were diseases of the heart, malignant neoplasm, accidents, cardiovascular disease and homicides.[59]

In each city, the disaggregated data showed that although many community centers were located in relative close proximity to the respondents,utilization of these centers was low. The explanations for low utilization were advanced in Chapter 2. Disaggregated data also revealed that blacks in metropolitan Atlanta tended to seek medical and dental care from the 103 black physicians and the 27 dentists in the city. Of special interest in terms of representation of health care practitioners in the general population was the observation that the black physician to black population ratio in Atlanta was 1:2,746 while the black dentist to black population ratio was 1:10,478. By contrast, 84 percent of the respondents in metropolitan Boston were served by non-black physicians when they sought health services. This situation reflected both the numerical problem (140 black physicians and 25 black dentists) as well as that of distribution.For instance, only 25 black physicians of the 140 were in private practice at the conclusion of the data collection process.[60]

According to field data, the Cleveland area has 64 black physicians and 49 black dentists. This apparent under representation of physicians and dentists helps to explain the higher utilization of non-black physicians and dentists reported by Cleveland area participants. A similar pattern was observed in Houston in which only 26.3 percent of the respondents stated that the medical services they received were most likely to be rendered by a black physician.

As mentioned in Chapter 2, the delivery of adequate health services is not merely a function of the location of community health centers in target areas. Good health services require adequate personnel, physicians, dentists, nurses and other health practitioners, in addition to good access of these services, via adequate transportation networks, to the targeted population. Without information and the means to take advantage of available services, delivery will be ineffective and health problems will remain.

Alienation, Distrust and Orientation to the Future

The alienation scale was not as successful in differentiating degrees of alienation as desired. This failure seemed apparent in the tendency of most responses to be grouped in the medium level on all scales. For example, 98.3 percent of all respondents in the Boston area were classified as "medium" with respect to alienation; 1.0 percent as *low* and less than one percent (0.7) as high in alienation. The low, medium and high percents for Los Angeles were 1.6, 95 and 3.5 percent, respectively. Among Houston area respondents these low, medium and high percents were 6.2, 88.5 and 5.3 percent, respectively. The next lowest ranks on the alienatiom scale were observed among Atlanta area residents with percents of 5.4 for low alienation, 87.3 for medium and 7.2 percent for high alienation. However, in the Cleveland area, the responses were classified as follows: 16.6 percent low alienation, 80.1 percent medium and 3.3 percent high alienation.

In Atlanta, blacks appeared to be somewhat but not highly alienated. They scored from medium (moderate) to high on the alienation scale. An inverse relationship was observed between rank on the alienation scale, and the annual income reported as well as with the degree of education attainment. In other words, the higher the annual income and the higher the degree of educational attainment reported the lower the sense of alienation. Conversely, highly alienated persons seemed to be persons with low incomes and less formal schooling.

Blacks in metropolitan Atlanta also scored from medium to high on the anomie and powerlessness scale but medium to low in the social isolation scale. Inasmuch as the tilt on the powerlessness scale appeared to be from medium (65 percent) to high (32.5 percent), and given the high unemployment rate and large numbers of persons who reported low incomes, the intervention of the class variable loomed large as a determinant of perceptions and feelings of powerlessness. Importantly, blacks in metropolitan Atlanta scored *low* on the sense of distrust of the power structure scale. This low sense of distrust may be explained by the high visibility of black leaders in public office.

At the time of the interviews in the Atlanta area, blacks held at least 28 elective positions. They included three Fulton County representatives, the mayor of Atlanta, the president of the Atlanta City council, seventeen members of the city council, one judge and five members of the school board. In the 1981 city-wide elections, former U.N. Ambassador Andrew Young was elected to succeed Maynard Jackson, who was forbidden by law to succeed himself, as mayor of Atlanta. According to the voting patterns reported by *The New York Times,* voting behavior reflected the racial composition of the city. White Atlantans, on the whole, tended to vote for the white candidate and black voters, by and large, tended to vote for the black candidate, Andrew Young.[61] This pattern may be interpreted as racial polarization. It may also be viewed as an expression of political power employed by blacks in much the same way that many ethnic groups have done and continue to demonstrate in various parts of the United States.

In addition to elected officials, a significant number of black persons hold appointive positions of presumed power and influence (e.g., the commissioner of public safety). Other blacks own prestigious business firms, banks, newspapers, construction enterprises and serve as college and university administrators.

Despite widespresd poverty and other social problems, blacks seemed to trust the power structure in Atlanta. This high sense of trust undoubtedly reflected a strong belief that the demonstrated political empowerment of blacks, as evidenced through their ability to elect blacks to important public positions, has begun to have positive benefits for blacks in Atlanta.

By contrast, the socio-economic status variables of education, income and occupation did not differentiate individuals in Boston and their ranks on the alienation scale. However, an inverse relationship was observed between educational attainment and rank on the anomie scale, as well as between a sense of powerlessness and income reported. In other words, the higher the number of years of schooling claimed, the lower the feeling of anomie expressed. Similarly, the higher the level of annual income stated by the respondents, the lower their sense of powerlessness. The same pattern was observed with respect to the relationship between rank on the social isolation scale, education and sense of community solidarity. Specifically, the higher the number of years of schooling reported and the greater the sense of commmunity solidarity, the lower the rank on the social isolation scale.

Blacks in metropolitan Boston, who ranked high on orientation to the future, also tended to rank low on both the alienation and the social isolation scale. With regard to rank on the orientation to the future scale, blacks in the Boston area concentrated their responses in the medium or moderate (72.3 percent) category and were almost evenly divided between low (14.6 percent) and high (13.1 percent) prospects for the future. Blacks in metropolitan Boston also ranked highest among all five cities in their sense of distrust of the power structure. Over one-half (54.4 percent) of all respondents scored high in their sense of distrust of the power structure. Over 40 percent (40.5) scored medium (moderate) and only 5.1 percent scored low in distrust of the power structure. This finding, as all others reported in this chapter, were statistically significant (See Table 20). As previously suggested, this high sense of distrust probably reflected the disaffection of blacks from the political life of the city. However, that perception may be changed by the ability of blacks to forge coalitions with white liberals and other minorities to elect more blacks to public offices. In the November 1981 elections, two blacks were elected to the school committee (board) for the first time in this century, including a re-elected black president. A black person was also elected to the city council for the first time since 1970. Nevertheless, there was confirmation for the hypothesis that the greater the distrust among blacks of the power structure, the greater their sense of powerlessness and higher their rank on alienation and anomie scales.

Because of the comparatively small number of respondents from Cleveland (N = 106), drawing generalizations from scale data was risky. However, it may be noted that responses on the alienation, anomie, powerlessness and social isolation scales tended to be concentrated in the medium and low categories. In fact, Clevelanders appeared to be lowest when compared to blacks in other metropolitan areas, in alienation and all of its variants. Over half (56.9 percent) scored low in their sense of distrust of the power structure. Only 3.1 percent scored high on the distrust scale.

Inverse relationships were found for therelationship between rank on the powerlessness scale and level of education and orientation to the future. Similarly, inverse relationships were observed between rank on the anomie scale and level of income and position on the occupational scale. Once again, although the number of respondents was small, the findings were statistically significant (Table 20 in Appendix One).

Among blacks in metropolitan Houston, the tilt was from medium (88.5 percent) to low (6.2 percent) on the alienation scale, from medium (77.0 percent) to low (18.9 percent) on the social isolation scale, and from medium (77.0 percent) to low (15.5 percent) on the orientation to the future scale. On the other hand, the tilt was from medium (75.7 percent) to high (19.3 percent) on the anomie scale and from medium (71.1 percent) to high (17.9 percent) on the powerlessness scale. In other words, a significant proportion of blacks in metropolitan Houston reported a high sense of anomie, and powerlessness but fewer reported a sense of alienation and social isolation. However, several did not express optimism about the future. This analysis also showed that high educational attainment was negatively correlated with educational level and occupational status. An inverse relationship was similarly observed between rank on the powerlessness scale, level of educational attainment and occupational status. Moreover, this analysis showed that, for Houston area blacks, high alienation was found among the least educated as well as persons with the lowest annual incomes.

The Los Angeles area sample was quite small, (N = 67), when compared to the samples of such cities as Atlanta, Boston and Houston. However, as was seen in other metropolitan areas, the respondents tended to concentrate their responses in the *medium* category of all scales. Nevertheless, variations in this pattern were also observed.

For instance, 95 percent of the Los Angeles area respondents scored *medium* in alienation, 3.5 percent scored *high* and 1.6 percent scored low on alienation. The distribution on the anomie scale was strikingly different. Over two-thirds (68.9 percent) scored "medium," about one-fourth (24.1 percent) scored "high" and about one-fourteenth (7 percent) scored low on the anomie scale. Slight variations from the distribution on anomie were observed on the powerlessness scale. On these items, somewhat more than two-thirds (71.1 percent) scored "medium" slightly less than one-fifth (17.9 percent) scored "high", and just above one-tenth (11 percent) scored low on powerlessness. However, a discernible shift in the direction of the low category was observed with respect to social isolation. In this case, while more than three-fourths (77 percent) scored "medium," almost one-fifth (18.9 percent) scored "low" and about one-twenty-fifth (4.1 percent) scored "high" on the social isolation scale.

Because of the small numbers in each category, it was not possible to perform the type of statistical analysis observed in such cities as Atlanta, Boston and Houston. However, the impressions drawn from scale distributions suggest that, even if one discounts the concentration in the medium category, certain tentative generalizations may be reached. In the first instance, a larger percentage of blacks in metropolitan Los Angeles scored "low" than "high" on the alienation scale. Second, a larger percentage scored "high" than "low" on the anomie scale. Third, almost twice as many scored "high" than "low" on the powerlessness scale. Fourth, almost five times as many scored "low" than "high" on the social isolation scale.

Briefly, this comparative analysis demonstrated the unique characteristics and special concerns reported by the respondents in each of the five cities studied. It also highlighted some of the serious problems and socio-economic conditions faced by black Americans. Clearly, there was a high degree of agreement among respondents in each city studied on the critical issues they faced as individuals and in their perceptions of issues of importance to black communities in cities and suburbs.

Although each city and each suburb is different in geographical location, cultural history and politcal economy, it is evident that, with respect to the black community, each has a great deal in common. This fact is especially evident in the dimensions of socio-economic status variables, priority ranks given to issues of apparent secondary concern, degrees of alienation, anomie, powerlessness and social isolation. It was also striking with respect to differences conveyed by respondents regarding orientation to the future and their level of trust in the existing power structure. Hence, geographical location may make a difference in some aspects of daily living among blacks but being black in American society is itself a far more salient determinant of their life chances.

Notes

1. Brown, Lee P., "Crime Specific Planning: The Atlanta Experience," *The Police Chief* (July, 1980), pp. 53-59.
2. For further discussion on this issue, cf. James E. Blackwell, *The Black Community: Diversity and Unity.* New York: Harper & Row, 1975.
3. *Op. Cit.*
4. *Ibid.*
5. *Ibid.*
6. *Ibid.*
7. Cf. *The Boston Globe*, "Spotlight Team Report." April 4-5, 1979 and December 13, 1980
8. *Ibid.*
9. *Ibid., (December 13, 1980), p. 68.*
10. *Ibid.*
11. Hart, Philip, *Feasibility Study for the Development of a Multi-Service Community Center in the Mattapan Section of the City of Boston.* Unpublished Manuscript Prepared Under the Auspices of the Boston Urban Observatory of the University of Massachusetts/ Boston, 1977, pp. 13-14.
12. *Ibid.*, pp. 157-159.
13. *Ibid.*
14. "Boston Major Crimes by Police District in 1979," *The Boston Globe*, December 13, 1980, p. 68
15. Baker, Andrea, On-Site Field Supervisory Report from Cleveland.
16. *Ibid.*
17. Blackwell, James E., and Marie Haug, "Relations Between Black Bosses and Black Workers," *The Black Scholar*, (January 1973), pp. 36-43.
18. Joint Center for Political Studies, *National Roster of Black Elected Officials.* Washington, D.C.: Joint Center for Political Studies, 1979.
19. Public Interest Advocacy Center of Houston, *Preliminary Deadly Force Study: Houston, 1970-78, Conclusions.* Houston, Texas: Public Interest Advocacy Center of Houston, 1979.
20. *Ibid.*
21. *Ibid.*
22. *Ibid.*
23. *Ibid.*
24. *Ibid.*

25. *Ibid.*
26. *Ibid.* Also, see U.S. Commission on Civil Rights, *Who Is Guarding The Guardians?* Washington, D.C.: U.S. Commission on Civil Rights, October 1981, Preface and Chapter 2.
27. Bernard, Ryan, "Deadly Force," *Texas Monthly,* October, 1980.
28. *Ibid.*
29. Coulter, Bill, "4 Incumbent Judges Lose Benches in Harris County," *The Houston Post,* November 6, 1980, p. 6.
30. "Tale of Three Cities," *Newsweek,* (October 1980), pp. 26-27.
31. Public Interest Advocacy Center, *Op. Cit.*
32. *Ibid.*
33. This information was provided by Dr. James Kelsaw, Field Supervisor in Houston.
34. Stancill, Nancy, "HISD Declining White Enrollment Hurts Integration Plan, Chief Says," *Houston Chronicle,* October 4, 1980
35. Burka, Paul, "Why Is Houston Falling Apart?" *Texas Monthly,* (November 1980), p. 189.

CHAPTER 8

The Reagan Administration and Black Americans

The election of Ronald Reagan as President of the United States in 1980 and the shift to the political right in the American Congress signaled a major turning point in American race relations. For the past 40 years, in general, black Americans looked to the White House and to the federal government for support in their quest for constitutional guarantees as citizens. During the decades of the fifties, sixties and seventies, they became even more dependent upon the federal government and the United States Supreme Court for legal remedies against racial inequities created by past and present patterns of segregation and discrimination.

Especially over the 30 year period between 1950 and 1980, the nation witnessed the obliteration of many barriers to equal opportunity and racial equality. There was a steady dismantling of other more resistant, deeply entrenched discriminatory patterns. For instance, the U.S. Supreme Court responded favorably to grievances registered by black plaintiffs in a number of important cases such as the *Brown v. Board of Education of Topeka, Kansas,* which desegregated public schools, *Sweatt v. Painter,* which attacked segregation in law schools, and *Adams vs. Richardson,* which called for the dismantling of the continuing dual systems of higher education in several southern and border states.[1]

Furthermore, Congress enacted a number of far-reaching pieces of legislation which affected the civil rights of black Americans. Among these were the Civil Rights Act of 1957 which established the U.S. Commission on Civil Rights, the Civil Rights Act of 1964 that paved the way for access to public accommodations, equal opportunity in jobs, and provided the leverage for attacks against discrimination in a variety of areas based upon race, sex and religion. Congress also enacted the Voting Rights Act of 1965 which effectively enfranchised millions of Americans, especially blacks and

181

other minorities, who had been denied the right to vote by virtue of barriers constructed by several state and local jurisdictions. In 1968, Congress passed the Omnibus Housing Act which expanded opportunities for blacks to purchase and rent housing. In addition to these impressive legislative Acts, several landmark Executive Orders were issued by Presidents Kennedy and Johnson in such areas as affirmative action, job opportunities and housing.[2] These actions, combined with effective and enlightened leadership among the black population and within the federal government, helped to shift the mood of the nation toward the goal of first-class citizenship for all Americans, irrespective of race, color, religion or creed.

It is precisely because of these accomplishments that many black Americans looked with anxiety, fear and trepidations upon the election of Ronald Reagan to the presidency. They did not and do not regard him as a friend. Nor is there reason to assume that they regard the Congress of the United States, as constituted in 1981, as particularly concerned with issues of paramount importance to black Americans. Almost 90 percent of the black electorate cast their votes in 1980 for President Jimmy Carter, probably because they believed that Carter would continue to demonstrate support for those issues and programs of special interest to black Americans. On the other hand, many blacks were alarmed by the lukewarm support given to the same causes by candidate Reagan and, in some instances, his direct opposition to them. Similarly, many blacks interpreted the rhetoric of many of Reagan's supporters as ominous signs of retrenchment in national support for civil rights and social programs.

Following the Reagan victory in 1980, it became evident that the Republican Party had gained control of the U.S. Senate and substantially increased its strength in the House of Representatives. Even though the Republican party was still the minority party in the House, the election of such a large number of Conservative Representatives of both political parties to the House of Representatives boded ill times ahead for minorities and the poor. A Reagan Plan, with respect to blacks, minorities and the white poor, began to unfold.

The Reagan Plan was evidenced by his Cabinet appointments, the elevation of Senator Strom Thurmond (R-South Carolina) to the chairmanship of the powerful Senate Judiciary Committee, the emergence of Senator Jesse Helms of North Carolina as an influential voice for the arch-Conservative forces in the United States, the rise of Senator Orrin Hatch (R-Utah) to a position of prominence in the Senate, and the appointment of David Stockman to the important position of Director of the Office of Management and Budget (OMB). The philosophical underpinnings of the

Reagan Plan for black America were evident in the rhetoric and behavior of members of this group reported in the media. For instance, Senator Hatch called for the discontinuation of affirmative action. Senator Thurmond sought to dilute the impact of the Civil Rights Act of 1964. Others, such as Senator L. Bennett Johnston of Louisiana, Jesse Helms and Orrin Hatch fought to eliminate busing as a viable tool for school desegregation, and David Stockman appeared to be the chief architect of that part of the plan which called for the discontinuation of federal support for a number of social programs from which minorities and poor whites had benefitted.

Hence, black Americans quickly concluded that newly elected President Reagan planned not only to stall the process of black American advancement toward racial, political and social equality, and to curtail their movement out of economic servitude, he intended, in their view, to "turn back the clock" to the pre-1954 period of black-white relations in the United States. In the view of black America, the Reagan Plan called for the systematic elimination of most of the Federal assistance programs and the withdrawal of national support for equality of opportunity which had been of tremendous importance during the 30 years prior to his inauguration as president.

Just as the majority of the white population appeared sanguine about the elevation of Ronald Reagan to the presidency, although for diverse political and social reasons, a relatively small number of black conservatives applauded that event.

In this chapter, attention is devoted primarily to the perceived and anticipated impact of the Reagan Plan on black America. Although some concrete evidence is now available to support the position outlined in this chapter, some of what is said is conjecture informed by past exprience and lessons of history. This discussion includes such topics as the black conservatives, the perceptions of black Americans about President Reagan, economic issues, affirmative action, school desegregation, voting rights, and the rising sense of distrust and alienation of black Americans in the 1980's.

Black Conservatives and the Reagan Plan

During the Reconstruction Era and for approximately two decades after the *Plessy v. Ferguson* decision ("separate-but-equal") killed it, the black electorate supported the Republican Party — the "party of Lincoln, the Great Emancipator."[3] Although any number of events resulted in the

shift of the black electorate to the Democratic Party, one of the most important was the Great Depression of the 1930's. To combat the serious,
devastating economic disabilities, and social traumas triggered by the
Depression, President Franklin D. Roosevelt's Administration initiated a
large and impressive array of social programs under the rubric of The New
Deal. Blacks and the working poor among the white population were able
to survive, "get back on their feet again," and to care for their families as a
result of New Deal Programs. In addition, President Roosevelt appointed a
number of blacks to important sub-cabinet positions. By so doing, he
created the impression that the Democratic Party was the party of "the big
people," of all citizens in the United States, irrespective of race or class.[4]
Therefore, the commitment of the black electorate to the Democratic Party
began, and has continued without significant interruption for approximately 50 years.

As a result of the Civil Rights Movement, the enunciation of major
federal policies in the areas of employment opportunity, access to higher
education, business opportunities, and affirmative action, the black middle
class expanded.[5] Its new members are recruited from among the young,
well-educated, the professionals, corporate executives and private entrepreneurs. Many in this group, though likely to deny it, gained entry into
college, graduate and professional schools, the labor market or built their
businesses primarily because of the expansion of opportunities created by
the very structures that some now denigrate. Others profitted under the
dual, segregated system which has characterized the United States
throughout most of its history. Their commitment to the Republican Party
is not necessarily recent in origin. However, it is largely from both groups
that the new black conservatives are drawn.

Lee Daniels maintains that the new black conservatives support many
of the elements of the Reagan Plan. For instance, they support the administration's plan to eliminate busing as a tool for school integration; they
are opposed to many of the major social programs established under the
New Deal and the Great Society legislation passed by Congress during the
Johnson administration. Many of them are opposed to affirmative action,
public welfare programs, and governmental intervention to foster racial
equality. Several claim to believe in free-market enterprise, and de-
regulation in private industry.[6]

According to Daniels, a distinction can be drawn between what he
perceives to be essentially two groups of black conservatives: (1) black conservative politicians, and (2) philosophical black conservatives. The black
conservative politicians, in this view, wish to "strengthen individual respon-

sibilities" among black Americans, to break the 50 year tie between blacks and the Democratic Party and thereby shift more blacks toward the Republicans. This view is predicated on the presumption of greater benefits derived from alliance with two parties than presently gained from Democrats. They seek to force blacks to be less dependent upon the federal government and to establish their own self-help programs. Representatives of this group are Gloria Toote, a New York based lawyer; William T. Coleman, Jr., who served as Secretary of Transportation during the Ford Administration; Arthur Fletcher, a Washington businessman who served as assistant secretary of labor during the Nixon Administration, and Nathan Wright, Jr., an established scholar of national prominence. Many in this group of black conservatives have long ties to the struggle of blacks for racial equality. Indeed, Arthur Fletcher was the architect of the Philadelphia Plan which set the tone for federal government enforcement of affirmative action guidelines.[7]

By contrast, the philosophical black conservatives, according to Daniels, have formulated a philosophy indistinguishable from those ideas espoused by the right wing of the Republican Party. Specifically, they support free-market enterprise; they are enamored by notions of rugged individualism. They are often vehemently opposed to affirmative action and busing for school desegregation, and they do not believe racial discrimination is a major determinant or impediment to the progress of black Americans. Included in this group are Tom Sowell of the Hoover Institute; Walter Williams, an economist at George Mason University in Virginia; and J. A. Y. Parker, President of the Lincoln Institute and Educational Foundation in Washington, D.C.[8]

There is a belief among many black Americans that the Reagan Administration is attempting to drive a wedge between the black leadership and the major civil rights organizations through inordinate attention to the views of the black philosophical conservatives.[9] Further, many black Americans feel that the print and electronic media are collaborating in this process. Consequently, few editorials denounce the view articulated by the philosophical black conservatives as unjustified because blacks are still a long way from gaining the kind of racial parity that would support claims of the insignificance of racial discrimination in determining the life chances of black Americans. It appears to many Americans that the Reagan Administration has been buoyed and become even more determined to initiate policies antagonistic to black aspirations in part as a consequence of public support from many black philosophical conservatives.

If the Reagan Administration assumes that the views expressed and the ideas espoused by the black philosophical conservatives represent the prevailing sentiments of the majority of the black population, and if it constructs social policies based upon such beliefs, it is not in touch with reality. It is likely to drive this nation inexorably toward a kind of racial turmoil not witnessed since the 1960's. It is folly to encourage people to pull themselves up by their own bootstraps when they have no boots to wear. It is unwise to withdraw national commitment to federal programs that have worked to elevate a significant proportion of the population from the depths of poverty. It is unconscionable to discontinue programs that will result in an increased number of unemployed without opportunities to earn a decent living. There is evidence that the anticipated disillusionment of black Americans with the Reagan Administration has already manifested itself in poll data.

Attitudes of Blacks Toward the Reagan Administration

According to poll data collected at strategic points in 1981, black Americans have become increasingly disenchanted and fearful of the policies proposed by the Reagan Administration. These sentiments cut across all social classes within the black community. Polls taken during 1981 by *Black Enterprise Magazine,* the Gallup Organization, Market Opinion Research of Detroit, *TheNew York Times*/CBS News, *The Washington Post* and others revealed widespread distrust of the Reagan Administration among black Americans. Distrust of the Administration appeared to deepen throughout 1981 as blacks became more knowledgeable of the actual and potential impact of Reaganomics on black Americans.

In February, 1981, a poll taken by the Gallup Organization for *Newsweek* magazine revealed that 62 percent of the blacks and only 9 percent of all whites in the sample expected things to worsen for them under the Reagan Administration.[10]

A *Washington Post*/ABC News poll released in March, 1981 showed that both blacks and whites felt that some progress had been attained in American race relations. However, blacks and whites differed dramatically with respect to their views on the continuing salience of discrimination in the United States for life chances among black Americans. Whites in the sample, on the whole, expressed the belief that anti-black discrimination was a thing of the past, "all but disappeared" from American society. Consequently, future economic and social progress was a responsibility of blacks themselves. On the other hand, black Americans rejected that view in their belief that racial discrimination remains a serious impediment to efforts by blacks to move into the mainstream of American life. Further, blacks expressed fear of a "political backlash and renewed racist violence" which could undo progress already attained.[11]

Other evidence about the feelings and suspicions that black Americans had of President Reagan were registered as early as late February and early March, 1981, in an ABC News/ *Washington Post* poll. According to these data, only 4 percent of blacks in the sample stated that they believed President Reagan would do more for them than did President Carter. However, slightly more than half (51 percent) stated that he would do less, and somewhat less than one-third (31 percent) said that Reagan would do about the same (an expression of cynicism or the belief that it really does not matter who is in the White House). The remainder stated no opinion.

By June, a *New York Times*/CBS News poll showed that, compared to results of their 1979 poll, the increase in the number of blacks who felt that their future would worsen under the Reagan Administration was noticeably sharp. Almost simultaneously, while blacks were becoming increasingly pessimistic about their future, white Americans were registering increasing optimism. In other words, while white Americans appeared satisfied with events occurring or anticipated under the Reagan Administration, black Americans were becoming increasingly alarmed, and their hostility toward President Reagan appeared to rise proportionately.[12] This poll also revealed that 76 percent of blacks and 38 percent of whites in the sample believed that the budget cuts proposed by the Reagan Administration would hurt them personally. Hence, blacks were twice as likely to express a deepening concern over future federal action than were whites.[13]

As more evidence about the impending Reagan budget cuts appeared in the media, or was revealed by representatives of formal organizations opposed to them, dissatisfaction among blacks increased. By November of 1981, data accumulated by *The Washington Post* showed a systematic "erosion of support" for Reaganomics among literally all sectors of the population. By that time, American whites and minority groups, had begun to articulate their grave concern over the rising rate of unemployment (8.4 percent for the nation as a whole and approximately 17 percent for black Americans). Almost three-fifths (57 percent) of all Americans polled expressed opposition to the Reagan economic plan and over half expressed dissatisfaction over proposals for additional budget cuts because of their perceived negative impact on needed social programs.[14]

Moreover, more than half reported that they believed that President Reagan favored the rich over the poor; therefore, he and his Administration were more concerned about protecting the interest of the rich than they were about problems affecting the poor, such as unemployment and social programs.[15] Undoubtedly, these feelings were considerably stronger among black Americans since the unemployment rate was twice as high for them than it was for whites. The staggering rate of joblessness among teenage blacks remained at an all-time high.

The failure of the President, his aides, the secretaries of labor, and health and human services to express publicly a sense of genuine concern over such problems convinced even the less cynical among the black population that blacks could no longer look to the White House and to the Congress for relief from economic and social discrimination. When Vice President Bush challenged black organizations to present "the government with a plan" for change, he seemed totally unaware of the constructive alternative budget proposed by the Congressional Black Caucus. Their plan would have spared the nation of some of the pain inflicted by Congress by virtue of the mis-directed advice given by David Stockman. The cavalier approach to the problems of persistent discrimination, economic and social injustice was not well-received by black Americans. Nor was President Reagan greeted with enthusiasm when he appeared before the annual convention of the National Association for the Advancement of Colored People in June, 1981. At that time, President Reagan offered nothing to allay suspicions among many blacks of his profound disinterest in the conditions of minorities and the poor in America. The feeling of distrust deepened as the Reagan Plan took concrete form.

Reaganomics and Black Americans

On October 1, 1981, the major components of the Reagan Plan for "economic recovery" went into effect. Several programs from which many minorities and poor white Americans benefitted were eviscerated. In order to fully understand the magnitude, complexity, and impact of this recovery program on blacks, it is necessary to describe some of the most seriously affected programs.

As a result of New Deal and Great Society legislation, the federal government utilized five broad categories of programs to facilitate the movement of the disadvantaged population from poverty and to promote equal educational and economic opportunity. These catgories were: (1) human resources development, (2) area development, (3) direct cash support, (4) in-kind goods and services, and (5) affirmative action.[16]

Human resources development programs include: (1) education programs, represented by Head Start, Compensatory Education, Basic Education Opportunity Grants (BEOG) to college students, and loan programs for college students; and (2) training programs which include Comprehensive Education Training Act programs (CETA), Job Corps, Neighborhood Youth Corps, On-The-Job-Training, Institutional and Classroom Training, and the Work Incentive Program (WIN), and others.[17]

Area development programs include Model Cities, Community Development Block Grants, Urban Development Action Grants, minority business and rural development programs, and Economic Development Administration grants. Their main purpose is to assist "economically distressed areas or communities" in their efforts to achieve overall economic betterment in their specific areas.[18]

There are two types of direct cash or income maintenance programs: (1) social insurance and (2) public assistance. The purpose of social insurance programs is to "provide supplemental income to individuals" irrespective of economic need. Included in these programs are Social Security or Old Age, Survival and Disability Insurance, workers compensation, federal retirement benefits, veterans benefits, and unemployment insurance. Public assistance programs are often called "welfare." They include Aid to Families with Dependent Children (AFDC), AFDC-Unemployed Parents as well as Supplemental Security Income (SSI). The latter type is designed "primarily for the blind, disabled and indigent elderly."[19]

In-kind programs include Medicaid, Medicare, food stamps, free school lunches, and such housing assistance programs as public housing and subsidized rent. Finally, the affirmative action programs have as their central function the reduction and elimination of discrimination based upon race, sex, religion and age. They encompass such areas as employment, education, public accommodations and housing. The primary federal agencies with direct responsibility for affirmative action policies and programs are the Equal Employment Opportunity Commission (EEOC) and the Office of Federal Contract Compliance (OFCC).[20] In addition to those programs and agencies, the U.S. Commission on Civil Rights monitors several of their activities and makes periodic, highly significant reports of its findings relative to the status of civil rights of all minority groups

Many of the programs mentioned above have become identified in the mind of the American public as essentially programs for blacks and other minority groups. Robert Hill points out that, although blacks do benefit from most of these social programs, they are by no means their largest beneficiaries. For example, blacks compromise only one-tenth of the 22 million recipients of Social Security and one-tenth of all recipients of unemployment compensation. Nevertheless, about one-third (31 percent) of all blacks do receive social security benefits and approximately one-sixteenth (6 percent) of all blacks receive unemployment benefits. He also maintains that 70 percent "of all unemployed blacks never receive any unemployment compensation."[21] Further, he shows that about three-fourths of all black families do not receive assistance from welfare. Nevertheless, blacks are over-represented in the welfare statistics.

Hill explodes the myth that the majority of recipients of in-kind program beneficiaries are black. He shows, for instance, that blacks compromise: (1) about 10 percent of the 18 million recipients of Medicare, (2) two fifths (39 percent) of the recipients of public housing, (3) about two-fifths (36 percent) of the "reduced price school lunches," (4) one-third of the 21 million food stamp recipients, and (5) about three-tenths of the 8 million Medicaid recipients. Nonetheless, these programs are essential to the economic life and health care of black Americans. For example, 28 percent of all blacks receive food stamps. The same percentage receive both public housing and Medicare, while 17 percent receive rent subsidies. Hill's data also showed that "there is relatively little multiple participation" among blacks in the seven major transfer programs established by the federal government for the poor. Nevertheless, approximately two-thirds of all black households participate in at least one of these programs.[22] Further, since there is little or no total dependence on federal largesse, many poor people do supplement federal benefits with other resources. The Reagan budget cuts will make it extremely difficult for any number of poor people to maintain a reasonable semblance of decent living.

The Reagan Plan resulted in the shift of 57 programs from administration by the federal government into nine block grants for the states. This action was accompanied by a 25 percent reduction in the appropriation for these 57 programs. Consequently, only $7.5 billion will be available for these programs in FY 82. Included in these block grants are such programs as those subsumed under education, health, community development and welfare. Before these reductions went into effect on October 1, 1981, President Reagan demanded an additional cutback by 12 percent on his persistent but fruitless effort to balance the federal budget by 1984.

The enormity of the impact of the budget cuts effectuated by October 1, 1981 can be gleaned in part from the following observations:

1. Cutbacks were concentrated in the following areas: public assistance (welfare), food stamps, medical programs, unemployment insurance, public housing, housing assistance, social services and public service jobs.

2. Federal aid for social services was reduced by 20 percent, or from $3 billion down to $2.4 billion for FY 82. This action resulted in the reduction of the number of children who could receive publicly financed day care services, the closing of several day care centers in many states and an increase in the fees charged for day care services charged by some states. It also forced many women who were enrolled in college, or who were gainfully employed to abandon education or work in order to remain at home to take care of their children. In other instances, some states reported that more and more children were left at home to "fend for themselves" since their parents were working (e.g., as in workfare programs in Massachusetts).[23]

3. It was estimated in September, 1981, by federal officials that, as a result of budget cutbacks in public welfare, about 687,000 of the 3.9 million families who received public assistance (welfare) would be removed from welfare rolls. Generally, removal from public welfare also meant a loss of Medicaid benefits.[24]

4. One program that suffered serious reductions in federal support was the Aid to Families with Dependent Children (AFDC). In fiscal year 1981, approximately 3.8 million families received AFDC benefits. More than one-third of them were black. Under the new regulations that governed the cutbacks in AFDC program benefits, approximately 408,000 families were scheduled to lose all such benefits and the benefits for another 279,000 were earmarked for reduction. Of the $7.9 billion appropriated for AFDC benefits in fiscal year 1981, approximately $2.5 billion went to black families. However, of the $1.2 billion in cutbacks scheduled for FY 82, poor black families would bear the burden of $400 million.[25]

5. Andrew Brimmer noted that one-fifth of the 22.5 million persons who benefitted from the Medicaid program during FY 81 were black. While the total cost of the Medicaid program that year was $16.5 billion, about $3 billion of that "amount was spent on medical services for blacks." However, he estimated that about $120 million of the $600 million lost in Medicaid services in FY 82 would directly affect the black community.[26] In addition, blacks would be seriously affected by reductions in the Medicare program for persons aged 65 and over.

6. During the 1981 fiscal year, the estimated cost of the food stamp pro-

gram to the federal government was about $11.3 billion. Assuming that blacks received an amount proportionate to their numbers in the food stamp program, approximately $4 billion went to the black community in food stamp outlays. This amount was distributed to 2.8 million black families, out of a total of 7.8 million families or 22.6 million persons who received food stamps in FY 81. The "New Federalism" budget which became effective on October 1, 1981, carried regulations that tightened eligibility requirements for food stamps. Consequently, Brimmer estimated that about 875,000 food stamp recipients, including about 400,000 blacks, were forced off the food stamp eligibility lists.[27]

7. The Reagan recovery plan also eliminated more than 300,000 CETA jobs — public service jobs subsidized by the federal government covered by the Comprehensive Employment Training Act (CETA). About one-third, or approximately 100,000 of those losses were black workers.[28] These losses occurred at a time when the unemployment rate among the black population approximated Depression levels and the number for the nation as a whole was estimated at about nine million persons. It was estimated that, during 1981, black unemployment *averaged* 20.3 percent of the total unemployment rate. This percent meant that, on the average, about 1.6 million of the *average* of 8 million unemployed persons in the total American labor force of 106.7 million persons during 1981 were black.[29] This general average was worse in such states as Michigan in which the unemployment rate among blacks exceeded 22 percent in 1981.

8. Federal reductions in Force (RIFs) took a heavy toll on black employees of the federal government, especially those blacks in professional, managerial and technical positions. These persons were part of a newly expanding black middle class and their annual earnings in these jobs ranged between $20,000 and $37,000. Fifty-five percent of all blacks employed by the federal government prior to the 1981 budget cutbacks were in that category. The remaining 45 percent comprised persons holding clerical and blue-collar jobs which paid lower wages. However, blacks represented only six percent of the professional-level and 9.4 percent of the administrative-level positions in the federal government. But, these were the areas hardest hit by the 6,000 jobs lost by all federal employees by September 30, 1981.[30]

It was estimated that more than half of the RIFs in 1981 and of these scheduled for 1982 were to be in the Department of Health and Human Resources. For instance, the Community Services Administration, once the centerpiece of the War on Poverty program, was completely abolished by the Reagan Administration. Approximately 60 percent of its staff of 900 were black. Hence, more than 500 jobs were lost to blacks with the elimination of this anti-poverty agency.[31]

The consequences of the Reagan budget plan were felt immediately in the black community. In city after city — all across the nation — job losses were staggering. More than a half million workers in Michigan, black and white, were jobless by November, 1981. As mentioned earlier on, the unemployment rate for the nation as a whole reached 8.4 percent in November, 1981. Official government rates for blacks were twice as high and unofficial rates were substantially higher for the black population. This pattern of escalating unemployment continued in December, 1981 when an additional 458,000 persons were added to the unemployment roll. Thus, as 1981 ended, nearly 9.5 million persons, or 8.9 percent of the labor force, were looking for work and unable to find it. As a result, the December 1981 unemployment rate was the highest rate since 1975 which was the worst recession in the United States since the beginning of the World War II era. Since this trend is likely to be unabated, the nation will experience its most serious recession since the 1930s by early 1982.

More than two million persons became unemployed between July and December 1981. Among blacks, the official unemployment rate reached an unprecedented high of 17.4 percent in December, 1981. This figure represents a 1.3 percent increase from November, 1981. Even President Reagan acknowledged that the unemployment situation would worsen "before it gets better" but by late Spring 1982 he anticipated that an upturn in the economy would occur. The economic trends observed at the end of 1981, however, do not support the President's optimism. If, in fact, his projections of a rapidly improving economy are not borne out by the Summer of 1982, serious problems in urban areas are highly likely during the Summer of 1982. The perceptions of the Reagan Administration as an anti-black and as an anti-poor administration may be given greater force and with far-reaching national implications.

The complexity of the unemployment situation is further observed in the reality that the same persons do not always remain in the unemployed list from quarter to quarter. It is also complicated by the fact that the unemployment rate fluctuated between seven and eight percent throughout the year and approximately 5-6 million entered the unemployed rolls each quarter; therefore, as many as 25 million or almost one-quarter of the entire American labor force could have experienced unemployment during the year. In 1981, young and old, black and white, defeated by their inability to find work, found some degree of temporary relief by becoming recipients of public assistance. Many laid-off persons had no choice but to accept public welfare even though they preferred a job that was unavailable to them. In state after state, as in Massachusetts, the Department of Welfare reported that as many as a third of all persons who lost their eligibility for welfare benefits under the new Reagan Administration regulations were expected to quit their jobs in order to qualify for welfare. Although many persons experienced unemployment for the first time in their adult lives, thousands of black youths continued relentlessly in their fruitless search for their very first job.

The unemployed sometimes become outraged as they seek to provide sustenance needs for themselves and their families. That desperation can manifest itself in crime — burglary, breaking and entering, robbery and drug trafficking — as despairing people take extreme action in a period of prolonged, personal, economic crisis. For others, the level of cynicism, distrust and alienation rises; their discontent increases and, finally, their consummate frustration boils over in destruction and violence. Although no one in America would like to witness the conflagrations that occurred in the nation's cities during the 1960's, it may very well happen again if voiceless, powerless poor people of all races begin to ventilate their increasing hostilities against Reaganomics in violent acts. The fact of the matter is that unemployed people, disqualified for jobs, food stamps and public assistance may not feel that they have the time to wait to see if the Reagan economic recovery program will work. The question often raised is: "What are they to do in the meantime?" Another equally compelling question is "What happens if David Stockman has his way and millions of other Americans from the white working poor are added to the roster of the unemployed, discouraged workers, and their futures are held captive by a plan installed under national suspicion?"

The cost of living increased during 1981. Inflation was not actually checked. The poverty level, according to the U.S. Department of Labor, rose from $7,412 in 1979 to $8,414 in 1980. Fifty-two percent of all poverty-level families were in public housing; 53 percent of all persons who received Medicaid benefits were in poverty; and 45 percent of all families who received reduced-price lunches were below the poverty level.[32] Cutbacks in these programs are likely to result in enormous problems for a substantial proportion of the American population.

Block Grants

The 57 programs transferred from the federal government to the states were merged into nine different block grants. The assumption of state responsibilities for such a wide array of social, educational and economic development programs was not well received by many black Americans. This feeling is deeply rooted in the past discriminatory practices of several states against black Americans. Consequently, a low level of trust and optimism is not unexpected. What the states will actually do toward equitable distribution of the services they assumed under the block grants is not clear.

The nine block grants and the amount authorized for each are as follows:[33]

1. Community development (for cities and towns with a population less than 50,000 persons) — $1 billion;
2. Health preservation and services — $95 million. This program now consolidates into one block all programs concerning rodent control, home health, emergency medical services, risk reduction, health incentive grants, public health, and flouridation;
3. Alcohol, drug abuse and mental health — $491 million. This block represents the merger of the three separate programs;
4. Primary care — $284 million. No consolidation is involved in this block. However, states are permitted to assume responsibilities for administering previously federally operated community health centers in 1982 if they match funds of 20 percent during the first year of operation and one-third by FY 84;
5. Maternal and child health — $373 million. Included in this block are such programs as maternal, child and crippled children programs, prevention of lead poisoning, teenage pregnancy services, hemophilia services, genetic diseases program, and sudden infant death syndrome (SIDS);
6. Social services — $2.4 billion. Two existing block grants are consolidated under the new regulations. Both come under the Social Security Act and cover a large number of social services. States now have more authority to determine how these funds will be used;
7. Community services — $354 million. Since the Community Services Administration was abolished, the program was converted into a block grant for states, in turn, the states are required to award 90 percent of the funds to the local governments for their control and re-distribution;
8. Low income energy aid — $1.9 billion. Under the existing block grant,

states are given increased flexibility in the administration of the program; and

9. Education — $589 million. This block consolidates about 33 separate programs including basic skills programs, gifted children, pre-college science teachers programs, the metric art and consumer education program, counseling, ethnic heritage and community schools.

The problems of the poor will worsen under the Reagan Administration cuts proposed for FY 83. According to media reports in November and December, 1981, David Stockman and the Office of Management and Budget proposed even deeper cuts in areas that would have a major impact on the American poor, including blacks and other minorities. For instance:

1. The remains of the CETA program would be wiped out.
2. The Job Corps would be reduced sharply from its 1981 enrollment of 40,000 to 23,000.
3. The Education Department would be required to reduce its spending from $14.9 billion to $7.7 billion resulting in heavy losses to college student aid programs and to the Title I program for disadvantaged elementary school pupils.
4. The largest aid program for cities (community development block grants and urban development action grants) for the poor would be eliminated by 1984. The discontinuation of subsidized housing would mean the elimination of Section 8 programs and public housing for the poor.[34] (President Reagan did not support the Stockman proposals with respect to urban development).

Because of the devastating consequences of such proposals on the cities, the "New Federalism" was labeled a "Bay of Pigs" by Governor Richard Snelling (Vermont Republican) and "a shame and a sham" by Mayor Edward Koch of New York City.[35]

Inasmuch as the black population is largely an urban population, any new reductions in appropriations for community development, urban development, subsidized housing, public housing and jobs will have a major impact on their lives.

The Reagan Plan and Education

The impact of federal budgetary cutbacks in higher education have already been felt and will continue to have a dramatic effect over the next several years. The original proposal from the Reagan Administration called for a 30 percent reduction in Federal assistance to education. After all the debates, maneuvering and trade-offs, Congress approved reductions in the area of 12 percent. However, these reductions do not only represent a curtailment of financial outlays by the federal government to higher education, they suggest a fundamental philosophical shift away from the established federal commitment to promote equality of access to higher education.

This philosophical shift is best represented, perhaps, in a testimony given by David Stockman in September, 1981, before the House Sub-Committee on Post Secondary Education. On this subject, Stockman said that he did not "accept the notion that the federal government has an obligation to fund generous grants to anybody who wants to go to college. It seems to me that if people want to go to college bad enough, then there is opportunity and responsibility on their part to finance their way through the best they can." This view is contrary to the long-established notion of the responsibility of the federal government to facilitate access to higher education for the disadvantaged population. As Edward B. Fiske points out, this philosophy "has its roots in the G. I. Bill of Rights." With the success of this bill, through which millions of young Americans were able to obtain a college education, the concept of "federal investment" arose. It was, therefore, in the nation's best interest to have a well-trained work force, a better educated populace capable of earning more money and, subsequently, of paying higher taxes into the federal coffers.[36]

The race to the moon and other space explorations triggered by the Soviet Sputnik success in 1957 also stimulated expansion of the concept of federal investment. As a result, a number of loan and other scholarship programs were established over the next few years. These programs offered assistance to students at all levels of higher education. Hence, not only were low income black students and the economically disadvantaged students of all races able to enroll in colleges and universities, they were able to become doctors, lawyers, physicians, dentists, nurses and teachers. Had it not been for the Basic Educational Opportunity Grants, now called Pell Grants in honor of the Senator from Rhode Island, the Guaranteed Student Loan program, and other financial assistance available to graduate and professional school students, most blacks and other minorities would not have received higher education. The same can be said for the tens of millions of white students who also benefitted from these programs. Yet, David Stockman does not accept this assistance as "a proper obligation of the taxpayer."[37] However, withdrawal from the existing obligation would mean a return to the days when higher education was limited to a relatively few persons in American society. This philosophical shift comes precisely at a time when technological demands require an increasingly well-educated society.

It was undoubtedly the success of the federal aid programs in higher education that made them such an easy target for those bent on balancing the budget in 1984.[38]

The budget rescissions and cutbacks in education affected training programs for graduate and professional students and resulted in reductions in the amount of money available for a wide range of additional programs. Consequently, thousands of needy students lost this source of financial support. Some examples[39] will illustrate this point.

1. Approximately 2.7 million students received Pell Grants (or BEOG's) prior to the policy changes initiated by the Reagan Administration and approved by Congress. Because of changes in eligibility requirements, it is estimated that approximately 250,000 students will be disqualified in 1982. Further, the awards granted to students were reduced by an average of $80.00, and the maximum award permitted was sliced from $1,750 to $1,650.

   Under the Pell Grants, many disadvantaged students also qualified for assistance through the campus-based programs: (1) Supplementary Educational Opportunity Grants (SEOG's), (2) College Work Study, and (3) National Direct Student Loans (NDSL's). Campus-based programs of necessity will be reduced drastically as a result of the reduced appropriations for higher education over the next several years.

2. About 750,000 students qualified for educational assistance through the Social Security awarded to their families. This program will be phased out by the Fall semester of 1982. Many of these students will attempt to obtain Pell grants, thereby straining a program whose funds were already substantially decreased.

3. In the past, the federal government paid the interest on guaranteed student loans for approximately 3.6 million students who could borrow up to $2,500 each at 9 percent interest. The approximate total of this program was $8 billion up to 1981. Initiated in the early 1970's for families whose incomes did not exceed $25,000 annually, this program was expanded in 1978, in the Middle Income Student Assistance Act, under intense congressional pressure, to include "middle-income families." Since there were broad-based allegations of abuse (e.g., able parents permitting their children to borrow money at a lower interest, then investing the same sums at a higher interest and receiving substan-

tial profits at the government's expense), this program was particularly vulnerable to cutbacks by its critics.

With the new regulations, automatic eligibility for GSLs is limited to those students who come from families whose adjusted gross annual income does not exceed $30,000. Students whose family income exceeds the $30,000 ceiling are now compelled to pass a so-called "needs test." The loans are now based also on a principle of "remaining need." This means that they represent the difference between the sums obtained from other sources and family contributions, and the educational cost at the institution in which the student is enrolled. In order to protect the federal government against defaults on interest payments, the new regulations imposed "an origination fee," (of 5 percent). This means that the cost of the initial interest on the loan taken by the student is deducted from the amount borrowed. For example, if a student borrowed the maximum of $2,500, that student would receive 5 percent less or $2,375 because the first year interest is automatically deducted.

4. The Parent Loan Program was given a new name, Auxiliary Loans to Assist Students. This program provides subsidized loans not exceeding $3,000 but the interest charged is raised from nine to fourteen percent.

Because of new regulations, beginning in 1982, it will be considerably more difficult for tens of thousands of college students and students enrolled in graduate and professional schools to continue their education. The total amount available will, of course, be considerably less. Regarding Pell Grants, a new sliding scale to determine the expected parents' contribution from their discretionary income will be raised from 10.5 percent in 1981 to as much as 40 to 55 percent in 1982. Changes in eligibility, as well as those resulting in workfare programs for welfare recipients, will result in a reduction in the number of minority students enrolled at all college levels as well as in the number of women with small children who had returned to college because of the availability of day care services.

It is estimated that about 40 percent of all black college students are currently enrolled in community colleges. Cutbacks in campus-based programs, such as work-study and SEOG's will inevitably restrict the number of students that a given institution can support. Consequently, this important base of access to higher education will be curtailed. In addition, there are approximately 105 historically black colleges in the United States. A significant proportion of students enrolled in these colleges are from homes in which the annual median family income is less than 50 percent of the annual median family income for the nation's college students as a whole. In excess of 90 percent of these students, particularly those at the private black colleges, may support their education through Pell Grants. The United Negro College Fund, which has a major responsibility for raising funds to support its 41 private college members, estimates that fully-implemented Reagan cutbacks will result in a loss of between $30 and $40 million to black colleges over the period between 1982 and 1986.[40]

The potential impact on graduate and professional students is enormous. Not only is there likely to be immense difficulty in financing their education, their indebtedness upon completion of their graduate and professional training will be staggering for many in this category. The great majority of professional school students of all races finance their training through various forms of loans and government scholarships.[41] Their indebtedness, which was already as much as $50,000 or more in some areas, such as medicine and dentistry, could skyrocket to as much as $106,000 on a $10,000 Health Assistance Loan over a ten year period of time.[42] The possibilities of an indebtedness of such monumental proportions may discourage highly qualified persons, who might serve the needs of people in depressed areas, from entering the health care professions.

Other aspects of higher education, which concern equality of educational opportunity, focus less on financial and more on the philosophical underpinnings that guide the Reagan Plan. Whereas previous administrations used the Justice Department and the Office of Civil Rights to *enforce* the law with respect to access to public school and higher education, the Reagan Administration has given notice that some significant changes will be made.

For instance, it does not seem inclined to support the established guidelines for dismantling dual systems of higher education as mandated in Judge John Pratt's orders with respect to the *Adams v. Califano case*. The Reagan Administration engaged in relatively secret negotiations with the University of North Carolina System to settle a long-standing suit over the government's earlier decision to withhold federal funds from that system due to its failure to comply with the mandate to dismantle its dual system of higher education. Even some of the Justice Department lawyers were unaware of the negotiations until their results appeared in the press. The NAACP-Legal Defense and Educational Fund was essentially presented with a *fait accompli* and given a short time span for responding to the settlement.

Among the essential questions that arise, with regard to the strategy employed by the Reagan Administration in the 19 jurisdictions subsumed by the *Adams v. Califano* decision are the following: (1) Will black students be enrolled at parity levels in the flagship institutions of these jurisdictions? (2) Will black students have equal access to all educational programs and support mechanisms (teaching and research assistantships, loans and scholarships) at the traditionally white colleges? (3) Will the traditionally white institutions in the 19 jurisdictions covered by *Adams v. Califano* recruit black faculty, promote and tenure them at levels beyond tokenism? (4) Will the traditionally white institutions recruit, hire and promote black administrators, executives and managers into positions of authority and influence beyond token levels? (5) Will black colleges be successful in strengthening their academic programs by virtue of agreements reached to settle disputes raised under *Adams v. Califano?* (6) Will the historically black public institutions be successful in their recruitment of white students and establish themselves as racially integrated institutions? or (7) Will the Reagan Administration strategy inevitably perpetuate "separate-but-unequal" publicly financed institutions for higher learning in the United States?

Busing For School Desegregation

As stated earlier on, the Reagan Administration is opposed to busing for school desegregation. This opposition is consistent with the views articulated by right-wing groups across the nation, by the Moral Majority, by some former "liberals," by black conservatives, and some other blacks but for entirely different reasons. This opposition is manifested in a number of ways:

1. Senator Orrin Hatch proposed a bill to the U.S. Congress that would prevent the courts from ordering busing even if proof of discrimination is found.[43]
2. By mid-November of 1981, as many as 200 of the 218 signatures needed had been obtained among members of the House of Representatives to force a vote on a proposed constitutional amendment that would prevent busing.
3. Senators J. Bennett Johnston (Louisiana) and Jesse Helms (North Carolina) proposed a bill that would restrict the courts form ordering busing of children to a school more than 15 minutes from their homes, or, essentially, from attending schools outside their immediate neighborhoods.

4. The Justice Department under President Reagan has decided to abandon the procedure of desegregating an entire school district when segregation is found to exist in part of the district. In other words, the Justice Department will no longer seek "system-wide remedies" to school segregation, even though this approach to litigation is viewed as essential by many civil rights lawyers. Instead, the Justice Department will focus on the specific schools in which sufficient evidence is mounted to prove *intentional segregation*. And, the burden of proof will be on the plaintiff(s).

   In effect, the U.S. Justice Department has decided to move in opposition to the decision handed down in 1973 by the U.S. Supreme Court in the *Keyes v. Denver School District* case. In that case, the U.S. Supreme Court found that whenever state-imposed racial segregation is found in one part of a school system, the presumption was that state action yields racial imbalance in other parts of the system. The U.S. Justice Department maintains that that "presumption" has been unfairly employed in the desegregation of segregated schools because of the lack of proof of "intent" to discriminate.[44]

5. A further evidence of the shift in federal policy with respect to public school desegregation is found in actions taken with respect to litigation which arose in the state of Washington. The Justice Department decided to join with the state of Washington against the Seattle school board in the case of *Seattle School District v. State of Washington*. Reversing previous positions taken by the Justice Department in other Administrations, the Justice Department in 1981 asked the U.S. Supreme Court to overturn the decisions rendered by two federal lower courts against an antibusing law that was adopted by voters in the state of Washington in 1978. That antibusing law was approved by Washington voters *after* voluntary and subsequently mandatory busing plans had been instituted by school districts in Seattle, Tacoma and Pasco. Neither of these cities had been found guilty of "intentional discrimination." Neither had these cities ever been ordered by a court to desegregate schools. In Seattle, various voluntary school desegregation strategies had been tried but failed to accomplish their purposes. Therefore, the school district in Seattle ordered mandatory busing in order to achieve racial balance in the system. A group called Citizens for Voluntary Integration (CIVIC) engineered the state-wide approval of an initiative that banned busing for racial purposes unless court-ordered. The Seattle school board sued, claiming this bill to be unconstitiutional. The oddity of the intervention of the Justice Depart-

ment under the Reagan Administration in this litigation is that the federal government has now opposed local school boards whose desegregation model appeared to have been working effectively. The Justice Department, in supporting the state of Washington, lent its support and prestige for legislation whose impact would be immediately "segregative." This is the view of civil rights lawyers and the School District of Seattle, Tacoma and Pasco. The Justice Department, in this instance, is asking the U.S. Supreme Court to decide whether or not a given state can "constitutionally prohibit local school boards" from institutionalizing a voluntary busing plan that promotes racial balance under conditions found in the three cities in Washington.[45] In October 1981, the U.S. Supreme Court voted to hear arguments in this case.

Similarly, the Justice Department reversed the position taken by the Department under other Administrations with respect to school desegregation in cities such as Chicago and Houston. In fact, in July of 1981, the Justice Department attacked as unacceptable the Chicago school board proposals for school desegregation because the plan would place an undue and unfair burden on black school children to accomplish desegregation. However, in August, 1981, the Reagan Administration rejected its own criticisms and characterized the position taken in July as ill-advised. The Justice Department also abandoned the plan to force cross-district school desegregation (a metropolitanization plan) between Houston and surrounding suburbs. The net result of these actions is to withdraw the power and influence of the federal government from efforts to establish workable school desegregation programs.

6. The Reagan Administration is in favor of *tuition tax credits* for parents who send their children to private schools. Such plans raise important constitutional issues. On the one hand, for example, is the constitutionality of using public funds to support private, sectarian schools. On the other hand, is the question of the right of parents to provide the best education they feel is available to their children. As determined by media reports, journalists, and various columnists, the position taken by the Reagan Administration in support of vouchers and tax credits is favored by conservative groups, the leadeship structure of private schools, and a number of parents who have all but given up on the possibilities of quality education in public schools.

Others take the view that the Reagan Administration's proposals will undermine the national tradition of public school education and that it represents a retrenchment of the national responsibility to provide access of all pupils to a good quality of education in the public sector.

The Reagan Administration may have underestimated the commitment of the public to protect the integrity of the public school system. In November, 1981, for instance, the voters of Washington, D.C. had to decide on Initiative 7 — tuition tax credits. This initiative had strong endorsement of the National Taxpayers Union. If it had passed, it would have enabled each taxpayer a reduction of as much as $1,200 from local taxes to cover either the cost of private school education or the costs of such things as books, field trips, gymwear and other items. This initiative would have also permitted childless couples to adopt a child of another person for tax purposes. It included similar arrangements for companies doing business in the District of Columbia. The initiative failed decisively. Almost nine of every ten voters (89.2 percent) voted NO while only one in ten (10.8 percent) voted YES. Hence, by a margin of about 8 to 1, the tuition tax credit initiative was defeated.[46] Hence, it may be that the average American citizen remains committed to the idea of free public school education for the nation's children.

Finally, the deepening fear that the ultimate objective of the Reagan philosophy of modern conservatism is to return this nation to a segregated, racially separate and unequal state, as a matter of national policy, was given significant momentum in January, 1982 by an action taken by the Internal Revenue Service. This agency, with the approval of the Secretary of the Treasury, the Attorney General of the United States and the "White House," revoked a twelve year policy of denying tax exempt status to private schools, colleges and nonprofit institutions that discriminate against blacks and other minorities. As a result, an estimated 100 institutions that practice racial discrimination will be awarded tax exempt status and, under this Administration policy shift, will be free to continue the practice of racial discrimination with what is tantamount to an endorsement by the highest levels of policy-making in the federal government. In effect, the U.S. Government and the people of the United States, through the governmental utilization of their tax dollars, will subsidize racial discrimination and segregation in private schools, colleges and nonprofit institutions. Although the President of the United States may assert that such institutional policies are abhorrent to him, the very fact that that radical shift in national policy was made, admittedly with his endorsement, gives apparent credence to the view that, in fact, the Reagan Administration is committed to "turning back the clock" to racial conditions of the pre-1954 era.

The Administration claimed that its primary motivation in revoking a policy that had been in existence since 1970 was to shift the enforcement function from the Internal Revenue Service to Congress with respect to such "social" problems. Hence, the Internal Revenue Service would be freed to perform its major function of collecting revenue. Irrespective of disclaimers and pronounced opposition against racial discrimination asserted by President Reagan in a press release on January 12, 1982, the action taken by the Internal Revenue Service was consistent with the President's philosophy. Shortly after Mr. Reagan took office, he stated his personal opposition to the utilization of the "taxing power of the Government . . . to regulate the economy" or to effectuate social change. The implementation of that philosophy is, however, quite selective. For instance, the average reader may recall that a considerable amount of time was spent by Mr. Reagan earlier on advocating transformations in tax laws for the expressed purpose of inducing fundamental changes in both economic and social behavior, and not expressly for the collection of revenue.

This policy reversal seems to have been skillfully designed to *assure*, once and forever, the withdrawal of the federal government from enforcement of such penalties against institutions and organizations that practice racial discrimination. The Administration was well aware of the conservative profile of the American Congress. The Congress as constituted in 1982, will probably not enact the kind of legislation required to remedy this situation without a major struggle, if ever. Further, it would be most surprising, indeed, if the U.S. Supreme Court, as constituted in January 1982, will provide the type of relief that may be sought by civil rights organizations and their dwindling friends in the Congress of the United States.

The Voting Rights Act of 1965

One of the areas in which "mixed signals" were given to the public by President Reagan during 1981 was with respect to his views on the Voting Rights Act of 1965. At various points throughout the year, by virtue of statements he made, such as before the annual convention of the NAACP in June, 1981, and other comments attributed to him by the press, he seemed uncertain about voting rights. (As this book goes to press, the House of Representatives has already approved, by an extremely wide margin, the extension of the Voting Rights Act through 1992. The Senate had not concluded its deliberations on the measure.)

The Voting Rights Act of 1965 was a federal government response (from its president and members of the Congress of the United States) against the continuing brutalities inflicted against black Americans in various parts of the South. The nation had witnessed bloodshed in Selma, Alabama, particularly, as blacks and white supporters marched between Selma and Montgomery. This act was designed to enfranchise black citizens by ending some of the practices which had precluded their participation in the political process. Specifically, it was meant to eliminate a number of barriers imposed by local registrars against the successful registration of potential black voters (e.g., literacy tests, poll taxes, changes of place for registration, re-locating voting machines over-night so that blacks could not vote, annexing other communities, without informing the federal government, when the black population exceeded the white population in a given community so that whites would continue to be in the majority).

As a result of the enactment of the Voting Rights Act in 1965, more than 1.5 million blacks in various parts of the South have registered to vote. Consequently, they have changed the face of local and state governments. Their representation in the state legislatures of such states as Mississippi, Alabama, Louisiana and Georgia, as examples, is impressive. Since 1965, Georgia has sent a black to the U.S House of Representatives. So have Texas, Missouri, and Tennessee. Black mayors now head municipal governments in several states that once comprised the "Old Confederacy." Black voters have often provided the balance of power in important local and state elections (e.g., the race for Governor in Virginia in 1981). The practice of gerrymandering (illegal re-districting) can now be controlled whether in New York City or in South Carolina. Increasing numbers of blacks and other previously disenfranchised groups in the nation have seized upon the opportunities provided under the Voting Rights Act of 1965 for political participation.

This act, unless extended, will expire in 1982. Persuading Congress to not only extend the act but to strengthen various sections of it became a matter of first priority for several civil rights groups. Perhaps, the most controversial section of the act is Section 5 which calls for "preclearance" of all electoral changes within a jurisdiction by the U.S. Department of Justice or by the Federal District Court in Washington, D.C. As of 1981, the preclearance section had special applicability to the states of Alabama, Florida, Georgia, Louisiana, Mississippi, North Carolina, South Carolina, Texas and Virginia because of the impediments to voting enforced against blacks in those states prior to 1965. In addition, 13 states or portions of them are also covered by the Voting Rights Act.

During the election campaign of 1980, candidate Ronald Reagan suggested that provisions of the Voting Rights Act should apply uniformly to all 50 states. When Senator Strom Thurmond assumed the chairmanship of the Senate Judiciary Committee in 1981, he also took the same position.

As stated earlier on, the House of Representatives approved of a ten year extension of the Act on October 5, 1981 by a vote of 389 for and only 24 against. The House version of the act set a "high standard of proof for states" that wished exemptions or "bail out" from further coverage. It also emphasized the actual manifestation of discrimination (that is, discriminatory result) instead of intentional discrimination needed only be proved by minorities when they aggrieved an election procedure. One immediate purpose of this section was to allow relief from discrimination which results from "at-large elections" such as found in the case of *Bolden v. Mobile, Alabama* which alleged that this procedure has kept blacks out of important elective positions. Hence, this section would increase the chances of blacks to be successful through district-wide elections as opposed to the at-large method.

The House version extends the requirement for bilingual elections in the covered areas beyond the expiration date of 1985 to 1992. This section is especially crucial in those areas of the country in which the Hispanic population resides.

The House version was subsequently opposed by President Reagan, upon a choice of recommendations made by Attorney General William French Smith. He stated that he was in favor of an extension of the act. However, the conditions he specified would seriously weaken the version approved by the House of Representatives by such a lopsided margin. For example, Mr. Reagan would require minorities to prove *intent* to discriminate in order to abrogate voting procedures deleterious to their objectives. He would weaken the "bail out" measure proposed by the House with respect to the preclearance provision.

(Undoubtedly, by the time this book is published, the Civil Rights Act will have been extended to 1992. However, one cannot be certain about its final form. The Republican-controlled Senate demonstrated unyielding loyalty to the Republican president in the struggle to enact the "New Federalism" budget or the Reagan Economic Recovery Plan. Without question, an attempt will be made to seriously weaken the House version of the act by those who feel threatened by the number of blacks who have registered to vote in their states, which could conceivably be reduced if a weakened act were appproved, and by those whose loyalty to the president supercedes the importance of eliminating all barriers to voting rights for minority groups.)

The Reagan Administration and Affirmative Action

Supreme Court Justice Harry A. Blackmun once wrote in an opinion that race must first be taken into account "in order to get beyond racism." It was precisely that motivation to move beyond racism in recruitment and hiring practices that various aspects of affirmative action were first initiated. The legal basis for affirmative action is found in various Executive Orders issued by Presidents dating back to 1941, statutes or bills enacted by the Congress of the United States, and important Supreme Court decisions.[47]

In 1941, President Franklin D. Roosevelt issued Executive Order No. 8802 which established equal employment opportunity as a national policy. Although the immediate concern was the right of blacks to be employed in the national defense program, the policy ultimately extended to other areas. As a result, the concept of fair employment practices (FEP) came into being. In 1951, President Harry S. Truman issued Executive Order No. 10308 which created a Committee on Government Contract Appliance. Its purpose was to handle complaints of discrimination in government contracts. In 1961, President John F. Kennedy issued Executive Order No. 10925 which established a Committee on Equal Employment Opportunity. It was designed to strengthen the federal government's commitment to equal employment opportunity throughout the nation.[48]

In 1964, a major Civil Rights Act was approved by Congress. Title VII of this act prohibited employment discrimination related to race, sex, religion or national origin. This act also made it possible for courts to order "affirmative action" as a remedy for past acts of discrimination. Several Supreme Court decisions rendered during the 1970's upheld other court decisions that supported the essential principles of affirmative action. In Weber v. Kaiser Aluminum (1979), the court upheld the right of private employers to give preferential treatment to black workers to overcome past acts of discrimination on jobs from which blacks were previously excluded. In the case of Bakke v. The Board of Regents of the University of California at Davis (1978), the U.S. Supreme Court rendered a mixed judgment. On the one hand, it decided against rigidly defined, set aside quotas for admission to universities and colleges. However, the Court also stated that the race variable could be legitimately considered in determining eligibility for admission to a professional school when a compelling state need was served.

President Reagan, the Attorney General of the United States, and the Assistant Attorney General for Civil Rights have taken positions in direct opposition to the fundamental principles of affirmative action. The Attorney General of the United States, William French Smith, claims that "reverse discrimination" (a euphemism for affirmative action policies) is no "cure" for discrimination in employment.[49] He, as other members of the Reagan Administration, opposed the use of quotas, numerical goals and timetables for hiring of minorities and women. His argument is that affirmative action "stigmatizes its beneficiaries." However, the Reagan Administration has offered no concrete proposals that would help to eliminate the continuing presence of discrimination in employment and access to other life chances. The Assistant Attorney General for Civil Rights asserts his intention to enforce antidiscrimination statutes but he also hopes that the Supreme Court will overturn its decision in the Weber case.[50] To follow his philosophy would return the nation to a court-enforced segregated society.

The attack on affirmative action extends into the U.S. Senate. Senator Orrin Hatch (R., Utah) has proposed a constitutional amendment that would prohibit the establishment of goals, timetables and quotas on the basis of race, color or national origin by the federal government and state agencies. Even if approved by Congress, it would probably take several years of challenge and litigation before such an amendment could take effect.

The lack of a consistent policy with respect to affirmative action in the Reagan Administration, one year after the 1980 election, is found in the somewhat contradictory positions taken by representatives of three departments. For instance, the Justice Department opposes such remedies employed in affirmative action as numerical goals and timetables for *hiring* but is not opposed to their use in *recruitment* of minorities and women. On the other hand, the U.S. Department of Labor favors the use of such devices but wishes to eliminate unnecessary paper requirements and "intrusive government regulations" on federal contractors. By contrast, the Equal Employment Opportunity Commission, through its Acting Chairman, J. Clay Smith, *advocates* affirmative action.[51]

Despite such divergent perspectives, it seems evident that the Reagan Administration is committed to shifting the burden for proof of discrimination onto the plaintiffs by its insistence on the utilization of the "intent test" for such determinations. That is to say, blacks and other minorities may now have to prove "intent to discriminate" as opposed to supplying the evidence of the result that discrimination has in fact occurred against blacks and other minorities when they pursue a complaint.

The U.S. Commission on Civil Rights has steadfastly supported affirmative action in hiring and in education. This Commission views affirmative action as absolutely imperative as a fundamental remedy against present and past acts of discrimination. In a report issued in December, 1981, *Affirmative Action in the 1980's: Dismantling the Process of Discrimination,* the U.S. Commission on Civil Rights criticized the Administration's stance on affirmative action as "inconsistent with . . . the principles . . . of civil rights law and policy."[52]

In all of the areas discussed in this chapter, it is not difficult to understand why it is that so many black Americans have such a high level of distrust of the white power structure. It is not incomprehensible for blacks to believe that the present Administration is neither supportive of the black population nor of minorities and the poor in general. It is easy to understand why it is that the alienation of a significant proportion of the black population will increase in the near future and that it may be necessary for blacks, minorities and the poor, in general, to join together in a concerted effort to combat the opposition against the achievement of their own rights of citizenship. However, if their concerns are not addressed, even greater strains in race relations are ahead.

Notes

1. Blackwell, James E., *Mainstreaming Outsiders: The Production of Black Professionals.* Bayside, New York: General Hall, Inc., 1981, Ch. 1.
2. Bardolph, Richard (ed.), *The Civil Rights Record: Black Americans and the Law, 1849-1970.* New York: Thomas Y. Crowell, 1970, passim.
3. Blackwell, James E., *The Black Community: Diversity and Unity.* New York: Harper & Row, 1975, Chapter 7.
4. *Ibid.*
5. Wilson, William J., *The Declining Significance of Race.* Chicago: The University of Chicago Press, 1978, pp. 18-22.
6. Daniels, Lee A., "The New Black Conservatives," *The New York Times Magazine.* October 4, 1981, p. 20 ff.
7. *Ibid.*
8. *Ibid.,* p. 22.
9. *Ibid.,* p. 54.
10. Clymer, Adam, "Blacks in U.S. Are Becoming More Pessimistic, Polls Hint," *The New York Times.* August 24, 1981, p. 1; and _____, "Poll Shows Concern Over Economy Cutting into Public Support for Reagan," *The New York Times.* September 29, 1981, p. 22.
11. Denton, Robert and Sussman, Barry, "Racial Strides Found by Poll," *The Boston Globe.* March 25, 1981, p. 11.
12. *Op. Cit.*
13. *Ibid.*
14. "Poll Says Public More Critical of Reagan," *The Boston Globe,* November 26, 1981, p. 18.

15. *Ibid.*
16. Hill, Robert B., *Economic Policies and Black Progress; Myths and Realities*, Washington, D.C.: National Urban League, 1981, p. 47.
17. *Ibid.*
18. *Ibid.*
19. *Ibid.*
20. *Ibid.*, p. 48.
21. *Ibid.*, p. 52.
22. *Ibid*, p. 53.
23. Cf. Pear, Robert "Shifts for Social Welfare," *The New York Times*, October 28, 1981, p. A22; _____, "Federal Cuts Forcing States to Curb Day-Care Services to the Poor," *The New York Times*, October 22, 1981, p. A19.
24. *Ibid.*
25. Brimmer, Andrew, "Economic Outlook: Reaganomics and the Black Community," *Black Enterprise Magazine*, (December 1981), pp. 40-44.
26. *Ibid.*
27. *Ibid.*
28. *Ibid.*
29. *Ibid.*
30. Pool, Isaih J., "Uncle Sam's Pink Slips," *Black Enterprise Magazine*, (December 1981), p. 29.
31. *Ibid.*
32. *Characteristics of Households Receiving Noncash Benefits.* Washington, D.C.: U.S. Government Printing Office, 1981.
33. This section represents a summary of information provided in Herbers, John, "States Lag in Planning Black Grant Programs," *The New York Times*, September 29, 1981, p. A16.
34. Cf. "Administration Considers Cutbacks in Urban Grants, Housing Subsidies," *The Boston Globe*, December 2, 1981, p. 10; and Rich, Spencer and Babcock, Charles, "New Cuts Planned for 1983," *The Boston Globe*, November 20, 1981, p. 5.
35. Carroll, James R., "Reagan Federalism Plan Called 'A Bay of Pigs' and Sham," *The Boston Globe,* December 2, 1981, p. 16.
36. Quoted by Fiske, Edward B., " Access for Disadvantaged in Peril," *The New York Times*, October 20, 1981, p. C-1.
37. *Ibid.*
38. *Ibid.*
39. This summary is based upon information reported in Fiske, Edward B., "After Reagan, A New Era in Paying for College," *The New York Times Education Supplement*, November 22, 1981, p. 1.
40. Claffey, Charles E., "Black Private Colleges: An Endangered Species," *The Boston Globe*, November 25, 1981, pp. 1, 17.
41. Blackwell, James E., *Mainstreaming Outsiders. Op. Cit.*, Chapters 4 and 5.
42. Rubin, Nancy, "Glum Reality of Borrowing for a Bright Future," *The New York Times Education Supplement*, November 22, 1981.
43. Roberts, Steven, "Action on Antibusing Bill Pressed in Congress," *The New York Times*, November 15, 1981, p. B-17.
44. Pear, Robert, "U.S. Alters Policy on Desegregation," *The New York Times*, November 19, 1981, P. A14.
45. Taylor, Stuart, Jr., "U.S. in Shift, Urges High Court to Back Antibusing Law," *The New*

York Times, September 11, 1981, p. D-1.
46. Shanker, Albert, "D.C. Voters Slam Door on Tax Credits," *The New York Times,"* November 8, 1981, p. E-9.
47. Bardolph, *Op. Cit.*
48. *Ibid.*
49. Pear, "U.S. Panel Report Backs Hiring Goals," *The New York Times,* December 9, 1981, p. A-21.
50. *Ibid.*
51. _____, "U.S. Agencies Vary on Policy Rights," *The New York Times,* November 16, 1981, P. 1.
52. *Ibid.*

APPENDIX A

Methodological Note

Sample Selection

As seen in the first chapter, the sample selection is a critical element in carrying out a survey research project. Sample selection is technical and demanding. Thus it is important to devote critical attention to this phase of the research. The Boston pilot study sample was drawn by co-author Philip Hart with technical assistance provided by Thomas Mangione, Center for Survey Research, a project of the University of Massachusetts-Boston, Harvard University and M.I.T.

As can be seen in the following Figure 1, for household sample selection focusing on black adults, we had to factor in the population, number of housing units, percentage of blacks in the geographic area, the number of households necessary to contact to secure 60 interviews, the sampling rate, cluster size, the number of blocks covered, and the interval. These assumptions used in determining the sample size served as a guiding framework for the sample selection work in the four other metropolitan centers included in this study.

The Scales

The pilot study and the resultant four city study were guided by the empirical research of McClosky and Schorr as reported in "Psychological Dimensions of Anomie," *American Sociological Review,* 30: 1(1965), 14-20 and Dean's study "Alienation: Its Meaning and Measurement," *American Sociological Review, 26,* October 1961, 753-758 because of the systematic procedure for investigating the dimensions of alienation and

Figure 1. Assumptions Used in Determining Sample Size — #C.S. Needed For

	Population	HU's	% Black	60 Interviews	Rate	Cluster Size	# Blocks	Interval
Mattapan	20,000	6,250	60%	165	1/38	8	28	288
Roxbury	60,000	18,750	70%	149	1/126	6	25	756
Dorchester	70,000	21,875	60%	165	1/133	6	28	798

$*(\text{\# Initial C.S.}) \times \left[\begin{array}{l} \text{Households} = (\text{Total} - \text{Vacancy},\\ \text{Business Addresses} \end{array} \right] \times (\text{Rate of Contact for Screening}) \times (\% \text{ Black}) \times (\text{Response Rate}) = \text{\# of interviews.}$

$*(\text{\# Initial C.S.}) \times {}^{.90} \left[\begin{array}{l} (\text{Mattapan, Dorchester})\\ (\text{Roxbury}) \end{array} \right] \times (.90) \times \left[\begin{array}{l} .60 \ (\text{Mattapan, Dorchester})\\ .70 \ (\text{Roxbury}) \end{array} \right] \times (.75) = 60$

anomie. Dean's alienation scale comprises three components: (1) powerlessness; (2) normlessness; and (3) social isolation. The reliability of the sub-scales, tested by the split-half method and corrected by the Spearman-Brown prophecy formula, was as follows: powerlessness - .78; normlessness - .73; social isolation - .84; and the total alienation scales, with items rotated to minimize a possible halo effect, had a reliability of .78. The intercorrelations among the alienation scale components ranged from .41 to .90. Validity was tested by correlating the Dean Alienation Scale with those of Srole and Nettler. In each case the correlations were in the .30s. The corrected split-half reliability coefficient for the anomie scale was .76.

In the Boston study, all three measures of alienation were included. However, due to the similarity of the normlessness scale and the anomie scale, it was decided to exclude the normlessness scale from the interview schedule used in the four city study. Conceptually, and by definition, anomie and normlessness are very similar, thus the decision to eliminate duplication. This decision also served to shorten the interview schedule.

Data Reduction and Analysis

As noted earlier, once the field work was completed, cover sheets and interview schedules were forwarded to Cambridge for coding, scaling, key punching, computer programming, computer runs, data analysis and storage. Key punching and verification services were purchased from Harvard University's Office of Information Technology (OIT). Computer facilities at Harvard University were also utilized under a long-standing contract with the computing center and the Solomon Fuller Institute. These computing facilities include the IBM 370 which can handle three different versions of the Statistical Package for the Social Sciences (SPSS) and which has a good turn-around time for data analysis purposes. SPSS is the package used in the programming. Once the data file was in proper order, the initial analytical activity focused on determining the validity and utility of the data. Comparisons between known population parameters and the sample characteristics served as measures of the sample validity. In instances where the population parameters and sample characteristics differed significantly, weighting techniques were employed to bring the sample in line with the population. Data utility was determined by ascertaining which items were differentiating and which were not. Frequency distributions and univariate statistics were run in this phase of the analysis.

The next phase involved data reduction activities. Scales were constructed for macro-community, micro-community, social participation, anomie, alienation, powerlessness, social isolation, orientation to the future, health utilization, health information, and distrust of the power structure. Composite indices were constructed for social participation and health utilization. Factor analysis was used to determine the dimensionality of a scale or index as well as the relative importance of the various items which comprise the scale or index. Guttman scaling techniques were used to examine scales which seem to be unidimensional. Multiple regression analysis was used in the data reduction phase in order to identify variables which show no relationship to the set of dependent variables and/or which may in fact be redundant. The multiple regression analysis had macro- and micro-community issues as dependent variables, with occupation, anomie, alienation, powerlessness, social isolation, social participation, orientation to the future and distrust of the power structure as independent variables. Urban-suburban comparisons were made across all variables by the total sample and by each city.

The procedures for determining degrees of alienation and anomie will follow the ones established by McClosky, Schorr, and Dean, respectively. They used a Likert scale format and a trichotomous classification of high, medium and low. This data was analyzed in a like fashion, though with the alienation scale the medium category was truncated, in that the pilot study revealed this scale to be less discriminating. Scores on the anomie scale were correlated with the pertinent variables contained in the stated hypotheses. Similar procedures were used in categorizing levels of alienation. In this way, it was possible to rank order the anomie scale and the various subscales of alienation, such as social isolation.

The pilot study results indicated that the scales used to measure macro-community concerns, alienation, and health information flow were the least discriminating. Thus the scale extremes of low and high were enlarged for the macro-community and alienation scales. The health information flow scale was dichotomized into low and high categories.

Weighting of Data

As described earlier, the household data collection phase of the survey included use of the Kish selection method in order to equalize the data in each metropolitan area by age and sex. This procedure worked well for the age variable. However, in the case of the sex variable, we found upon inspecting the data that there was an over-representation of females. This is a chronic problem in survey research dealing with black adults. In order to adjust for this over-representation of females, we added a case weight factor in order to readjust the male-female ratio in such a way as to approach the actual proportion in the metropolitan area's total black adult population. The strength of our data collection procedure is evident in that we only found it necessary to weight the sex variable. All other variables approximate the black adult population profile for each metropolitan area sampled.

Thus, for Atlanta, the case weight we factored in was 1.4, for Boston it was 1.8, and for Houston it was 2.0.* What this case weight factor did was give more weight to a male response equal to the case weight factor for each metropolitan area. This case weight was then included in the SPSS reanalysis of the original data with the goal being to have the sample approximate the male-female proportions for each metropolitan area. The larger the case-weight factor introduced, the larger was the sample dispersion from the actual male-female population distribution. Also, the case weight factor increased the sample size used for analysis and interpretation. The final total sample size, and that for each metropolitan area, reflects the use of the case-weight factor.

---

*Cleveland and Los Angeles required no caseweighting.

APPENDIX B

Table 20 Summary of Statistical Findings (p ≤ 0.05)

CHAPTER FOUR = MACRO/MICRO/HEALTH/NATIONAL PROFILE

Finding	Statistical Information
Younger persons are more likely to be concerned with macro-community issues than are older persons	$X^2 = 8.87$ $p = 0.054$
Older persons are more anomic than are younger persons	$X^2 = 23.62$ $p = 0.0001$
All age groups are in medium range of powerlessness	$X^2 = 10.08$ $p = 0.04$
Younger age group reported lower social isolation than did persons in the older age group	$X^2 = 12.47$ $p = 0.01$
Family heads attach greater importance to micro-community issues than did non-family heads	$X^2 = 14.73$ $p = 0.02$
Divorced, single, never married, and married differed significantly from widowed persons on macro-community concerns	$X^2 = 18.64$ $p = 0.02$
Higher income means a higher priority for micro-community issues	$X^2 = 37.66$ $p = 0.000$ $r = 0.12$ $p = 0.000$
Higher combined family income means higher priority given to micro-community issues	$X^2 = 19.73$ $p = 0.0006$
Higher a person's annual income, the greater is the priority for macro-community issues	$X^2 = 21.01$ $p = 0.0003$ $r = 0.14$ $p = 0.0000$
Higher combined family income means higher priority for macro-community issues	$X^2 = 19.78$ $p = 0.0006$
Employed persons have highest priority for macro-community issues	$X^2 = 46.08$ $p = 0.000$

Employed persons also have highest priority for micro-community issues	$X^2 = 26.58$ $p = 0.008$
Persons on fixed incomes are more likely to be concerned about micro-community issues than are unemployed persons	$X^2 = 26.58$ $p = 0.0008$
Higher education implies higher importance given to micro-community issues	$X^2 = 12.91$ $p = 0.01$
Higher the rank on a scale of occupational prestige, the greater will be the concern for macro-community issues	$X^2 = 46.08$ $p = 0.000$ $r = 0.10$ $p = 0.002$
Persons in suburbs have a higher concern for macro-community issues than do urban residents	$X^2 = 117.2$ $p = 0.0000$ $r = 0.37$ $p = 0.000$
Suburbanites also show a higher concern for micro-community issues than do urban residents	$X^2 = 11.69$ $p = 0.0000$
High macro-community concern is significantly related to low health information flow	$X^2 = 165.58$ $p = 0.00$
There is a significant relation between concern for micro-community issues and "never used health services."	$X^2 = 5.76$ $p = 0.05$
As the urgency for macro-community issues increases there is a corresponding lack of information about health services available in their neighborhoods	$r = 0.46$ $p = 0.000$
Those who claim macro-community issues are of highest priority also tend to be more highly anomic than those who do not make such a claim	$r = 0.34$ $p = 0.000$
There is an inverse relationship between high priority given to macro-community issues and the degree of social isolation	$r = -0.35$ $p = 0.000$
A high priority given to micro-community issues means a similar concern is expressed for macro-community issues	$r = 0.45$ $p = 0.000$
There is a significant positive correlation between high micro-community concerns and good health access	$r = 0.37$ $p = 0.000$
There is a significant, negative correlation between high micro-community concern and health information flow	$r = -0.18$ $p = 0.000$
Concern with micro-community issues is accompanied by a high state of anomie	$r = -0.08$ $p = 0.02$
Persons who are concerned about community-specific issues do not seem to feel powerless to do anything about them	$r = 0.08$ $p = 0.02$

Similarly, an inverse relationship exists between concern with community-specific issues and social isolation. In other words as the concern for micro-community issues increases, the feeling of social isolation diminishes

$r = -0.10$
$p = 0.000$

However, those who have high concern for micro-community issues have high orientation to the future

$r = 0.36$
$p = 0.000$

There is a significant relationship between the disemmi-nation of health information and the use of health services for accidents

$X^2 = 5.73$
$p = 0.02$

There is also a significant relationship between health access index and "never used" health services

$X^2 = 15.05$
$p = 0.0005$

There is a significant relationship between health access index and use of health services for mental illness

$X^2 = 9.91$
$p = 0.007$

CHAPTER FIVE: ALIENATION OF BLACK AMERICANS/ A NATIONAL PROFILE

Alienated persons can expect to have limited faith in prob-ability that life will get better in the future

$r = -0.12$
$p = 0.000$

Persons who have a high sense of powerlessness seem to rank micro-community issues comparatively low

$r = -0.08$
$p = .02$

Those with high sense of powerlessness rank low on health index

$r = -0.08$
$p = 0.000$

A sense of powerlessness is positively correlated a high rank on social participation

$r = 0.10$
$p = 0.03$

Among variants of alienation, the weakest correlation with anomie is with social isolation

$r = 0.06$
$p = 0.04$

Anomie has a relative weak, yet significant, correlation with micro-community concerns

$r = 0.08$
$p = 0.02$

Anomie has a stronger correlation with macro-community concerns

$r = 0.34$
$p = 0.000$

Yet, anomic persons tend to have a low orientation to the future and little faith in their capacity to affect change

$r = -0.16$
$p = 0.000$

High anomic individuals rank low on the health index

$r = -0.16$
$p = 0.001$

High anomic individuals feel that they do not receive a sufficient amount of information about health services available to them

$r = -0.35$
$p = 0.000$

Persons with high sense of social isolation tend to be less concerned about macro-community issues	$r = -0.10$ $p = 0.000$
Data suggests that a high concern with micro-community issues is accompanied by a low sense of social isolation	$r = 0.10$ $p = 0.004$
Persons who rank high on social isolation also assert that they receive an adequate amount of health information	$r = 0.23$ $p = 0.000$
Persons who tend to be optimistic about the future and have clearly defined goals tend to have a high concern for micro-community issues	$r = 0.36$ $p = 0.000$
Optimistic persons tend to believe the delivery of health care services is adequate	$r = 0.26$ $p = 0.000$
High distrust of power structure is accompanied by a positive orientation to the future	$r = 0.61$ $p = 0.000$
High distrust of power structure also means high social isolation	$r = 0.25$ $p = 0.000$
High distrust of power structure also means low anomie	$r = -0.33$ $p = 0.000$
High distrust of power structure also means low feelings of powerlessness	$r = 0.09$ $p = 0.003$
High distrust means individuals have a low concern for macro-community issues	$r = -0.56$
The higher the rank on occupational scale the lower the apparent concern for macro-community issues	$r = -0.23$
High occupational status also has a negative correlation with micro-community issues	$r = -0.26$
High occupational status is negatively correlated with orientation to the future	$r = -0.27$
High occupational status is negatively correlated with distrust of the power structure	$r = -0.15$
High occupational status is negatively correlated with the health index	$r = -0.15$
High occupational status is negatively correlated health information index	$r = -0.10$
Persons in high status occupations tend to be anomic, have a sense of powerlessness, and are alienated	$r = 0.20$ $r = 0.24$ $r = 0.17$
Older persons are higher on the anomic scale than are younger persons	$X^2 = 23.62$ $p = 0.0001$

All age groups are medium in powerlessness	$X^2 = 12.47$ $p = 0.01$
The higher a person's income, the lower the sense of powerlessness	$X^2 = 14.33$ $p = 0.006$
The higher the level of educational attainment the lower is the sense of powerlessness	$X^2 = 57.53$ $p = 0.000$
High income persons have a low sense of anomie	$X^2 = 13.94$ $p = 0.008$
Highly educated persons also have a low sense of anomie	$X^2 = 17.67$ $p = 0.001$
Highly educated persons have a low sense of social isolation	$X^2 = 22.06$ $p = 0.0002$
Higher the education, the lower will be alienation	$X^2 = 23.03$ $p = 0.0001$
High distrust of the power structure implies a high health access score	$X^2 = 27.51$ $p = 0.0000$
Anomie is significantly related to high health information	$X^2 = 31.62$ $p = 0.000$
Low health information flow is significantly related to feelings of powerlessness	$X^2 = 24.78$ $p = 0.000$
There is also a significant relationship between health information and distrust of the power structure	$X^2 = 113.16$ $p = 0.000$

CHAPTER SIX: SOCIAL PARTICIPATION

Black persons are likely to identify close friends from within the black population itself	$X^2 = 146.79$ $p = 0.000$ $N = 643$
Suburban blacks are more likely to count as many as fifteen neighborhood white persons as among their close neighborhood friends than are urban blacks	$X^2 = 37.65$ $p = 0.000$ $N = 643$
Younger persons are more likely to have close white friends in their neighborhood than are older persons	$X^2 = 21.94$ $p = 0.005$ $N = 639$
Persons with medium or low educational attainment are more likely to indicate the absence of close white neighborhood friends	$X^2 = 106.19$ $p = 0.000$ $N = 643$

The higher the annual income the larger the number of white friends in the neighborhood and the lower the income the fewer the close white friends in the neighborhood

$X^2 = 60.09$
$p = 0.000$
$N = 624$

Northern and West Coast cities (e.g. Cleveland and Los Angeles) have a greater degree of within home social integration than would Southern and Southwest cities

$X^2 = 119.82$
$p = 0.000$
$N = 618$

Suburban blacks are more likely to have racially integrated social guests, however, most of them are black from their old neighborhood

$X^2 = 9.99$
$p = 0.04$
$N = 618$

All age groups are about equal in their proclivity to have blacks from the old neighborhood as social guests in their homes

$X^2 = 21.7$
$p = 0.007$
$N = 614$

Black suburbanites twice as likely to report that they have been invited by their white neighbors into their homes for social activities than were urban counterparts

$X^2 = 44.07$
$p = 0.0000$
$N = 641$

Urban blacks are more likely to participate in black clubs and organizations in their present neighborhood. Suburban residents are more likely to participate in clubs and organizations which are black in old neighborhood or black and white in present neighborhood

$X^2 = 23.4$
$p = 0.0004$
$N = 630$

Urban residents more likely to have black leisure time friends in present neighborhood. Suburban residents more likely to have black leisure time friends in old neighborhood

$X^2 = 19.6$
$p = 0.002$
$N = 609$

More than half of children attend school in present neighborhood

$X^2 = 38.85$
$p = 0.0001$
$N = 514$

More highly educated blacks are more likely to report having integrated social gatherings in their homes

$X^2 = 53.53$
$p = 0.0000$
$N = 618$

Those with low education levels are more likely to have black social guests from the old neighborhood

$X^2 = 53.53$
$p = 0.0000$
$N = 618$

The higher the income the more likely is it to entertain guests in the home of both races

$X^2 = 25.68$
$p = 0.001$
$N = 602$

Blacks in Atlanta much more likely to never have home social contact with white friends

$X^2 = 193.09$
$p = 0.00$
$N = 641$

Urban residents more likely to report never having home social contacts with white friends

$X^2 = 44.07$
$p = 0.0000$
$N = 641$

Older persons are more likely to report never having home
social contacts with white friends

$X^2 = 29.90$
$p = 0.0002$
$N = 637$

Persons of high education more likely to report social
contacts within homes of white friends

$X^2 = 126.04$
$p = 0.0000$
$N = 641$

High education more likely to have children in private
school

$X^2 = 15.84$
$p = 0.04$
$N = 514$

Young blacks are less likely to be church-goers than middle
age or older

$X^2 = 38.53$
$p = 0.0000$
$N = 619$

Males are more likely not to be church-goers

$X^2 = 16.28$
$p = 0.003$
$N = 621$

High education less likely to be church-goers

$X^2 = 49.78$
$p = 0.0000$
$N = 623$

High income blacks slightly less likely to be a church-goer

$X^2 = 16.86$
$p = 0.03$
$N = 603$

CHAPTER SEVEN: A COMPARATIVE ANALYSIS

Boston blacks show lower concern for macro-community
issues than other cities

$X^2 = 662.77$
$p = 0.000$
$N = 871$

Cleveland and Houston were higher in their concern for
micro-community issues

$X^2 = 186.27$
$p = 0.00$
$N = 769$

Cleveland is lowest in terms of alienation

$X^2 = 55.05$
$p = 0.000$
$N = 911$

Atlanta and Los Angeles black residents report highest
feelings of powerlessness

$X^2 = 154.14$
$p = 0.0$
$N = 926$

Boston blacks report highest orientation to future

$X^2 = 103.74$
$p = 0.000$
$N = 921$

Boston blacks report highest distrust of the power structure

$X^2 = 396.75$
$p = 0.0$
$N = 922$

Name Index

Subject Index

Adams v. Califano, 200, 201
Adams v. Richardson, 181
Alienation, 9-14, 85, 102-115, 194, 210, 215
  correlates of, 107-110
  definitional problems, 104
  degrees of, 104
  hypotheses, 110-114
  in cities, 108-110

Blacks and Police, 78-79, 145-148, 150-151, 159, 161-164, 168-170
Black Conservatives, 183, 184-186
Black Elected Officials, 26, 37, 77-78, 150, 158-160, 164, 171, 175-177
Black Enterprise Readers Survey, 7-8, 49, 52
Black Pulse Survey, 7, 52, 75-76
Black Population of
  Atlanta, 14-15, 26
  Boston, 14-15, 29
  Cleveland, 14-15, 32
  Houston, 14-15, 33-34
  Los Angeles, 14-15, 36-37
Block grants, 190, 195-196
Bolden v. Mobile, Alabama, 207
Brown v. Board of Education, 2, 181
Busing for School Desegregation, 29, 33, 95, 130, 145, 154, 158, 168, 183, 185, 201-205

Characteristics of Participants by City, 137-141
Civil Rights Act of 1964, 2, 181, 204
Civil Rights Act of 1968, 2, 78, 181
Community Research Review Committee, 18, 22n
Crime, 22n, 24, 25, 29-30, 55-58, 60, 62, 64, 66, 69, 78-79, 96-97, 145, 148, 151-152, 159, 161-164, 168-170, 194
Critical Issues in Black Community, 40-81

and characteristics of participants, 40-50
  age, 42-43
  education, 43
  employment, 43-45
  family structure/authority, 42
  health problems, 49-50
  home ownership, 48-49
  household size, 45-46
  income, 46-47
  occupations, 43
  residential distribution, 40-41
  sex and marital status, 41-42
  unemployment, 47-48

Data Black/Public Opinion Poll, 8
Distrust of Power Structure, 86, 105-107, 109, 112, 186-188, 194, 210

Equal Employment Opportunity Commission, 2-3, 189, 209

Health Access Index
  definition, 84
  scale characteristics, 84
Health Information
  scale characteristics, 83
Health Issues/Problems, 49-50, 172-174
Hypotheses
  discussion of, 86-94, 109-112

Macro-Community Issues, 82-100
  by city, 141-142
  correlates of, 91-93
  definition of, 2, 83
  national profile, 83
  scale characteristics, 83
Micro-Community Issues, 82-100
  by city, 142-143
  correlates of, 93-95
  definition of, 2, 83
  national profile, 83

227